The Limits
of Free Will

Selected Essays

PAUL RUSSELL

OXFORD
UNIVERSITY PRESS

OXFORD
UNIVERSITY PRESS

Oxford University Press is a department of the University of Oxford. It furthers the University's objective of excellence in research, scholarship, and education by publishing worldwide. Oxford is a registered trade mark of Oxford University Press in the UK and certain other countries.

Published in the United States of America by Oxford University Press
198 Madison Avenue, New York, NY 10016, United States of America.

CIP data is on file at the Library of Congress
ISBN 978–0–19–062760–7

1 3 5 7 9 8 6 4 2

Printed by Sheridan Books, Inc., United States of America

In memory of Bernard Williams

One monkey stares and listens with mocking disdain,
the other seems to be dreaming away—
but when it's clear I don't know what to say
he prompts me with a gentle
clinking of his chain.

WISLAWA SZYMBORSKA ("Bruegel's Two Monkeys")

Contents

PART IV. *Pessimism and the Limits of Free Will*

Acknowledgments

ALTHOUGH EACH PAPER in this collection includes its own set of acknowledgments I would like to take the opportunity to thank a few friends and colleagues who have been especially important in shaping and directing my work in this general area over the past few decades: John M. Fischer, Derk Pereboom, Dave Shoemaker, Saul Smilansky, Angie Smith, Andras Szigeti, R. Jay Wallace, Susan Wolf and, especially, Michael McKenna. All of the above have influenced and improved my own understanding on these topics not only through our conversations and correspondence but also through my reading of their own significant and influential contributions to the field. My most substantial intellectual and personal debt is indicated in the dedication.

For financial and research support that gave me the opportunity to bring the papers in this collection together I would like to thank the University of British Columbia, the University of Gothenburg, as well as the Social Sciences and Research Council of Canada and, especially, the Swedish Research Council/*Vetenskapsrådet* for an award for the international recruitment of leading researchers (2014–2024: Ref: 2014–40).

Finally, I am grateful to Peter Ohlin and his colleagues at OUP for all their support and help and in bringing this collection into print.

Sources

"Sorabji and the Dilemma of Determinism," *Analysis*, 44 (1984), 166–172.

"Causation, Compulsion and Compatibilism," *American Philosophical Quarterly*, 25 (1988), 313–321.

"Strawson's Way of Naturalizing Responsibility," *Ethics*, 101 (1992), 287–302.

"Compatibilist-Fatalism: Finitude, Pessimism and the Limits of Free Will," in Ton van den Beld, ed., *Moral Responsibility and Ontology* (Dordrecht: Kluwer, 2000), 199–218.

"Pessimists, Pollyannas and the New Compatibilism," in Robert Kane, ed., *The Oxford Handbook of Free Will* (Oxford University Press, 2002), 229–256.

"Responsibility and the Condition of Moral Sense," *Philosophical Topics*, 32 (2004), 287–305. [Special Issue on Agency, ed. J. M. Fischer].

"Practical Reason and Motivational Skepticism," in Heiner F. Klemme, Manfred Kuehn, Dieter Schönecker, eds., *Moralisch e Motivation. Kant und die Alternativen*. Kant-Forschungen 16.2006. VIII, 350 Seiten. (Hamburg: Felix Meiner Verlag, 2006), 287–296.

"Free Will, Art and Morality," *The Journal of Ethics*, 12 (2008), 307–325. Invited contribution to special edition on *Metaphysics and Moral Responsibility*; guest ed. Joseph Campbell.

"Selective Hard Compatibilism," in Joseph Campbell, Michael O'Rourke, and Harry Silverstein, eds., *Action, Ethics and Responsibility: Topics in Contemporary Philosophy*, Vol. 7 (Cambridge, MA: MIT Press, 2010), 149–73.

"Moral Sense and the Foundations of Responsibility," in Robert Kane, ed., *The Oxford Handbook of Free Will*, 2nd ed. (Oxford: Oxford University Press: 2011), 199–220

"Responsibility, Naturalism and 'the Morality System,'" in David Shoemaker, ed., *Oxford Studies in Agency and Responsibility* (Oxford University Press: 2013), 184–204.

"Free Will Pessimism," in David Shoemaker, ed., *Oxford Studies in Agency and Responsibility IV* (Oxford University Press: 2017), 93–120.

Introduction

I

This collection is composed of a selection of chapters that represents work I have done on the topics of free will and moral responsibility. Most of the chapters have appeared over the past decade or so but I have also included a few older chapters that continue to be relevant to the current debate and discussion. The issues and problems addressed in these chapters are, of course, deeply rooted in the history of the subject and concern matters that are of perennial interest and importance in philosophy. The various issues addressed are not only intimately related to each other, but also of immediate relevance to neighboring fields, including subjects such as law and criminology, theology, moral psychology and, more recently, neuroscience. During the period that these chapters were written and first published this area of research has become increasingly active and vibrant. It has expanded and evolved well beyond the narrow and restrictive confines established by the methods and techniques of "analytic" philosophy as it was understood and practiced in the middle decades of the twentieth century. Although this collection does not reflect every aspect of the field, and some important problems and issues are not covered, most of the significant developments and changes that have taken place are well represented.

Among the various ways in which the contemporary debate has advanced and made progress there are four that are especially significant for the purpose of the chapters in this collection. First, the specific forms and varieties of compatibilist and libertarian positions have evolved and developed enormously over the past three or four decades.[1] The positions

---

1. Relevant selections of these contributions can be found in Russell & Deery, 2013. See also the Introduction for a discussion and account of these developments, along with a brief survey of the key positions and strategies in the contemporary free will debate.

taken are not only more subtle and complex, they deal more effectively and convincingly with the familiar problems and objections. Even though these accounts have not settled or put an end to the debate, they serve as clear evidence of the degree to which our understanding and evaluation of these matters has advanced. Second, consistent with developments elsewhere in philosophy, there is a greater concern to offer accounts or theories that are empirically better grounded and more informed. This trend is apparent in libertarian theories but it is especially pronounced in contemporary compatibilist thinking and theorizing. This "naturalistic turn" in recent work has, among other things, taken the form of insisting on the particular relevance of moral psychology for our understanding of the normative framework within which these issues and problems arise. No serious theory or account of free will and moral responsibility can simply ignore the way in which justificatory issues are themselves embedded in and structured by the psychological attitudes and dispositions that are at work in this sphere.[2]

The other two important developments are closely connected to each other, as well as being related to the two developments just described. One of these is the increasing seriousness with which the skeptical challenge to the whole edifice of free will and moral responsibility is now taken (e.g., Pereboom 2001; Waller 2011; Levy 2011; Harris 2012; Miles 2015). Only a generation or so ago it would be rare to find any serious theorizing about free will and moral responsibility from a skeptical point of view—the real debate was between the libertarian and compatibilist positions. This is no longer the case and one question that must, therefore, be taken more seriously is what is the significance of skepticism and what is involved in abandoning our self-image as free and responsible agents? Can we, for example, really *live* our skepticism in practice—is this something human beings are even capable of (Strawson, 1962)? The fourth development, related to the issue of skepticism, concerns our metaphysical attitudes of optimism and pessimism. It has been widely held that skepticism would commit us to a bleak and troubling understanding of the human predicament with respect to these matters and that, conversely, the defeat of skepticism serves to vindicate a more optimistic view. Several recent defenses

---

2. The naturalistic turn in recent years is, of course, itself something of a return to views articulated and defended by earlier figures, such as Hume. Contributions by Strawson (1962) and Williams (1965), among others, were especially influential in launching this process. For an account of the particular importance of Strawson's contribution in relation to this see the Introduction in McKenna & Russell (2008).

of the skeptical view have, however, denied this linkage or association between skepticism and pessimism and have argued, instead, that the skeptic can sustain a coherent and plausible optimistic picture of human life, without the illusions and confusions involved in regarding ourselves as free and responsible agents (see, e.g., Pereboom 2001; Honderich 2002; Sommers 2007; Waller 2011)

The four developments outlined above provide the broad framework within which the chapters included in this collection have been written. Each chapter draws upon one or more of these developments and, taken together, they reflect these important changes in the free will debate over the past few decades. There are, of course, some significant and substantial developments in the contemporary debate that are not covered or discussed in these studies. For example, over the past two or three decades—as with philosophy more generally—considerable effort has been made to include and accommodate the findings of science into this debate. The sort of "armchair" approach that was encouraged by the methodology of analytic philosophy is now generally resisted and repudiated. A number of prominent philosophers and scientists have attempted to employ and apply the methodologies and data of science as a way of resolving the free will problem. Some interesting and stimulating research has certainly been generated along these lines—especially as it concerns the experiments and discoveries of neuroscience and social psychology. At the same time, this process has also encouraged some extravagant and excessive claims. This includes the skeptical claim that we have (decisive) "empirical evidence" to prove that free will is an illusion and there is no basis for moral responsibility, and so on. Just as some scientists and philosophers have embraced and endorsed these extravagant claims, others have played an important and valuable role in challenging and discrediting them. My own work, however, has not engaged in any detail with these particular debates, interesting and influential as they may be. One reason for this is that I am less enthusiastic—and perhaps more skeptical—than most of my colleagues about the extent to which these controversies, in the final analysis, serve to clarify or elucidate the core issues. I believe that we need to look elsewhere if we are to make significant and substantial progress on these issues and problems.

One way in which my own methodological approach differs from the dominant contemporary paradigms is that my approach to these issues has been deeply embedded in and combined with historically oriented studies. In contrast with this, contemporary investigations not only tend to place heavy emphasis on the techniques and findings of science, but also generally neglect or even dismiss the value of historical studies and sensibilities in relation to this topic (this being the reverse side of an attitude that relies narrowly on the model and methods of science).[3] With this in mind, it is worth pointing out that the chapters that are included in this collection not only are intimately connected with these historically oriented studies of the free will problem, but also in a number of cases they have arisen directly from them. This relationship is especially obvious and pronounced with regard to several studies that I have presented concerning Hume's philosophy and the way in which it is of (multiple) relevance to the contemporary free will debate (Russell 1995; Russell 2015). None of this is flagged in detail in the chapters that follow but it should be evident to those who are familiar with the philosophy of Hume, along with the other historical figures I draw from.

With regard to the set of chapters included in this collection some are mostly critical in character, presenting critiques and commentary on major works or contributions in the contemporary scene. Others are primarily constructive, aiming to develop and articulate an alternative compatibilist theory—a theory, as I explain further below, that is deeply rooted in Strawson's naturalistic program but diverges from it (and other important and more recent variants of it) in significant respects. There is, nevertheless, no simple division between the critical and constructive tasks, as these two aspects of my work are fused together and serve to unite the collection into a coherent whole.

Finally, each chapter in this collection is self-standing and can be read in isolation from the others. There is, nevertheless, a core set of themes and issues that unite and link them all together. This collection is arranged and organized in a format that enables the reader to appreciate and recognize these links and the core themes that unite them. This is a key rationale or justification for the whole project. The collection, considered as a whole is, I believe, much more than simply the sum of its parts. Presented in this format, the collection reveals the deep and significant structural relationships that hold between the discussions in these chapters and shows how they are relevant and connected to each other—something that is otherwise obscured, even for the careful and interested reader.

---

3. On this see, for example, Williams, 1994; Williams 2000; and Williams, 2002. Williams wrote several pieces concerning the relevance of history for philosophy and for ethics in particular. He also expressed skepticism about the "scientistic" tendencies that are present, if not prevalent, in contemporary philosophy

II

It may be helpful if I provide a few further details about the structure and content of this collection. This volume is divided into four parts, with twelve chapters in total. Each part is arranged around a core theme and most of the themes and chapters overlap and are interrelated in terms of their content and concerns. (These themes are related to but distinct from the four developments described in the section above.) Among the key topics taken up are the relevance of the metaphysics of causation for free will; the nature and credibility of the (Strawsonian) naturalistic program, which draws on the role of moral sentiment considered as a solution to the free will problem; skepticism about practical reason; the relevance of free will for art and morality; the adequacy of reason-responsive theories of moral agency; the manipulation argument; and, finally, pessimism about the limits of agency.

The following is a brief summary and review of each of these four parts and of the particular chapters that have been assigned to them.

I. Free Will and Causal Relations

There is an obvious sense in which the metaphysics of causation is central to the problem of free will and, according to some, it can serve as the relevant basis for its solution. The basic idea common to these approaches is that the difficulties we encounter in this area have been generated by faulty assumptions about the nature of causation and how it relates to human action and conduct. The solution, therefore, rests with identifying and removing the source of the relevant metaphysical confusion. It is significant that both libertarians and compatibilists have sought solutions along these lines—despite the very different conclusions that they aim to draw from it. In the two chapters that are included in this part of the collection I take up an approach from each side of this debate—both of which have been extremely influential and continue to command support. I argue that neither strategy is successful. The failure of approaches of this kind suggests that a satisfactory solution likely has to be found elsewhere.

Lying at the heart of these approaches to the free will problem through the metaphysics of causation is the question about the nature of causal *relations*. Two questions that are especially important are: (1) do causes always necessitate their effects? and (2) do causal relations involve metaphysical powers or forces of some kind or are they to be analyzed simply in

terms of regularities or constant conjunctions of events? Over the past few
decades a number of libertarians have advanced an "event-causal" theory
that grounds libertarian metaphysics in explanatory but non-necessitating
causal relations. The most prominent representative of this strategy is
Robert Kane, who has presented and defended a particularly subtle and
detailed theory along these general lines (Kane 1996). However, a similar view was also advanced and defended, a few years earlier, by Richard
Sorabji (Sorabji 1980). In developing his own account, Sorabji drew on his
interpretation of Aristotle. In the first chapter I offer a critique of Sorabji's
event-causal theory and argue that it runs into difficulties and objections
located on both sides of the dilemma of determinism. I have included a
brief "addendum" to explain the relevance of my critique to the contemporary debate (i.e.. particularly as it concerns the debate around Kane's
model). The second chapter offers a critique of the classical compatibilist strategy, the central features of which originated with Hume but were
further developed and defended by leading figures of nineteenth- and
twentieth-century empiricism, such as Mill, Russell, Schlick and Ayer. The
aim of this strategy was to dissolve the (pseudo-) problem of free will by way
of diagnosing incompatibilist concerns as rooted in confusions about the
nature of causation. I argue that these efforts to ground the compatibilist
position in the regularity theory of causation not only manifest confusion
about the original insights relating to the caused/compelled distinction,
which is central to the compatibilist approach, but also threaten to generate some awkward problems for compatibilism by eroding the metaphysical bonds or ties between agent and action.[4]

II. Responsibility, Skepticism, and Moral Sentiment

Arguably the most important and influential contribution to the free will
debate in the last half of the twentieth century has been P. F. Strawson's
"Freedom and Resentment" (Strawson, 1962). The second group of chapters pursues themes and issues arising out of Strawson's contribution
and the substantial discussion and debate it has generated. Strawson's
approach involves turning away from the more familiar and dominant

---

4. Classical compatibilism is, of course, associated primarily with the central figures of
the British empiricist tradition (viz. Hume, Mill, Russell, Schlick, Ayer et al.) but it still
commands strong support and has influential defenders. See, e.g., Berofsky, 2012; and
Berofsky, 2017.

debates of the twentieth century concerning alternative possibilities and the interpretation of the concept of freedom, to a close examination and description of the role that reactive attitudes or moral sentiments play in circumstances where we hold agents responsible for their actions. (These are concerns that follow similar lines of argument that can be found in Hume's philosophy, which has been the focus of much of my attention in my more historical studies.) In "Strawson's Way of Naturalizing Responsibility," I am concerned with a key aspect of Strawson's strategy; namely, his claim that no reasoning of any sort could lead us to abandon or suspend our commitment to the "reactive attitudes." This is a claim that aims to discredit all radical, skeptical conclusions about moral responsibility based on concerns about the implications of determinism. I argue that Strawson fails to distinguish two very different forms or modes of naturalism and that he is constrained by the nature of his own objectives (i.e., the refutation of skepticism) to embrace the stronger, less plausible, form of naturalism. The critique provided suggests that there are significant gaps in Strawson's effort to reconstruct compatibilism along these lines and that while his (neo-Humean) strategy has significant merits, it is not acceptable or convincing as it stands.

The chapter that follows, "Responsibility and the Condition of Moral Sense," presents a thesis about necessary conditions of responsible agency that arise at the interface between (compatibilist) reason-responsive theories and Strawsonian naturalistic approaches. Contemporary compatibilists have suggested that Strawson's theory has a significant gap, that it lacks an adequate theory of moral capacity (a point I also argue for in "Strawson's Way"). A number of these critics have tried to plug this gap with an account of rational self-control or reason-responsiveness that does not involve any reference to moral sentiments and our ability to *hold* agents responsible. The thesis argued for in this chapter is that the responsible agent (i.e., one who is capable of *being* responsible) must also be one who is capable of holding herself responsible. Where moral sense is lacking, I maintain, rational self-control is seriously impaired or compromised. The third chapter in this part of the collection is a critical summary and account of Strawson's approach to moral responsibility and free will, along with a discussion of several of the key responses it has generated. After reviewing Strawson's core arguments and identifying several significant weaknesses in it, I turn to R. Jay Wallace's effort to recast Strawson's program and amend and modify it in ways that avoid various objections that have been directed against it (Wallace 1994). Wallace's theory involves two strands, a

Strawsonian account of holding people responsible and a Kantian account of moral agency. I argue that both these strands run into major difficulties. My discussion then turns to an analysis of Angela Smith's distinction between being and holding responsible, which she uses to criticize the whole Strawsonian program (Smith 2007). Contrary to Smith I argue, building on the discussion in the previous chapter, that there is a more complex and intimate relationship between these two aspects than her critique allows for or can accommodate. My discussion concludes with reflections on the relevance of an agent's history for our reactive attitudes and moral sentiments and whether or not such considerations license skeptical conclusions about the possibility of moral responsibility (e.g.. as per Derk Pereboom's "hard incompatibilism"). In this context I also provide a sketch of "critical compatibilism" and "free will pessimism" (which are discussed at greater length in various chapters in Part IV).

The last chapter in Part II returns to a critical discussion of Wallace's effort to provide a "narrow construal" of moral responsibility in terms of a modified Strawsonian approach. My particular concern in this chapter involves an elaboration and expansion of my earlier critiques. While I endorse and share many of Wallace's objections to Strawson's way of naturalizing responsibility, I reject his effort to reconstruct and compress our understanding of moral responsibility into the restrictive framework of what Bernard Williams has described as "the morality system"—an understanding that places heavy and exclusive emphasis on the notions of obligation, voluntariness and blame in accounting for moral responsibility. In opposition to the narrow construal, I suggest we should embrace a broader conception that can accommodate more varied modes of moral sentiment and the diverse forms of moral responsibility that go with them. One of the significant benefits of taking this route is that it blunts or deflates the (global) skeptical challenge to responsibility, along similar lines to Strawson's original program.

III. Practical Reason, Art, and Manipulation

The chapters grouped together in Part III are more loosely related than the other parts of this volume but they are, nevertheless, thematically connected with the volume as a whole. The issue of practical reason is closely connected with problems of freedom and responsibility, since different views about the nature of moral freedom and moral capacity presuppose very different accounts of the powers of practical reason and its manner of operation and influence. The first chapter in this part of the collection takes up a crucial debate between Christine Korsgaard and Bernard Williams on this subject. Korsgaard defends a broadly Kantian view of practical reason against William's modified Humean view. It is Korsgaard's particular concern to argue that if reason can itself identify substantive ends for our actions, independent of our existing desires, then there is no genuine or distinct motivational problem about how reasons can move (rational) agents to action. In this chapter I argue that Korsgaard's argument fails and the motivational problem cannot be resolved along the lines that she proposes. In "Free Will, Art, and Morality" I consider the relevance of the free will problem for our evaluation of artistic achievement and merit. I argue that with respect to both issues, creativity and merit, incompatibilist worries about the implications of determinism are groundless and misplaced. On this basis I consider the implications of these conclusions in light of the significant analogies that hold between art and morality. I argue that whether incompatibilists accept or reject the analogy they face a series of intractable problems and dilemmas that tell against the incompatibilist position. The implications of all this for compatibilism, however, are in no way "comfortable" or confirming of "optimism." On the contrary, the relevance of the art and morality analogy highlights the extent to which moral evaluation is inescapably permeated by background conditions of luck. In this respect, there is an important sense in which we may say morality is unfair. The last chapter in Part III takes up a well-known objection to the compatibilist position, which is "the manipulation argument" and related arguments based on covert control. In this chapter I reject soft compatibilist responses to cases of this kind, which rely on considerations of "history" to exclude manipulated or covertly controlled agents from responsible agency. Instead I defend a modified form of hard compatibilism, one that grants there is something problematic about cases of this kind but rejects the claim that agents in these conditions are not responsible. The issue is not, I suggest, that these agents are not responsible but that their manipulators or covert controllers are not entitled to hold them responsible. In this way, selective hard compatibilism maintains that what is compromised in these circumstances is not the moral responsibility of the agent (where robust compatibilist conditions of a relevant kind are satisfied) but the participant stance or moral standing of their manipulators. It is these distinct considerations that account for the (limited) intuitive force of incompatibilist counterexamples of this general nature.

IV. Pessimism and the Limits of Free Will

The previous parts of this collection include several contributions that suggest some proposals for how a broadly Strawsonian, compatibilist approach to free will and moral responsibility should (or should not) be amended and modified, with a view to meeting various objections that may be leveled against it. The final group of chapters in this collection, building on this, aims to articulate a distinctive account of compatibilism. Although it rejects any form of unqualified or radical skepticism, critical compatibilism insists that a plausible compatibilism has significant and substantive implications about the limits of agency and that this licenses a metaphysical attitude of (modest) pessimism on this topic. The first chapter, "Compatibilist Fatalism," argues that compatibilists require a richer conception of fatalistic concern, one that recognizes the legitimacy of (pessimistic) concerns about the origination of character and conduct. On this basis I argue that compatibilists must allow that determinism has fatalistic implications of a significant and relevant kind, even if they are not responsibility undermining. This mode of fatalistic concern, I maintain, licenses a distinct form of pessimistic concern grounded in concerns about the limitations or finitude and contingency of human agency. No credible form of compatibilism can hope to evade this form of pessimism and, thus, all forms of compatibilism that aspire to metaphysical optimism in this respect are guilty of evasion and superficiality. In the chapter that follows I pursue this general line of thought with particular reference to the "new compatibilism" and theories of reason-responsiveness associated with it (Dennett 1984 is a particular target of my criticism). I argue that although compatibilism, in its various forms, may defeat immediate skeptical threats relating to the powers of agents to guide and control their conduct in light of reason and deliberation, we eventually reach a point where the way in which these powers and abilities are acquired and exercised falls outside the agent's (ultimate) control. These reflections and observations, I argue, serve to justify "pessimism at the horizon." This mode of pessimism is not, however, as explained before, rooted in skepticism about freedom and responsibility but rather in our understanding of the way in which the abilities and powers involved in the operation and exercise of rational self-control are themselves limited and reveal us to be agents who are subject to finitude and contingency, a reflection that is at least disconcerting, although not one that justifies any form of deep despair.

The last chapter in this volume weaves together the core arguments relating to critical compatibilism (which was also briefly mentioned above in the summary of Part II). This chapter draws a basic distinction between "free will skepticism" and "free will pessimism." While any acceptable form of compatibilism cannot be skeptical it has, nevertheless, pessimistic implications relating to fate and luck. The source of strong resistance to this conclusion is rooted, I suggest, in "the morality system" and its aspiration to metaphysical optimism. Any plausible form of compatibilism must embrace free will pessimism and take the form of critical compatibilism (i.e., reject the optimistic aspirations of complacent compatibilism). Incompatibilists may welcome this conclusion and present it as an effective *reductio* of the compatibilist position. I argue, however, that incompatibilism, whether it takes the form of libertarianism or skepticism, encounters its own distinct difficulties when it comes to dealing with these broad concerns relating to fate and luck and the role they play in moral life. The conclusion that is drawn from all this is that although all the major parties in the free will debate reject (the very possibility of) free will pessimism, this is, nevertheless, the most truthful and accurate account of human agency and moral life. Critical compatibilism, I maintain, does not aim to solve the free will problem in terms that will satisfy the demands of the morality system. What we have is not a problem that needs to be solved but rather a troubling predicament that needs to be recognized and acknowledged.

REFERENCES

Berofsky, Bernard. 2012. *Nature's Challenge to Free Will*. Oxford: Oxford University Press.

———. 2017. "Classical Compatibilism." In Meghan Griffith, Neal Levy, Kevin Timpe, eds. *Routledge Companion to Free Will*. New York & London: Routledge.

Dennett, Daniel. 1984. *Elbow Room: Varieties of Free Will Worth Wanting*. Oxford: Oxford University Press.

Harris, Sam. 2012. *Free Will*. New York: Free Press.

Honderich, Ted. 2002. *How Free Are You? The Determinism Problem*. 2nd ed. Oxford: Oxford University Press.

Kane, Robert. 1996. *The Significance of Free Will*. New York & Oxford: Oxford University Press.

Levy, Neil. 2011. *Hard Luck: How Luck Undermines Free Will & Moral Responsibility*. Oxford: Oxford University Press.

McKenna, Michael & Paul Russell, eds. 2008. *Free Will and Reactive Attitudes*. Aldershot, UK: Ashgate Press.

Miles, James. 2015. *The Free Will Delusion: How We Settled for the Illusion of Morality.* Kibworth Beauchamp, Leics.: Matador.

Pereboom, Derk. 2001. *Living Without Free Will.* Cambridge: Cambridge University Press.

Russell, Paul. 1995. *Freedom and Moral Sentiment: Strawson's Way of Naturalizing Responsibility.* New York & Oxford: Oxford University Press.

Russell, Paul, 2015. "Hume's 'Lengthy Digression': Free Will in the *Treatise,*" in *Hume's Treatise: A Critical Guide,* edited by A. Butler and D. Ainslie (Cambridge: Cambridge University Press), 230–51.

Russell, Paul, & Oisin Deery, eds. 2013. *The Philosophy of Free Will: Essential Readings from the Contemporary Debates.* New York & Oxford: Oxford University Press.

Smith, Angie. 2007. "On Being and Holding Responsible." *Journal of Ethics* 11: 465–84.

Sommers, Tamler. 2007. "The objective attitude," *Philosophical Quarterly* 57: 321–41.

Sorabji, Richard. 1980. *Necessity, Cause and Blame.* London: Duckworth.

Strawson, P.F. (1962). "Freedom and Resentment." Reprinted in Russell & Deery, 2013.

Wallace, R. Jay. 1994. *Responsibility and the Moral Sentiments.* Cambridge, MA: Harvard University Press.

Waller, Bruce. 2011. *Against Moral Responsibility.* Cambridge, MA: MIT Press.

Williams, Bernard. 1965. "Morality and the emotions." Reprinted in *Problems of the Self.* Cambridge: Cambridge University Press.

———. 1994. "Descartes and the Historiography of Philosophy." Reprinted in *The Sense of the Past: Essays in the History of Philosophy.* Edited and introduced by Myles Burnyeat. Princeton: Princeton University Press.

———. 2000. "Philosophy as a Humanistic Discipline." Reprinted in *Philosophy as a Humanistic Discipline.* Edited and introduced by A.W. Moore. Princeton: Princeton University Press.

———. 2002. "Why Philosophy Needs History." Reprinted in *Essays and Reviews 1959–2002.* Foreword by Michael Wood. Princeton: Princeton University Press.

PART I

Free Will and Causal Relations

I

Sorabji and the Dilemma of Determinism

WITH AN ADDENDUM, 2016

IN *NECESSITY, CAUSE and Blame* (London: Duckworth, 1980) Richard Sorabji attempts to develop a notion of moral responsibility which does not get caught on either horn of a well-known dilemma. One horn is the argument that if an action was caused then it must have been necessary and therefore could not be one for which the agent is responsible. The other horn is the argument that if the action was not caused then it is inexplicable and random and therefore not something which the agent can be responsible for. Sorabji denies that what is caused is always necessitated. Causes are primarily explanatory rather than necessitating. This established, Sorabji hopes to show that action open to moral scrutiny may be caused without being necessitated and the dilemma collapses. I will argue that this strategy runs into serious difficulties.

I

Sorabji argues that desires and beliefs are causes of action, and clearly he means to suggest that they are *efficient* causes of action (cf. p. 40). These desires and beliefs, it is implied, have weights which may or may not be "equally balanced" when they oppose one another (I use the term "weight" here to correspond with Sorabji's metaphor of "scales," cf. pp. 30–31). Sorabji offers two examples in support of his claim that human action may be caused without being necessitated. In Chapter Fourteen he considers the case of a child who has equal but opposing desires. On the one hand the child wants to take another child's toy which appeals to him but on the other hand he equally wants to please and obey his parents. As it happens the child takes the toy but *"in the very same circumstances* the child could have acted in the other way" (p. 232n—my emphasis). We can, however, give an explanation and cite a cause of the child's action; namely, "that set of incentives which favoured taking the toy." Thus, while there is "no answer available for someone who . . . wants to be told why the child acted on the one set [sc. of incentives] rather than the other" there is neverthe-less an explanation for why the action occurred. In this way, it is argued, the problem of randomness may be overcome.

In Chapter Two Sorabji offers an example "in which the case for and against a decision does not seem equally balanced." An agent may have "overwhelming" reason for attending a lecture and "nine times out of ten in such circumstances a man may act accordingly." However, the agent also has some reason for not attending the lecture and therefore may sometimes not attend. (If "scales" are balanced at a ratio of 9:1 they *always* go to the weightier side—not at a ratio of 9:1. How, given the analogy, does Sorabji account for the exceptional case? If the "scales" do not always come down on the weightier side how do we establish the relative weight of rival sets of incentives? This sort of difficulty suggests that the metaphor of "scales" is perhaps not a very happy one.) In other words, Sorabji sug-gests that under identical circumstances C an agent may usually do X (i.e., attend a lecture) for given reasons, say R_1, but he may occasionally do Y for other conflicting reasons, say R_2. Hence under the said circumstances nei-ther X nor Y was necessitated, though doing X was more probable because R_1 was weightier than R_2. Nevertheless, whether X or Y occurs they will be explicable; X in terms of R_1 and Y in terms of R_2. However, a serious prob-lem remains and one which curiously does not seem to trouble Sorabji very much.

Sorabji admits that what cannot be explained is why the agent does X (acts on R_1) rather than Y (acting on R_2) or vice versa. "But then ought we to expect," he continues, "that there will be an explanation available cor-responding to every contrast that we care to choose?" (p. 31). Perhaps we need not be able to answer the question which asks why an agent does one given action rather than *any* other action. But there is another distinct question which does seem more pressing: given that the agent has a set of *actual* rival desires and beliefs (R_1, R_2, . . ., R_n) why, in any given case, does the agent act on some and not others? Let us call this the *comparative ques-tion*. In effect the comparative question asks if the agent can determine which set of incentives become his will. (The notion of will I use here is that of an *effective* set of incentives—one that moves the agent to undertake an action.) Sorabji seems to think not, and in this he certainly parts company with traditional libertarianism. What matters, it seems, is that when we do act there is some set of incentives which explain the action but do not necessitate it.

II

It seems clear, then, that the crucial issue is whether or not Sorabji is right in claiming that we need not be concerned about being unable to explain why an agent acts on one set of incentives rather than others which are also actually his. That is to say, can we ignore the comparative question and dismiss it as irrelevant to the issue of moral responsibility?

Let us assume that the difference between X and Y is morally significant. Action X, let us suppose, is some morally repugnant action (e.g., pushing an old lady in front of a bus) explicable in terms of a given set of incentives, R_1 (e.g., a dislike of old people, and a belief that this lady is one such person). Action Y, by contrast, is some morally commendable action (e.g., helping the old lady across the road) explicable in terms of another distinct set of incentives, R_2 (e.g., a love of one's fellow human beings, a pleasure in helping people and a recognition that help was required). Under conditions C the agent has overwhelming reason to do Y and, let us assume, 99 times in 100 would act on R_2. Despite this he does X and R_1 thereby becomes his will. Sorabji's argument suggests that because X was not necessary, is explicable in terms of R_1, and the agent could categorically have done Y he is (ceteris paribus) responsible. It does not matter, so it seems, that the agent had other much stronger and wholly different beliefs and desires which he did not act on. Nor does it matter, apparently, that he was unable to determine whether he acted on R_1 or R_2—in other words, determine whether R_1 or R_2 became his will.

It may be argued that if the agent did in fact act on R_1 rather than R_2 then he must have opted for R_1 in preference to R_2—thereby determining X in preference to Y. That is to say, when we act on R_1 rather than R_2 there must have been some "new rival temptation or force" which "tips the scales" in favor of R_1. This assumption of the determinist is, Sorabji claims, simply a "declaration of faith" (pp. 30–31). We require no new rival temptation or force to distinguish cases where we do X from those where we do Y. In identical circumstances (i.e., C) either R_1 or R_2 could be efficacious. There is no further influence of the agent which accounts for the occurrence of one action rather than the other.

Consider the following contrast. Suppose that in given conditions C we have two sets of incentives, R_1 and R_2. In one case both R_1 and R_2 are causally determined, and R_1 in turn necessitates action X. In the second case R_1^* and R_2^* may cause but cannot necessitate actions X^* and Y^* respectively—either alternative being quite possible. Given that X^* occurs it will have been caused, but unlike the first case (i.e., X) it will not have been necessitated. Sorabji would deny that the first case is an instance of morally free or responsible action because although the action was caused by the agent it was "necessary all along." How, then, would he regard the second case? As an action that was caused by the agent but not necessitated he would seem to regard it as one for which the agent is responsible. There is, however, no greater scope for agency in this case than in the first. The agent cannot determine whether he acts on R_1 or R_2 and so he no more determines which set of incentives becomes his will in this case than in the first case. That is to say, the opening up of possible actions in the second case does not increase the agent's influence over what he does. In both cases the agent fails to act on R_2 (or R_2^*). In the first case necessarily, in the second case because of chance. Accordingly, the lack of necessity in the second case does not contribute to the agent's moral freedom.

What is disturbing about Sorabji's account of the agent's conduct in these circumstances is that it suggests that what the agent does *within the range presented by* C (i.e., R_1, R_2, ..., R_n) is simply a matter of chance. The *nature and character* of the actions which the agent produces in these circumstances will be as random and subject to chance as the *"rate and route"* of radioactive emissions (Sorabji, it should be noted, uses this analogy between radioactive emissions and human conduct; cf. pp. 28–30). While it is certainly true that such actions are produced by the agent's will, it is equally clear that the agent can no more determine which set of incentives he will act on (i.e., which course of action he will pursue) than "the lump of radioactive material" can determine the rate and route of its emissions. Thus, clearly in these circumstances it is not up to the agent how he *wills*.

It may be suggested that Sorabji's position can be defended against this line of criticism if we simply assume that "a man is responsible (excusing conditions aside) for what he does by will, regardless of the origin of his will." However, for Sorabji's purposes this argument proves too much; it would serve equally well as a defense of the compatibilist position (a position which Sorabji explicitly rejects). That is, if we adopt this defense for

Sorabji's position then an agent could be justifiably held responsible for an action which was *necessitated,* as long as it was the agent's will that brought that action about.

The above considerations establish that acting on R_1 does not of itself adequately eliminate the problem of randomness as Sorabji thinks. He has limited the range of randomness (i.e., by excluding those actions with no causal connection with C and by establishing a causal connection between the action in question and C) but within C the randomness persists. In other words, within the range presented by C (R_1, R_2, ..., R_n) it is simply a game of roulette as to what action will follow. That I do X rather than Y, and therefore that I am condemned rather than praised, becomes a matter of chance (whether the "odds" are 1:100, 1:10, or 1:2 does not matter).

III

There is no denying that at first glance Sorabji's attempt to resolve the dilemma of determinism would seem to satisfy the demands of both libertarians and compatibilists. On the one hand his account gives libertarianism the categorical freedom (i.e., the possibility of doing otherwise in identical circumstances) which it seeks while, on the other hand, it meets the compatibilist demand that action be caused by the (antecedent) willings of the agent and not mere random happenings. However, despite this initial plausibility, I believe that both the traditional libertarian and the orthodox compatibilist would argue that Sorabji's theory suffers from serious defects. Their dissatisfaction, I suggest, is indicative of the fact that, for different reasons, neither party would accept that the comparative question is irrelevant to the difficulties which the dilemma of determinism presents us with.

From the traditional libertarian point of view Sorabji's thesis suffers from the same fatal flaw as the compatibilist's position. Namely, on Sorabji's account the agent cannot determine which of the pre-established alternative sets of incentives he acts on. While libertarians, notoriously, find it difficult to give much coherent content to the notion of a non-phenomenal "self," or the notion of how the will is "determined" by this "self," it is nevertheless quite clear why they believe that we need to appeal to these (obscure) notions. Moral responsibility, they argue, requires *moral autonomy*; and moral autonomy requires *self-determination*.

The traditional libertarian cannot accept that the comparative question is irrelevant to the issue of moral responsibility because it is clearly relevant to the issue of moral autonomy. For the traditional libertarian an agent is responsible in so far as *he* (i.e., a non-phenomenal "self") determines his *antecedently* undetermined will. Thus the explanation for why an agent in circumstances C does X rather than Y is that he (i.e., the "self") *chose* to act on that set of incentives. To be able to answer the comparative question is to establish that such an agent had moral autonomy and was capable of self-determination. Hence, to dismiss the comparative question as irrelevant to the issue of moral responsibility is to dismiss the issue of moral autonomy and self-determination as irrelevant to the issue of moral responsibility.

From the orthodox compatibilist perspective Sorabji's thesis suffers from a serious defect common to all libertarian theories: it allows too much scope for the play of chance. Given Sorabji's account of the explanation of human action agents may frequently and inexplicably act contrary to their dominant inclination. This claim raises a number of difficulties from a compatibilist point of view. In particular, in these circumstances how could we accurately infer anyone's character or disposition on the basis of his actions? If agents frequently and inexplicably act out of character and contrary to their stronger inclinations, we would find ourselves unable to anticipate their future actions reliably. In general, it may be argued that human motivation is more consistent and more coherent than Sorabji's model suggests. Indeed, it may be psychologically impossible to survive in a world in which people are randomly acting on rival sets of incentives. (Imagine how difficult it would be to live in a world in which everyone acts as if they had multiple personalities.) In this way, it seems clear that Sorabji's thesis suffers from the same sort of difficulties which compatibilists have found in other, traditional, libertarian theories.

For the compatibilist the only way in which the unacceptable play of chance can be eliminated is if the strongest set of incentives is the effective set of incentives and vice versa. As long as this is the case we can answer the comparative question. That is, the explanation for why an agent in circumstances C does X rather than Y is that the effective set of incentives (i.e., R_1) was stronger than the alternative set of incentives available to him (i.e., R_2).

In short, it is not evident that Sorabji's thesis succeeds in avoiding all the major difficulties associated with the dilemma of determinism. Indeed it may be argued that in some important respects his theory gets impaled on *both* horns of the dilemma at once. At the heart of these difficulties lies the issue of whether or not the comparative question can be dismissed as irrelevant to the issue of moral responsibility. Sorabji *assumes* that it is irrelevant. However, as we have noted, to assume this is simply to beg some of the key issues that are in dispute. At the very least, therefore, we require independent arguments in support of this assumption.

In my view the dilemma of determinism is not likely to be resolved by Sorabji's suggestion that what is caused need not be necessitated. However, the fact that Sorabji's rather ingenious attempt to resolve this dilemma runs aground on the same rocks as its predecessors is itself of considerable interest. The regular failure of this sort of project suggests that philosophers approach the issue of moral responsibility with the wrong set of questions in mind. If we want to avoid running aground on these rocks we must chart a new course—we must ask different questions. Most philosophers, Sorabji included, approach the issue of moral responsibility by way of trying to provide some adequate account of how a responsible agent "could have acted otherwise." Their problem then becomes: how are those *actions* for which we are justifiably held responsible *caused*? The intractable nature of the dilemma of determinism suggests that there is something fundamentally wrong with this entire approach.[1]

Addendum 2016

Sorabji's theory, as was mentioned in the Introduction, is a version of event-causal libertarianism. My criticisms of Sorabji were presented before Robert Kane published his own important and highly influential account of event-causal libertarianism (Kane, 1996; Kane, 1999; and Kane, 2005. See, esp., Kane, 1996, 33–34, where Kane briefly discusses Sorabji and Aristotle in relation to his own concerns.) Kane's model is both elaborate and sophisticated and it addresses several of the objections that I raise against Sorabji's account. In my view, however, although the terminology varies somewhat, these basic objections still stand and apply to Kane's model. The core objection I present against Sorabji takes the form of what is now commonly referred to as "the luck objection"—which concerns the lack of control that an agent has, on the event-causal model, over the way in which her will is actually exercised (given the available incentives or reasons). I argue that severing the connection between causation and necessity, along the lines pursued by both Sorabji and Kane, does not enable the

1. I am grateful to G. A. Cohen, B. A. O. Williams, S. Makin, the editor, and especially to Richard Sorabji for helpful comments on this chapter.

libertarians to avoid familiar weaknesses in their theories. This core objection may take a stronger or a weaker form. The weak criticism is that the event-causal model fails to *enhance* or expand an agent's freedom beyond what is provided by compatibilist theories—which are rejected by libertarians on the ground that they are inadequate. The stronger criticism maintains that event-causal models actually *diminish* or reduce control over her conduct by leaving the agent vulnerable to acting on weaker motivations and (routinely) acting out of character, in a way that would make her unreliable and unpredictable.

Much of the pressure of the luck objection turns on the demand that proponents of the event-causal view have something more convincing to say in answer to what I call the "comparative question," which is now generally described as "contrastive explanation." The demand here is to explain why an agent acts on some but not other available reasons or incentives (any of which, according to the model, could have actually moved the agent to act in the same situation). Kane's model attempts to defuse this objection by appealing to the role of competing "efforts," which are tied to available reasons. According to Kane an effort may indeterministically succeed while another opposing effort may fail, but whichever way it goes the upshot results from the agent's own effort. Although Sorabji's model, as presented in *Necessity, Cause and Blame*, does not mention or appeal to the role of "efforts," Sorabji (in private correspondence, April, 1982) did consider the possibility of "second-order desires" or "reflective choices" as providing a similar source for dealing with objections of this general kind (i.e., relating to lack of control and luck). In reply, I expressed doubt about this proposal on the ground that it would simply introduce another causal "loop" to the model, without eliminating the basic worry that agents operating with deliberative mechanisms of this kind could not adequately and effectively control which efforts would or would not actually move them to action. In all these ways, the difficulties that Sorabji's event-causal model encounters resurface in Kane's related proposals.

BIBLIOGRAPHY

Kane, Robert. 1996. *The Significance of Free Will*. New York: Oxford University Press.
———. 1999. "Responsibility, Luck, and Chance: Reflections on Free Will and Indeterminism." *Journal of Philosophy*, 96/5, 217–40.
———. 2005. *Free Will: A Contemporary Introduction*. New York: Oxford University Press.

2

Causation, Compulsion, and Compatibilism

IN THIS CHAPTER I will be concerned to examine certain salient features of the influential compatibilist position which is widely associated with the views of Thomas Hobbes, David Hume and various other leading figures of the empiricist tradition. The arguments which these philosophers have marshalled in defense of the compatibilist position constitute what I shall refer to as the traditional or orthodox "empiricist-compatibilist strategy." The historical and contemporary significance of the empiricist-compatibilist strategy has recently been described by John Searle in the following terms:

> One would think that after 2000 years of worrying about it, the problem of the freedom of the will would by now have been finally solved. Well, actually most philosophers think it has been solved. They think it was solved by Thomas Hobbes and David Hume and various other empirically-minded philosophers whose solutions have been repeated and improved right into the twentieth century.[1]

1. Searle, *Minds, Brains and Science* (Cambridge, MA; 1984), p. 86. Searle goes on to state that he does not believe that the free will problem has been solved by Hobbes, Hume and their empirically minded followers. The more important works by the philosophers in this tradition include Hobbes, *The Questions Concerning Liberty, Necessity, and Chance* [selections reprinted in S. Morgenbesser and J. Walsh, eds., *Free Will* (Englewood Cliffs, 1962), pp. 41–51]; Hume, *Treatise of Human Nature*, 2nd rev. ed. (Oxford: 1978), II, iii, 1–2; J. S. Mill, *A System of Logic*, Bk. VI, Ch. 2. [reprinted in W. Enteman, ed., *The Problem of Free Will* (New York, 1967), pp. 255–63.]; Bertrand Russell, "On the Notion of Cause," reprinted in *Mysticism and Logic*, 2nd ed. (London, 1917); Moritz Schlick, "When Is a Man Responsible?" [reprinted in Enteman, ed., *The Problem of Free Will*, pp. 184–95]; A. J. Ayer, "Freedom and Necessity" [reprinted in G. Watson, ed., *Free Will* (Oxford, 1982) pp. 15–23].

It is, I think, a matter of some debate whether or not the *majority* of con-temporary philosophers believe that Hobbes and Hume have provided us with a "solution" to the free will problem. However, there can be no doubt that a number of contemporary philosophers do take the view that an ade-quate solution to the free will problem lies along the lines that Hobbes and Hume pursued.[2] Clearly, then, to the extent that the empiricist-compatibilist strategy continues to enjoy some degree of influence among contemporary philosophers, so to that extent it continues to be of some contemporary, as well as historical, philosophical interest.

Throughout this chapter I will be concerned with the major features of the empiricist-compatibilist strategy *as it is generally understood.*[3] In this respect, therefore, I am simply taking for granted the account of the empiricist-compatibilist strategy which is current in the contemporary lit-erature on this subject. This account of the empiricist-compatibilist strat-egy presupposes that we may interpret the philosophers in this tradition as pursuing a common strategy.[4] It is important to emphasize in this context that the accuracy of such interpretations is not my concern. Accordingly, in order to circumvent any problems of detailed exegesis I will base my discussion around my own account of what I take to be a standard inter-pretation of the empiricist-compatibilist strategy.

The empiricist-compatibilist strategy falls, essentially, into two distinct stages of argument. Historically speaking, the first stage was initiated by Hobbes and the second stage was initiated by Hume. The first stage, which I shall refer to as the "compulsion argument" seeks to describe the general significance of the distinction between causation and compulsion for the "free will" dispute. The second stage of the empiricist-compatibilist

---

2. See, e.g., Donald Davidson, "Freedom to Act," reprinted in *Actions and Events* (Oxford, 1980), p. 63: "Hobbes, Locke, Hume, Moore, Schlick, Ayer, Stevenson, and a host of others have done what can be done, or ought ever to have been needed, to *remove the confusions that can make determinism seem to frustrate freedom*" [my emphasis].

3. Some standard accounts of this position can be found in Richard Taylor, "Determinism," an article in Paul Edwards, ed., *The Encyclopedia of Philosophy* (New York, 1970), Vol. 2, pp. 363–68; D. J. O'Connor, *Free Will* (Garden City, 1971), Ch. 9; and Barry Stroud, *Hume* (London, 1977), pp. 141–54.

4. Jonathan Glover, for example, states "that almost identical versions of this doctrine [sc. compatibilism] are to be discovered in Hobbes, Hume, Mill, Russell, Schlick, and Ayer" *Responsibility* (London: 1970), p. 50n. (For references to the works of these philosophers see note 1 above.) Note also that it is not unusual to find references to the "Hobbes-Hume-Schlick doctrine" (Isaiah Berlin) or to the "Hume-Mill-Schlick-Ayer theory" (Paul Edwards and John Hospers).

strategy, which I shall refer to as the "regularity argument," endeavors to reconstruct the compulsion argument on the foundation of the regularity theory of causation. My primary concern in this chapter will be to examine the relation between these two stages of the empiricist-compatibilist strategy. Proponents of this strategy claim that the regularity argument strengthens the compatibilist position. I will argue, on the contrary, that the regularity argument generates serious difficulties for the compulsion argument and that it therefore *weakens* the compatibilist position. In this way I will be concerned to show that the traditional empiricist-compatibilist strategy suffers from significant internal tensions and that these tensions indicate that the regularity theory of causation does not serve as a particularly secure or congenial metaphysical foundation upon which to rest the compatibilist position as it is generally understood.

I

Let me begin by describing the basic structure of the two stages of the compatibilist strategy. The compulsion argument seeks to show that there is in fact no incompatibility between, on the one hand, an action being caused or determined and, on the other hand, that action being a free action for which the agent may be held responsible. Freedom, it is argued, is opposed not to determinism or causal necessity but rather to *compulsion*. Free actions are those which are *caused by our desires or willings*. In these circumstances the agent is connected to his actions through his willings. Responsibility for action depends on the existence of some such causal link between the agent and his actions. Without any such causal link or connection between the agent and his actions it would be impossible to attribute the actions to the agent.[5] By contrast, an action which is unfree is brought about by "external" causes rather than by the agent's will. In these circumstances, the agent is forced or compelled to act and therefore he is not responsible for his actions.[6] In short, the compatibilist seeks to

---

5. Thus Stroud reports Hume's position as follows: "We only praise or blame someone for something *he* does. The action must be *his* action, not somebody else's, and it must not be something that merely happens to him but otherwise has no connection with him at all . . . But if an 'action' does not proceed from a man's character, wants, desires, motives, etc., then there is no connection between the 'action' and the man who is said to have done it" (*Hume*, p. 149; Stroud's emphasis).

6. "Freedom means the opposite of compulsion; a man is *free* if he does not act under *compulsion*, and he is compelled or unfree when he is hindered from without in the realization

establish that free action is to be distinguished from unfree actions, not by an *absence* of cause, but rather by a different *type* of cause.[7] We are responsible for our actions in virtue of the fact that it is our willings or desires which produce or bring about our actions.

So described, the "compulsion argument" involves two important conditions—one "positive" and the other "negative." The positive condition requires that a free or responsible action must be one to which the agent is "linked" or "connected" through his willings or desires. This condition is a positive requirement of freedom and responsibility insofar as in the absence of this requirement the agent cannot be said to produce or bring about his actions at all. That is to say, without the appropriate causal link between the agent and his actions such actions simply "happen to" or "befall" the agent: they are not *his*. The negative condition requires that a free or responsible action be one which was not compelled or constrained by "external" forces. This condition is "negative" in so far as it is concerned to establish that in the presence of such compelling or constraining external forces the agent cannot be said to be acting freely and, therefore, cannot be responsible for the action in question. In this way, according to the compatibilist, in order to determine whether or not the agent is acting freely we must first identify the *nature of the cause of his actions* (i.e., were his actions the product of his own will?). Clearly, then, the fundamental distinction drawn by the compulsion argument between causation and compulsion serves as the basis of the compatibilist's account of the relevant "positive" and "negative" conditions of freedom and responsibility. This general argument, whatever its merits or inadequacies, constitutes the first stage of the empiricist-compatibilist strategy.[8]

---

of his natural desires. Hence ... a man will be considered quite free and responsible if no such external compulsion is exerted upon him" (Schlick, "When is a Man Responsible?," sect. 4; Schlick's emphasis).

7. "It is not when my action has any cause at all, but only when it has a special sort of cause, that it is reckoned not to be free" (Ayer, "Freedom and Necessity," p. 21). Along these lines Paul Edwards explains the "Hume-Mill-Schlick theory" as follows: "In distinguishing between free and unfree actions we do not try to mark the presence or absence of causes but attempt to indicate the *kind* of causes that are present" (Edwards, "Hard and Soft Determinism," in S. Hook, ed., *Determinism and Freedom* [New York, 1961], p. 118; Edwards' emphasis). Similarly, Jonathan Bennett notes that for "both Hume and Schlick, the question of whether there is accountability in a given case depends upon *what* natural cause the action had" (*Kant's Dialectic* [Cambridge, 1974], p. 195; Bennett's emphasis).

8. There are, of course, numerous well-known objections to this argument as it stands. Perhaps the most important of these objections is that the argument does not provide us with an adequate account of what constitutes an ("external") compelling or constraining

The second stage of the compatibilist strategy, the regularity argument, was first put forward and developed by Hume (*Treatise*, II, iii, 1–2). Hume, according to the orthodox interpretation of his position, sought to reconstruct the overall compatibilist strategy by placing the compulsion argument on the foundation of the regularity theory of causation. The regularity theory maintains that the causal relation must be understood in terms of a regular succession or constant conjunction of like objects (i.e., objects resembling the cause followed by objects resembling the effect). Beyond this regularity we discover no further "tie" or "necessary connection" between cause and effect. That is to say considered on its own we can discover no "power," "force," or "agency" in *any* cause (*Treatise*, I, iii, 14). Hence, all that we can discover of causation as it exists "in the objects themselves" is constant conjunction.[9] Hume's successors in the empiricist tradition—however they may differ over points of detail—have generally accepted the basic tenets of Hume's regularity theory and have, following Hume, built it into their compatibilist position.

What is the significance of Hume's regularity theory of causation for the compatibilist position? It would appear that Hume's successors have interpreted the significance of the regularity argument for the compatibilist position largely in terms of Hume's suggestion that causation or necessity seems "to imply something of force, and violence, and constraint, of which we are not sensible" (*Treatise*, p. 407). In other words, traditional "metaphysical" theories of causation, it is suggested, have encouraged a fundamental confusion between the notion of an event being caused and that of an event being compelled. The source of this confusion lies with the misleading assumption, implicit in traditional metaphysical theories of causation, that a cause somehow compels or constrains its effect. On the basis of such an erroneous conception of causation many philosophers have arrived at the equally mistaken conclusion that there must be an incompatibility between determinism and freedom. The regularity theory of causation, it is argued, identifies and removes the source of this confusion in the free will dispute by way of challenging the deep-seated

---

cause. Lying behind this objection is the more fundamental concern that the compulsion argument presupposes a wholly inadequate understanding of the nature of excusing and mitigating considerations. This, however, is not an issue which is directly relevant to my present concerns and therefore I will not pursue it in this chapter. (See note 11 below.)

9. For a detailed account of Hume's views on causation and necessity see my "Hume's 'Two Definitions' of Cause and the Ontology of 'Double Existence,'" *Hume Studies*, vol. 10 (1984), 1–25.

assumption that there is something more to causation than mere constant conjunction or regular succession.

Clearly, as I have said, Hume's successors vary somewhat in the particular way in which they articulate the "regularity argument." They are, nevertheless, agreed on the fundamental strategy described above. We find, therefore, that Hume's effort to reconstruct the compatibilist strategy on the foundation of the regularity theory of causation has, over the past two centuries, become an integral part of the general compatibilist strategy.[10] The significance of the regularity argument for the empiricist-compatibilist strategy may be interpreted in terms of the "positive" and "negative" requirements of the compulsion argument. Free, responsible action, it is suggested, must be *both* uncompelled and caused (by the agent's willings). Traditional theories of causation, however, confuse or conflate causation and compulsion and thus generate an ineradicable conflict between these positive and negative requirements. It is, therefore, the great merit of the regularity argument that it shows how the positive and negative requirements of freedom and responsibility can be reconciled, and how the ("pseudo") conflict generated by traditional theories of causation can be overcome.

II

In presenting the compatibilist strategy I have shown that the regularity argument is intended to strengthen the compulsion argument by exposing and eliminating a source of potential confusion. That is to say, once we recognize that causation involves nothing more than regular succession or constant conjunction then, it is argued, we will be less tempted to assume erroneously that what is caused is somehow compelled or forced to occur. Compatibilists have made this point in a variety of ways and we can trace the argument back through the centuries. Ayer, for example, notes that the word "determinism" tends to suggest that "one event is somehow in the power of another, whereas the truth is merely that they are *factually correlated*" ("Freedom and Necessity," p. 22; my emphasis). One source of this confusion, says Ayer, "is the survival of an animistic conception of causality, in which all causal relationships are modelled on the example of one person's exercising authority over another" (ibid). In a similar vein, Schlick suggests that because we confuse "descriptive" laws (of nature)

---

10. See, for example, Ayer's remarks: "Freedom and Necessity," pp. 21–22.

with "prescriptive" laws (of society) we mistakenly confuse natural necessity with compulsion ("When is a Man Responsible?" sects. 2, 3, 4, and 7).
It is this confusion which encourages us to identify freedom with determinism and to regard it as being opposed to causality. Russell argues the
same point as follows:

> The subjective sense of freedom, sometimes alleged against deter-
> minism, has no bearing on the question whatever. The view that it
> has a bearing rests upon the belief that causes compel their effects, or
> that nature enforces obedience to its laws as governments do. These
> are mere anthropomorphic superstitions, due to the assimilation of
> causes with volitions and of natural laws with human edicts ... it is
> one of the demerits of the traditional theory of causality that it has
> created an artificial opposition between determinism and the free-
> dom of which we are introspectively conscious.
>
> "On the Notion of Cause," p. 206

According to Russell a volition "operates" when there is "some law in virtue of which a similar volition in rather similar circumstances will usually
be followed by what it wills" (ibid., p. 192; my emphasis).

The above remarks, it may be noted, leave us with the firm impression that were the causal relation to involve some stronger "bond" or
"union" than that of mere "uniformity of sequence" then causes would
indeed (somehow) compel or constrain their effects. This view of the matter is stated more explicitly by Mill. Mill suggests that people are reluctant
to accept that "there is nothing in causation but invariable, certain, and
unconditional sequence." He continues:

> There are few to whom mere constancy of succession appears a
> sufficiently stringent bond of union for so peculiar a relation as that
> of cause and effect. Even if the reason repudiates, the imagination
> retains, the feeling of some more intimate connection, of some
> peculiar tie or mysterious constraint exercised by the antecedent
> over the consequent. Now this it is which, considered as applying
> to the human will, conflicts with our consciousness and revolts our
> feelings. We are certain that in the case of our volitions, there is not
> this mysterious constraint. We know that we are not compelled, as
> by a magical spell, to obey any particular motive.
>
> *A System of Logic*, VI, ii, 2

On the basis of these remarks Mill proceeds to argue that a stronger conception of causation than that of mere regularity may lead us into full-
blown fatalism. That is to say, traditional theories of causation seem to
imply that a cause has some "irresistible" power over its effect. This leads
to the fatalistic conclusion that there is "no use in struggling against
it" (ibid., VI, ii, 3). The event in question "will happen however we may
strive to prevent it." Mill, like others in the empiricist-compatibilist tradition, maintains that an understanding of causation in terms of regularity
enables us to steer clear of these pitfalls.

What are we to make of this aspect of the compatibilist strategy?
Considered as an attempt to *strengthen* the compulsion argument the regularity argument, I suggest, must be deemed a failure. It suffers from two
closely related shortcomings. First, the regularity argument gives credence
to the view that if there were some stronger "bond" or "tie" between cause
and effect beyond that of mere regularity then causes would (somehow)
compel or constrain their effects. A close examination of the compulsion
argument, however, reveals that this assumption is itself confused. The distinction which is fundamental to the compatibilist position is that between
those actions which have external causes (i.e., compelled or constrained
actions) and those actions which have causes internal to the agent.[11] This
crucial distinction between actions that originate from the agent and those
that do not is not compromised by "metaphysical" (i.e., non-regularity)
views of causation. (Hobbes and Locke, for example, consistently adhere to
metaphysical accounts of causation without undermining their compatibilist positions.) What is relevant to whether an action was compelled or
not is the nature of the *cause*, not the nature of the *causal relation*. Nothing
about the metaphysical conception of cause when applied to human action
need suggest that we do not act according to our will and could not act
otherwise *if* we so willed. Clearly, therefore, proponents of the regularity
argument are mistaken when they suggest that metaphysical theories of
causation would pose a threat to the compulsion argument. To concede

---

11. Of course, notoriously, this sharp divide is difficult to maintain. Thus, for example, Ayer
allows ("Freedom and Necessity," p. 20) for psychologically compelled behavior (e.g., that of
a kleptomaniac). This concession, however, generates serious difficulties for the orthodox
compatibilist. It is no longer clear, for example, given this concession, just which "internal"
causes should be regarded as "constraining" or "compelling" and which should not. A useful
approach to this general issue, along somewhat different lines, may be found in Harry G.
Frankfurt, "Freedom of the Will and the Concept of a Person," reprinted in Watson, ed., *Free
Will*, pp. 81–95.

this point to the incompatibilist is to be confused about the very force or significance of the compulsion argument itself.

This brings us to the second and closely related shortcoming of the regularity argument. The regularity argument suggests that our (supposed) tendency to confuse causation with compulsion has its source in mistaken views regarding the nature of the causal relation. This, quite simply, makes the wrong point against the incompatibilist. The point at issue, as I have noted, concerns the nature of the cause, not the nature of the causal relation. If incompatibilists are confused about *this* issue then so too are proponents of the regularity argument. Confusion about the significance of the caused/compelled distinction cannot be eliminated by trying to describe "non-compelling" causal relations in terms of regularity or constant conjunction. Causal relations, as such, are neither compelling or non-compelling. It is the nature of the *cause* (i.e., the object) which determines whether or not a given action was compelled. In this way, it seems clear that the strategy of the regularity argument is fundamentally misconceived. It involves, ironically enough, a failure to grasp the significance of the compulsion argument. We must conclude, therefore, that it is not obvious that the regularity view of causation strengthens the compulsion argument. On the contrary, as it stands it seems clear that traditional theories of causation pose no threat to the compulsion argument, and the regularity theory, therefore, has no claim to be especially congenial to the compatibilist position.

III

In the foregoing section I have argued that the regularity argument does not strengthen the compatibilist position. In this section I will argue that the regularity argument in fact weakens the compatibilist position by undermining the metaphysical foundation of the compulsion argument.[12] According to the compulsion argument it is a fundamental requirement of freedom and responsibility that the agent caused or determined his actions. Without this causal link or connection between agent and action, as has been noted, the action could not be attributed to the agent. In other words, the existence of a causal connection between the agent and his

---

12. For a related discussion, which is concerned primarily with the *interpretation* of Hume's compatibilist position, see my "On the Naturalism of Hume's 'Reconciling Project'," *Mind*, vol. 92 (1983), pp. 593–600.

action is, for the orthodox compatibilist, essential to the "positive" requirement of freedom and responsibility. The regularity argument, I would
suggest, deals a severe blow to this metaphysical requirement of the compatibilist position.

The damage which the regularity argument inflicts upon the compulsion argument varies somewhat depending upon how we interpret the
regularity argument. On one interpretation it straightforwardly torpedoes
the compulsion argument. On another interpretation it generates some
rather awkward—though perhaps not fatal—difficulties for the compulsion argument. More specifically, we may interpret the regularity argument as being either "skeptical" or "revisionary" in nature. According to
the skeptical interpretation, the regularity argument should be understood as seeking to establish that there are no causal "connections," "ties,"
or "bonds" of *any sort* between cause and effect. It is, on this account,
a mistake to conclude that there exists any power, agency or force in a
cause whereby it "produces" its effects. All that we can discover is uniform sequence—one event being *followed* by another event. This regularity enables us to infer one event from another but we must not allow our
"anthropomorphic superstitions" to lead us into the erroneous conclusion
that the cause possesses some kind of power or force whereby it somehow
"brings about" its effect. The remarks which Hume and Russell make on
this issue seem, quite clearly, to accord with this "skeptical" interpretation
of the regularity argument.[13]

The regularity argument, understood in terms of the skeptical interpretation, cannot, I suggest, be rendered consistent with the metaphysical
requirements of the compulsion argument. That is to say, if it is true that
all we discover when we look at the causal relation is "uniform sequence"
or "regular succession," and that we discover no "bond" or "tie" between
cause and effect, nor discover any "power" or "agency" in any cause, then
it must follow that *no cause* can, strictly speaking, be said to "produce"
or "bring about" its effect. Clearly, however, if we accept this (skeptical)
account of the causal relation then it follows that no agent (i.e., person)
"produces" or "brings about" his *actions*. Nor is any agent "connected" or

---

13. In a number of very important respects Russell's skepticism about causation is far more
radical than that of Hume's. Indeed, in suggesting that we should abandon the "traditional
theory of causality," Russell *includes* the regularity theory itself. In his view we should replace
concern with regular sequences of events with a "theory of functional relations." It may be
argued, however, that Russell's view of causation can be understood in terms of the regularity theory. On this issue see J. L. Mackie, *The Cement of the Universe* (Oxford, 1973), Ch. 6.

"linked" to his actions through his willings. These metaphysical bonds have been dispensed with by the regularity theory. In these circumstances, therefore, given the stated requirements of the compulsion argument, there can be no free and responsible actions. The skeptical interpretation of the regularity argument suggests that the "positive" requirement of the compulsion argument (i.e., that an agent must be "connected" with his actions through his willings) simply cannot be met.

In response to this criticism defenders of the regularity argument may argue that this skeptical interpretation—however faithful it may be to Hume's and Russell's intentions—is too stringent and fails to make the most of this wider aspect of the compatibilist strategy. The revisionary account of the regularity argument maintains that regularity or constant conjunction is *constitutive* of the causal connection which holds between cause and effect. On this interpretation free agents do possess the power to produce or bring about their actions, but this relationship between an agent's willings and his actions must be understood in terms of regularity or a uniform sequence of events. There exists no *further* bond or union between agent and action. This revisionary account of the regularity argument succeeds in removing the immediate danger which the skeptical interpretation generates for the compulsion argument.

There remain, however, at least two further difficulties to be considered. First, while we grant that the revisionary version of the regularity argument is not *intended* to generate skeptical doubts about the sufficiency of the causal connection between agent and action it may nevertheless lead us in precisely this direction. (This is a point which Mill, for example, as has been noted, frankly acknowledges.) More specifically, it may be argued that the relation of one event simply "being followed by" another event cannot possibly suffice as an adequate ground upon which to *attribute an action to the agent*. Surely, we may ask, the compulsion argument requires something stronger than this? A mere regularity between events, whereby one type of event is uniformly "followed by" another type of event seems to lack the metaphysical "cement" or force which is required by the compulsion argument.[14] The compatibilist position placed on the foundation of the regularity argument (so interpreted), seems to drain away the force

---

14. In other words, the relation of one event being regularly "followed by" another event may be *called* a "connection" between two such events—but does such a relation *constitute* the sort of connection which we require?

or power which connects an agent with his actions. Given this account of causation, it may be argued, we are left with an impoverished and some-what flimsy account of human freedom and responsibility. It is in this way that skeptical doubts may start to creep back in and gradually undermine the foundations of the compulsion argument.

Second, even if we accept the "revisionary" account of the regularity argument—and refrain from indulging in skeptical anxieties—it still seems clear that the regularity argument serves only to *weaken* the compulsion argument. That is to say, even if we grant that the regularity argument, so interpreted, does not entirely *remove* the metaphysical "cement" between agent and action it most certainly loosens it.[15] The whole weight of the compulsion argument rests with the demand that an agent must be tied to or connected with his actions, that the agent must have brought about or produced his actions (if they were truly free and responsible actions). By watering down the strength of the causal connection, and the causal power of agents, the regularity argument appears to erode the very foundation of the compulsion argument. So interpreted the regularity argument may not collapse these foundations but it certainly suggests that they are less "solid" and secure than the early adherents of the compatibilist position had supposed. A world in which every event is entirely "loose and separate" from every other event, and in which events have no tighter bond or union than that of one following another, is a world in which the compulsion argument begins to lose its grip. By weakening the causal fabric in this way the regularity argument inevitably undermines the overall compatibilist position. In short, even on the most generous interpretation, the regularity argument presents awkward difficulties for the compulsion argument and thus weakens rather than strengthens the compatibilist strategy.[16]

---

15. "So that, upon the whole, there appears not, throughout all nature any one instance of connexion which is conceivable by us. *All events seem entirely loose and separate.* One event follows another; but we can never observe any tie between them" (Hume, *An Enquiry Concerning Human Understanding*, sect. VII, Pt. 2 [Selby-Bigge, ed., p. 74]; my emphasis).

16. Arguably, *some* of these difficulties can be met if we are willing to adopt the sort of highly revisionary ("forward-looking") account of responsibility which Schlick describes ("When is a Man Responsible?" sect. 5). Schlick recommends that we interpret responsibility entirely in terms of the efficaciousness of punishment. Suffice it to note, however, that this entire approach to responsibility encounters a number of well-known difficulties. See, for example, C. A. Campbell's classic discussion of Schlick's views in "Is 'Freewill' a Pseudo-Problem?," *Mind*, vol. 60 (1951), pp. 446–65 (esp. sect. III), and Bennett, *Kant's Dialectic*, sect. 63.

IV

By way of conclusion let me, first, summarize the points which I have been especially concerned to establish in this chapter and, second, make a few brief remarks about their wider significance. According to the regularity argument traditional theories of causation have given rise to a conflict between what I have described as the "positive" and "negative" requirements of freedom and responsibility. The regularity argument seeks to overcome this conflict by developing a conception of causation which involves no suggestion of compulsion or constraint. This entire strategy, I have argued, is misguided. In particular, I have argued that traditional theories of causation generate no such conflict. The view that they do so involves a failure to appreciate a point which is crucial to the compulsion argument: namely, that the distinction between action which is free and action which is compelled must be understood in terms of the *nature of the cause of the action* (rather than in terms of the causal relation). In this way, the regularity argument fails to identify the real source of the incompatibilist's (supposed) "confusion" because the regularity argument is itself confused on this issue. By way of its misguided effort to articulate a "non-compelling" mode of causation the regularity argument, ironically enough, produces its own difficulties for the compulsion argument. The regularity argument, by weakening—if not removing—the causal "cement" between agent and action, tends to undermine and erode the metaphysical foundation of the traditional compatibilist position.

The final irony, therefore, is that the regularity argument not only fails to strengthen the compatibilist position but actually generates some rather awkward and embarrassing difficulties for the compatibilist and to this extent it brings the entire strategy into question. Accordingly, we may conclude that the regularity theory of causation, contrary to the opinion of several of the leading figures of the empiricist tradition, is not a particularly secure or congenial foundation upon which to rest the compulsion argument.

By way of criticism, it may be suggested—contrary to Searle's remarks cited above—that the empiricist-compatibilist strategy is now rather "dated" and therefore the conclusions which we have reached in this chapter are of limited *contemporary* philosophical interest. In answer to this criticism I would like to make three points:

(1) As I indicated in my introductory remarks, even if the empiricist-compatibilist position is no longer the *dominant* position it once was, it

certainly continues to command some degree of support and influence among contemporary philosophers. Many "empirically minded philosophers" continue to embrace *both* the regularity theory of causation and some variant of the compatibilist strategy associated with Hobbes and Hume. Moreover, they regard these two positions as complementary or mutually supporting. Clearly the conclusions reached in this chapter cannot be ignored by philosophers of this general persuasion.

(2) The *historical* significance of the empiricist-compatibilist strategy is, I take it, not in dispute. Moreover, it seems equally clear that this strategy continues to play an important role in initiating students to philosophy of the "free will problem." To this extent the empiricist-compatibilist strategy continues to play an important role in shaping the very way that we think about, or frame, the free will problem. Given this, it is incumbent on those philosophers who reject or dismiss this strategy to identify and articulate their *reasons* for doing so. Indeed, this is, obviously, a precondition for making progress on this subject.

(3) The points which I have been concerned to establish in this chapter are, I believe, of wider significance for the free will problem. It is a deep assumption of the empiricist-compatibilist strategy—as it has been developed since Hume—that the key to resolving this dispute lies with arriving at a more adequate account of the nature of the causal relation. The motivation behind this strategy can perhaps be best understood in terms of the framework of the dilemma of determinism. That is to say, the regularity argument purports to show that we may find a middle way between, on the one hand, "metaphysical" necessity, understood in terms of compulsion, and, on the other hand, chance understood as the absence of causation and necessity. In other words, we may interpret the regularity argument as an attempt to show that the dilemma of determinism, as it is usually conceived, misconstrues our alternatives.

This general approach to the free will problem is not unique to the empiricist-compatibilist strategy. In recent years several defenders of the incompatibilist position have suggested that an adequate solution to the free will problem requires that we develop an account of causation which involves no suggestion of *necessitation*.[17] The motivation behind this

---

17. Arguments of this nature have been put forward by, for example, Peter Van Inwagen (*An Essay on Free Will* [Oxford, 1983], pp. 138–42), and, in considerably more detail, by Richard

strategy is, once again, to find a middle-way between the horns of necessity and chance. In important respects, therefore, the general strategy remains the same: it is hoped that we may find an acceptable "solution" to the free will problem by way of developing a suitably amended account of the nature of the causal relation whereby we may slip through the horns of the dilemma. The repeated failure of this sort of project suggests that there is something fundamentally flawed about this general strategy. In light of these considerations it may be argued that no "solution" to these problems is likely to be discovered along these lines and that we should, therefore, look for an alternative approach to these problems.

Granted that we should turn our attention away from concern with the nature of the causal relation and the general framework of the dilemma of determinism what, if any, alternative presents itself? It is beyond the scope of this chapter to describe or map out any alternative approach. Suffice it to note, however, that at least one alternative approach to the problem of responsibility may be found in another, much neglected, aspect of Hume's "reconciling project": namely, in his discussion of the role that moral sentiment plays in human life. The significant features of this strategy have recently been restated and further articulated by P. F. Strawson in his well-known paper "Freedom and Resentment."[18] According to this account, responsibility must be understood in terms of our natural, psychological reactions to the moral qualities and character traits of our fellow human beings. That is to say, we find that the attitudes and intentions of other people towards ourselves or others inevitably generate emotional responses or reactions in us (i.e., moral sentiments). On the basis of these observations it is argued that responsibility must be viewed as a "given" of our human nature. In order to understand the nature and circumstances of responsibility, therefore, it is essential that we develop a clearer understanding of the role that moral sentiment plays in human life.

Sorabji (*Necessity Cause and Blame* [London, 1980], Parts I and V). I have expressed doubts about this alternative strategy in "Sorabji and the Dilemma of Determinism," *Analysis*, vol. 44 (1984), pp. 166–72.

18. Reprinted in Watson, ed., *Free Will*, pp. 59–80. See my "The Naturalism of Hume's Reconciling Project' " for an interpretation of Hume's position which accords with Strawson's approach.

Whether or not an alternative approach to the problem of responsibility can be successfully constructed along these ("naturalistic") lines remains to be seen. My immediate concerns in this chapter lie elsewhere. That is, throughout this chapter it has been my particular objective to show that whatever merits are to be found in the traditional empiricist-compatibilist strategy they do not rest with the efforts of its proponents to place that strategy on the foundation of the regularity theory of causation.[19]

19. Versions of this chapter have been read to audiences at the University of British Columbia and Simon Fraser University. I am grateful to those who attended for their helpful comments. I am particularly grateful to Don Brown, Ed Levy and Tom Patton.

PART II

Responsibility, Skepticism, and Moral Sentiment

3

*Strawson's Way of Naturalizing Responsibility**

Where Nature thus determines us, we have an original non-
rational commitment which sets the bounds within which,
or the stage upon which, reason can effectively operate.

P. F. STRAWSON, *Skepticism and Naturalism*, p. 39

IN THIS CHAPTER I am concerned with a central strand of Strawson's well-known and highly influential essay "Freedom and Resentment."[1] One of Strawson's principal objectives in this work is to refute or discredit the views of the "Pessimist." The Pessimist, as Strawson understands him (or her), claims that the truth of the thesis of determinism would render the attitudes and practices associated with moral responsibility incoherent and unjustified. Given this, the Pessimist claims that if determinism is true, then we must abandon or suspend these attitudes and practices altogether. Against the Pessimist, Strawson argues that no reasoning of any sort could lead us to abandon or suspend our "reactive attitudes." That is to say, according to Strawson responsibility is a "given" of human

* I would like to thank Dick Sikora, Jim Dybikowski, and especially Jerry Cohen for helpful comments and suggestions concerning this article, and also Jonathan Bennett and Peter Remnant, who provided stout defense for Strawson's position. I am grateful to the editor and reviewers of *Ethics* for further comments and suggestions concerning the final draft of this chapter. Work on this chapter was done while I held a Mellon Fellowship at Stanford University (1989–90) and a (Canadian) Social Science and Humanities Research Council research grant (1990–91).

1. P. F. Strawson, "Freedom and Resentment," reprinted in *Freedom and Resentment and Other Essays* (London: Methuen, 1974), pp. 1–25, and also in Gary Watson, ed., *Free Will* (Oxford: Oxford University Press, 1982), pp. 59–80. References to this chapter will be to the Strawson edition and will be abbreviated in these notes and in the text as FR. I will also refer to P. F. Strawson, *Skepticism and Naturalism* (London: Methuen, 1985), abbreviated as SN.

life and society—something which we are inescapably committed to.[2] In this article I will argue that Strawson's reply to the Pessimist is seriously flawed. More specifically, I argue that Strawson fails to distinguish two very different forms or modes of naturalism and that he is constrained by the nature of his own objectives (i.e., the refutation of Pessimism) to embrace the stronger and far less plausible form of naturalism. On this basis I conclude that while there is something to be said for Strawson's general approach to these matters, we nevertheless cannot naturalize responsibility along the specific lines that he suggests.[3]

I

Strawson develops his analysis of the nature and conditions of moral responsibility on the basis of what he takes to be a "commonplace" observation: the attitudes and intentions which individuals manifest to each other are of great importance to human beings, and we react to each other accordingly (FR, pp. 5–6). Strawson claims that perplexity has been generated on the subject of moral responsibility largely because philosophers have been unable or unwilling to recognize or acknowledge the significance of "reactive attitudes and feelings" in this sphere. (Hereafter, I will

2. This is a theme which Strawson emphasizes repeatedly, both in "Freedom and Resentment" and in his more recent work *Skepticism and Naturalism*. Whatever we may think of this claim, it cannot be dismissed as an unnecessary or inessential aspect of Strawson's general position. On the contrary, as I will show, it plays a crucial role in Strawson's effort to refute or discredit the views of the Pessimist. In a highly sympathetic discussion of "Freedom and Resentment" Jonathan Bennett has distanced himself, in this respect, from Strawson's position. Bennett claims that Strawson places too much emphasis on the claim "that we could not possibly relinquish all reactive feelings" (Jonathan Bennett, "Accountability," in *Philosophical Subjects*, ed. Zak van Straaten [Oxford: Oxford University Press, 1980], p. 30). Whatever Bennett's views on this subject may be, however, Strawson does not show any sign of withdrawing any emphasis on this claim. See, e.g., Strawson's remarks to the contrary in his reply to Bennett: "What I was above all concerned to stress . . ." (P. F. Strawson, "Replies," in van Straaten, ed., p. 265). More critical discussions of Strawson's views, closer to my own position in this article, can be found in A. J. Ayer, "Free Will and Rationality," in van Straaten, ed., pp. 1–13; and Thomas Nagel, *The View from Nowhere* (Oxford: Oxford University Press, 1986), chap. 7, sec. 4.

3. On my interpretation, the core of Strawson's naturalism in regard to responsibility is contained in the claim that moral responsibility is in some way a "given" or inescapable feature of human life and existence—and it is this claim that I am especially concerned with. However, the naturalistic approach may be described, in more general terms, as involving two closely related principles. First, it insists upon an empirical, descriptive approach to this issue—one which has an informed and plausible moral psychology. Second, the naturalistic approach emphasizes the role of emotion or feeling in this sphere. Clearly, the narrower claim has its foundations in the more general principles guiding the naturalistic approach.

refer simply to "reactive attitudes.") More specifically, it is our reactive attitudes, Strawson claims, which are essential to, or constitutive of, the whole framework or fabric of moral responsibility. It seems clear, then, that we must consider the arguments of the Pessimist from this general perspective.

There are two different claims which are constitutive of the Pessimist's outlook.[4] The Pessimist maintains, first, that if the thesis of determinism is true, then we have reason to reject and repudiate the (established) attitudes and practices associated with moral responsibility on the ground that they are incoherent and unjustified. Beyond this, the Pessimist supposes that if we have reason to suspend or abandon the attitudes and practices associated with moral responsibility, then we are, psychologically or practically speaking, capable of doing so. Strawson rejects both Pessimist claims. In reply to the Pessimist he weaves together two quite distinct lines of argument, each of which corresponds to the two key claims of the Pessimist noted above. I will distinguish these lines of argument as the "rationalistic strategy" and the "naturalistic strategy." Strawson believes that his anti-Pessimist strategies, although independent of each other, are nevertheless consistent and mutually supportive. I will show that their relations with each other are not as straightforward as Strawson supposes.

Let us consider these strategies in more detail. The Pessimist believes that if determinism is true, excusing considerations will (somehow) apply to all human action and thus hold universally. It follows that in these circumstances no individual is ever responsible for anything. Strawson's rationalistic strategy counters by way of an analysis of excusing considerations. Under what circumstances, he asks, do we "modify or mollify" our reactive attitudes or withhold them altogether? There are, he maintains, two different sorts of excusing consideration (FR, pp. 7–9). The first sort—which I will refer to as "specific" considerations—in no way suggests that the agent is (either temporarily or permanently) an inappropriate object of reactive attitudes or one of whom it is not reasonable to demand some degree of goodwill and regard. Rather, in these cases (e.g., accident, ignorance, etc.) "the fact of injury [is] quite consistent with the agent's attitude

---

4. There is, of course, a large literature defending the Pessimist outlook—particularly from a libertarian perspective. The classic statement in this century is given by C. A. Campbell: "Is 'Freewill' a Pseudo-Problem?" reprinted in *Free Will and Determinism,* ed. Bernard Berofsky (New York: Harper & Row, 1966), pp. 112–35. Strawson's asides concerning "contra-causal freedom" suggest that he has Campbell primarily in mind; cf. FR, p. 24, with Campbell's remark that "moral responsibility implies a contra-causal type of freedom" (p. 126).

and intentions being just what we demand they should be." By contrast, the second sort of excusing consideration—which I will refer to as "global" considerations—invites us to withdraw entirely our reactive attitudes in regard to the agent on the ground that the individual is not one from whom we can make the usual demand of goodwill. Such individuals may be placed in abnormal circumstances (e.g., stressed, drugged, etc.) or, more important, they may be either psychologically abnormal or morally underdeveloped. In situations such as these we must adopt what Strawson describes as the "objective attitude."

> To adopt the objective attitude to another human being is to see him, perhaps, as an object of social policy; as a subject for what, in a wide range of sense, might be called treatment; as something ... to be managed or handled or cured or trained. ... *But it cannot include the range of reactive feelings and attitudes which belong to involvement or participation with others in inter-personal human relationships.*
>
> FR, *p. 9; my emphasis*

It is important to be very clear about how the objective attitude relates to excusing considerations. The following distinction is especially important. (*a*) Where excusing considerations of the second sort apply ("abnormality," etc.) we must—that is, we are rationally and morally required to—adopt the objective attitude (FR, pp. 9–11 and SN, pp. 39–40). In other words, as Strawson's rationalistic strategy would have it, there are circumstances in which the objective attitude is not merely an option for us, regarding certain individuals but it is, rather, demanded of us (at least, insofar as we are "civilized"; cf. FR, pp. 11–12).[5] (*b*) There are other circumstances, it is argued, when the objective attitude is an available option, which we may choose to adopt if we wish, though we are not required to do so. That is to say, the objective attitude may sometimes be adopted even when we are dealing with "the normal and mature" because we want, for example, to use it as a "refuge from the strains of involvement" or an "aid to policy" (FR, pp. 10, 11, 12, 17; and SN, p. 34). However, in these cases (i.e., circumstances where we are dealing with normal adults) there are strict limits to the extent to which we can adopt the objective attitude. More specifically,

5. Strawson, it should be noted, speaks of the objective attitude as being a *consequence* of viewing the agent as one in respect of whom global excusing considerations apply (FR, p. 12). This indicates the strength of the demand that we withdraw reactive attitudes in these circumstances.

being human, Strawson says, "we cannot *in the normal case,* do this for long or altogether" (FR, p. 10; my emphasis).

In what way are Strawson's observations concerning excusing considerations supposed to refute the Pessimist? Strawson maintains that nothing about the thesis of determinism implies that we always act accidentally, or in ignorance, or without forethought. Nor does the thesis suggest that we are all (somehow) rendered psychologically abnormal or morally undeveloped. In short, considerations of determinism, however they are interpreted, do not, as such, provide us with any reason to modify or suspend our reactive attitudes. The grounds on which we do suspend or alter our reactive attitudes are of a wholly distinct and independent nature (FR, pp. 10–11, 18). We have, accordingly, no reason whatsoever to suspend or abandon our reactive attitudes entirely even if the thesis of determinism is true. This is the essence of Strawson's rationalistic reply to the Pessimist.

The rationalistic strategy does not, by itself, convey the real force or power of Strawson's position. The most interesting and most controversial aspect of Strawson's reply to the Pessimist is contained in the naturalistic strategy. The heart of the naturalistic strategy is the claim that it is psychologically impossible to suspend or abandon our reactive attitudes entirely. Our "human commitment" to the whole framework of reactive attitudes is so "thoroughgoing and deeply rooted" in our nature that it is "practically inconceivable" (though perhaps not self-contradictory) that we should simply "give them up" or entirely abandon them. A sustained objectivity of attitude to all people through time "does not seem to be something of which human beings would be capable, *even if some general truth were a theoretical ground for it*" (FR, pp. 11–12; my emphasis). Our "commitment" to reactive attitudes is, on this account, insulated from skeptical doubts by our inherent nature or constitution. It is, therefore, "useless" and "idle" to ask whether or not it would be rational to suspend or abandon our reactive attitudes if the thesis of determinism is true. On any interpretation, no such option is available to us. If reason were to point us in this direction, Strawson argues, we would be constitutionally incapable of following its lead. Clearly, then, we cannot expect to follow reason in an area where it is nature that must be our guide (FR, pp. 18, 23).[6]

6. The same themes are pressed by Strawson with, perhaps, even greater vigor in *Skepticism and Naturalism.* Arguments and counterarguments concerning whether it would be rational for us to suspend the whole framework of our reactive attitudes (given the truth of some general metaphysical thesis) are both, equally, "inefficacious and idle." Such arguments are

Contrary to what Strawson seems to suppose, there are, I suggest, significant strains between his two anti-Pessimist strategies. That is to say, on the face of it, the naturalistic strategy appears to imply that the rationalistic strategy, considered as a response to the Pessimist, is fundamentally mistaken or misguided. To reason with the Pessimist, to endeavor to meet his arguments with counterarguments, is, according to the naturalistic strategy, to share the Pessimist's mistaken views about the nature of our commitment to reactive attitudes. That is, insofar as the rationalist strategy is understood as an effort to show that we have no reason to suspend or abandon our reactive attitudes (if the thesis of determinism is true), it suggests that without some adequate philosophical or rational defense our reactive attitudes may indeed (have to) be abandoned altogether. From the point of view of the naturalistic strategy, such an approach is wholly mistaken. This observation suggests that something has gone amiss in Strawson's twofold reply to the Pessimist. A more detailed analysis of Strawson's specific arguments will reveal where the trouble lies.

II

Lying at the heart of Strawson's naturalistic strategy is, I have argued, the claim that it is psychologically impossible altogether to suspend or abandon our reactive attitudes (i.e., such reactions are an inescapable feature of human life). This claim is, of course, intimately bound up with the related but distinct claim that responsibility must be understood or interpreted in terms of our emotional reactions or responses to the attitudes and intentions which we manifest to one another. Strawson speaks of "reactive attitudes and feelings" but he points out that the phrase "moral sentiments" would be a good name for the network of emotions that he is concerned with (FR, p. 24). When we recognize the parallels between our reactive attitudes and other emotions, then it seems that much of what Strawson is claiming falls into place. The fact that the whole framework of reactive attitudes "neither calls for nor permits, an external 'rational'

---

beside the point because our reactive attitudes are "neither shaken by skeptical argument nor reinforced by rational counter-argument" (SN, p. 39). In other words, reason simply does not operate at this level of moral life. In respect of these matters, Strawson claims to follow "Hume the naturalist against Hume the skeptic." "According to Hume the naturalist," Strawson says, "skeptical doubts are not to be met by argument. *They are simply to be neglected*" (SN, pp. 12–14, 38–39; my emphasis).

justification" is easily understood once we recognize that the reactive attitudes (or moral sentiments) are simply a species of emotion. No species or type of emotion requires an external rational justification. Nor
is there any question of us suspending, abandoning, or giving up the
various emotions (e.g., love, hate, fear, grief, etc.) of which we are susceptible. Within the framework of these emotions there may be, as Strawson
suggests, considerable scope for criticism, modification, redirection, and
justification. Clearly, however, "questions of justification are internal to
the structure [of any particular species of emotion] or relate to modifications internal to it." It is, as Strawson suggests, useless to ask whether it
would or would not be rational to "suspend" a particular species or type of
emotion. Someone who presses such a question reveals that he or she has
failed to grasp the fact that our "commitment" to a given kind of emotion
is simply founded upon human nature. Further, someone who presses
this sort of question reveals that he has failed to grasp the role which
reason plays in justifying our emotions. Our questioner has, as Strawson
puts it, "over-intellectualized" the facts and, consequently, his whole line
of questioning proceeds from presuppositions which are themselves seriously mistaken.

Consider, for example, the emotion of fear.[7] When we are afraid, there
are many considerations which may be brought to our attention which
will "modify or mollify" this emotion (i.e., particular instances or given
tokens of this emotion). Sometimes, for example, we may recognize, in
the light of new information, that our being afraid is unjustified or unreasonable. At other times, we may recognize that we actually have good
reason for being afraid. Clearly, then, we all recognize in day-to-day life
that this emotion may be deemed reasonable or unreasonable, justified
or unjustified, depending on the circumstances. Thus, on any particular
occasion, if relevant considerations are brought to our attention, we may
either cease to be afraid or become afraid. Beyond this, however, the question of justifying the fact that we are susceptible to this species of emotion
does not arise. The whole framework of the emotion of fear, obviously,
comes with our human nature. Nor is there any question of us giving a
reason for the fact that this species of emotion is "retained." We no more
need to, or can, justify the fact that we are susceptible of fear than we need
to, or can, justify the fact that the human being is born with a heart and

7. The analogy between reactive attitudes and fear is suggested by Strawson; see his "Replies,"
p. 265.

two kidneys.[8] In short, an appreciation of the parallels between reactive attitudes and other emotions provides considerable support for the view that reactive attitudes require no external, rational justification and are, at least in some sense, a given of our human nature.[9]

Strawson, as I have indicated, believes that these naturalistic observations constitute an effective way of refuting or discrediting Pessimism. I believe that he is mistaken about this. Consider, again, the parallels between reactive attitudes and the emotion of fear. Suppose that we encounter a pessimist with respect to fear—the counterpart of the Pessimist with respect to reactive attitudes. There are, I suggest, two very different sorts of pessimism which we may be presented with. The first, type-pessimism, focuses on the supposed need for an (external, rational) justification for the fact that we are susceptible or liable to fear. Having failed to identify any satisfactory justification of this nature, the fear-type-pessimist maintains that we can and must free ourselves of this (irrational) disposition to fear. The appropriate response to this mode of pessimism is provided, in general terms, by the naturalistic argument or observations outlined above. Let us refer to this response as type-naturalism. Type-naturalism claims that our liability to fear is natural to humans and requires no general justification of any sort. It is not possible for us to disengage from fear at this level.

8. Consider what may happen if we fail to grasp this point: namely, that the emotion of fear requires no external rational justification. More than likely, some philosopher (e.g., a "one-eyed utilitarian") will suggest that this emotion is justified by its social utility. Without fear, it may be argued, man would not respond so effectively in dangerous situations and this would threaten our species. Thus, it may be suggested that this emotion can be "justified" in terms of considerations regarding our individual well-being and the interests of human society. It is, I think, obvious that this line of reasoning is mistaken. Were we to discover, e.g., that the emotion of fear is of little value to man, we could hardly reason ourselves into "abandoning" this emotion altogether (although, no doubt, we would do our best to inhibit it).

9. The inclination to justify the fact that we are susceptible to various species or types of emotion is perhaps encouraged by certain theological doctrines. In particular, once it is assumed that God made humans the way we are with some reason or purpose in mind, then it is not entirely unnatural to ask for a general, external rationale for the emotion in question. Thus Bishop Butler, e.g., in his sermon "Upon Resentment," asks: Why, for what end, is "so harsh and turbulent" a passion as resentment "given" to man? Butler argues that the passion, "as implanted in our nature by God," has a good influence "upon the affairs of the world." Men, he suggests, "are plainly restrained from injuring their fellow-creatures by fear of resentment; and it is very happy that they are so, when they would not be restrained by a principle of virtue" (Joseph Butler, *Fifteen Sermons* [London: Bell & Sons, 1949], p. 131, sermon 8). The important point here is that while it, perhaps, makes some sense to ask for God's justification for "giving" man some species of emotion, it is senseless for men to demand of each other that they justify their own emotional make-up as if they created themselves *ex nihilo*.

The fear-pessimist may reply, at this point, that his concerns have been misunderstood. The fear-pessimist should be interpreted as claiming only that given our circumstances we are never justified in being afraid (i.e., we are never justified in entertaining any tokens of fear). This claim may be in itself highly implausible, but it cannot be dismissed on the ground that it commits the fear-pessimist to type-pessimism (i.e., the demand for external, rational justifications, etc.). On the contrary, the fear-pessimist, on this account, insists on being interpreted as a token-pessimist and rightly points out that this is consistent with being a type-naturalist. In other words, it is at least consistent to maintain that while we may be (naturally) prone or liable to fear, we are nevertheless capable of altogether ceasing to feel or experience fear if and when we judge that, given our circumstances, this emotion is never justified.

What, then, is the appropriate (naturalistic) reply to this distinct form of pessimism? The most obvious strategy is to establish that, contrary to what has been claimed, we regularly and inevitably encounter circumstances in which fear is entirely appropriate or reasonable and, hence, feelings or experiences of fear will continue to be an inescapable part of human life. It is important to note, however, that this reply turns, crucially, on the claim that we do regularly and inevitably encounter the relevant or appropriate circumstances or conditions required to render fear reasonable or appropriate. The naturalist of a Strawsonian disposition may regard such a response as conceding too much to the fear-pessimist. Accordingly, a stronger line may be pursued. It may be argued that no reasoning of any sort could ever lead us to cease altogether entertaining or feeling this emotion. That is to say, on this strong naturalistic account, it is claimed that no reasoning or theoretical considerations of any sort can prevent us entirely from having or experiencing tokens of fear. Whatever considerations are brought to our attention regarding our circumstances—whatever reason may suggest to us—we will nevertheless continue to experience fear as an active force in our lives. No matter what arguments the fear-token-pessimist may present us with in an effort to show us that fear is never in order or called for, the fact is that we will continue to feel and experience fear. Nature, according to the token-naturalist, insulates us from the skeptical arguments of the token-pessimist no less than it insulates us from the skeptical arguments of the type-pessimist. We do not need to reason against token-pessimism any more than we need to reason against type-pessimism. Fear is natural to human beings not only in the sense that we are inescapably liable to this emotion but in the further, stronger, sense that we will inescapably or inevitably continue to entertain or feel this emotion, whatever reason suggests to us.

In respect of fear-pessimism, both type- and token-pessimism are equally implausible—but they are implausible for very different reasons. Type-pessimism, as I have suggested, misrepresents the way in which our disposition to fear is embedded in our human nature. There is no scope for skeptical anxieties at this level. Things are very different, however, with regard to token-pessimism. What is implausible about token-pessimism is the claim that circumstances are never such that fear is in order or justified. Clearly, we have good reason to be skeptical about this claim. Note, however, that if the token-pessimist were right about this, then it is not implausible to suggest that in these circumstances we should cease, and are capable of altogether ceasing, to entertain or feel (tokens of) fear. From this perspective it seems evident that the token-naturalist (unlike the type-naturalist) puts forward the wrong sort of reply to his pessimist counterpart. More specifically, the token-naturalist, in an effort to discredit the token-pessimist, makes claims that seem suspect in point of fact and which, in any case, do nothing to lift or remove the wholly legitimate concerns of the token-pessimist (i.e., that in the circumstances fear is inappropriate and uncalled for). The claims advanced are suspect in point of fact because it is far from obvious—indeed, it seems simply untrue—that we are constitutionally incapable of entirely ceasing to entertain or feel fear in circumstances where we believe that it is never appropriate or called for. Similarly, the claims advanced by the token-naturalist do nothing to lift or remove the (wholly legitimate) concerns of the token-pessimist because they do not even address the justificatory issue which is the focus of the token-pessimist's concerns.

The parallels between pessimism in respect of fear and pessimism in respect of reactive attitudes are, I believe, quite straightforward. The crucial questions are: What sort of naturalism does Strawson embrace? and—on the other side of the same coin—What sort of pessimism is he trying to discredit? Given our analysis of fear-pessimism it seems clear that Strawson's position is much more plausible if he is interpreted as a type-naturalist who is seeking to discredit type-pessimism in respect of reactive attitudes. Much of what Strawson says suggests that this is how he understands his own position (insofar as he draws the distinction at all). On this view of things the Pessimist who is the target of Strawson's remarks in "Freedom and Resentment" is a type-pessimist—one who believes that if determinism is true, then we are not justified in being disposed or prone to reactive attitudes and that we must, therefore (somehow) rid ourselves of this type or species of emotion.

This interpretation of the Pessimist's position, I believe, misrepresents the nature and character of his (or her) concerns. That is to say, the Pessimist may argue that the issue which ought to concern us is whether (granted our liability to reactive attitudes) we can or cannot reasonably or appropriately entertain or engage these attitudes. Strawson acknowledges that we may find ourselves in circumstances where our reactive attitudes are not called for or are inappropriate. Accordingly, at this level—the level of entertaining or engaging our reactive attitudes—emotional reactions of this nature can and must be withdrawn or suspended altogether when this is required of us. Clearly, then, while we may remain prone to reactive attitudes, they are, with us, in these circumstances, wholly inactive and disengaged (because they are acknowledged to be inappropriate and uncalled for). These straightforward observations—which Strawson readily accepts in the context of his rationalistic strategy—may be further extended by the Pessimist and applied to the question of determinism. The Pessimist does not (or need not) claim that we are capable of suspending or abandoning our disposition or liability to reactive attitudes—much less that the thesis of determinism requires us to do so. This is not the level at which his concerns arise. Rather, the Pessimist claims only that we can and must cease to entertain reactive attitudes toward any and all individuals who are morally incapacitated and that we are capable of ceasing altogether to engage or entertain reactive attitudes insofar as we have reason to believe that *everyone* is incapacitated in the relevant ways. If the thesis of determinism is true, the Pessimist argues, then we are, indeed, all morally incapacitated.[10] It is important to note that the Pessimist may be wrong in claiming or supposing that determinism implies that we are all so incapacitated and yet, nevertheless, still right in maintaining that if the truth of determinism does have these implications, then we are capable of ceasing altogether to entertain or engage our reactive attitudes. In order to assess independently Strawson's (distinct) rationalistic and naturalistic arguments, it is crucial that we distinguish these issues. The Pessimist, then, should be interpreted as claiming only that if the thesis of determinism is true,

---

10. The relevant capacity, according to libertarian-Pessimists at any rate, is "free will" or "contra-causal freedom" (see n. 4 above). Strawson objects to this aspect of the (libertarian) Pessimist's position on the ground that it involves "obscure and panicky metaphysics" (FR, p. 25; cf. sec. 6, passim). I will return to this issue below.

then (disposed as we may be to reactive attitudes) the fact is that our circumstances are such that we are never justified in entertaining or feeling (tokens of our) reactive attitudes. Moreover, in these circumstances, the Pessimist claims, we both can and must cease altogether to entertain such emotions. Clearly, then, so interpreted, the Pessimist is a token-Pessimist.

This analysis indicates that, from any perspective, Strawson's naturalistic reply to the Pessimist is seriously flawed. That is to say, if Strawson is embracing type-naturalism, then he does nothing to refute or discredit the Pessimist. If, on the other hand, he is embracing token-naturalism, then, worse still, he is embracing a position that is committed to suspect and disturbing factual claims and which, moreover, does not even address itself to the (legitimate) concerns of the Pessimist. The most plausible interpretation of Strawson's remarks in "Freedom and Resentment" (and *Skepticism and Naturalism*), I suggest, is that Strawson is putting forward both type- and token-naturalism (but fails entirely to distinguish adequately between them). Indeed, it seems clear that Strawson has to be arguing for (stronger) token-naturalism given his objectives. Strawson is fundamentally concerned to deny the Pessimist's supposition that we are capable of adopting the "objective attitude" toward everyone all of the time. To take up the objective attitude, as Strawson understands it, involves ceasing to entertain (tokens of) reactive attitudes toward some or all individuals. It does not, clearly, involve giving up our disposition or proneness to such attitudes (i.e., objectivity does involve giving up our "commitment" to this type of emotion). Only token-naturalism, therefore, stands opposed to the Pessimist's claim that we are capable of taking up the "objective attitude" toward everyone. That is to say, while a universal objectivity of attitude is compatible with type-naturalism, it is not compatible with token-naturalism. Strawson, then, can discredit the Pessimist's position by means of token-naturalism alone. If he withdraws from his token-naturalist claims, then he has no effective naturalistic reply to the Pessimist at all (keeping in mind that the Pessimist can readily embrace type-naturalism). In this way, we may conclude that Strawson is constrained by the nature of his own objectives to embrace token-naturalism and that this approach to the problem of responsibility entirely misfires.

In light of these observations it seems clear why the Pessimist finds Strawson's naturalistic reply both misguided and disturbing. What is particularly disturbing about Strawson's naturalistic strategy, expressed in more general terms, is that it casts doubt on our ability or capacity to curb or control our emotional life according to the dictates of reason.

More specifically, it seems clear that, despite disclaimers to the contrary, Strawson's naturalistic strategy invites us to accept or reconcile ourselves to reactive attitudes (and their associated retributive practices) even in circumstances when we have reason to repudiate them.[11] Given this, it seems evident that we have good reason to reject Strawson's suggestion that we dismiss the Pessimist and refuse to take his arguments seriously. We have, on the contrary, every reason to take the Pessimist seriously, and this puts greater weight on Strawson's rationalistic strategy. I will argue, however, that Strawson's rationalistic strategy, as he presents it, cannot bear this weight.

III

Strawson's effort to discredit Pessimism by means of naturalistic claims leads, or compels, him, I maintain, to embrace an implausibly strong form of naturalism. The Pessimist cannot, I have argued, be refuted or discredited by means of a strategy or approach of this nature. It may be, however, that it is possible to refute or discredit the Pessimist's position by means of the rationalistic strategy which Strawson independently advances. More specifically, it may be argued that the Pessimist is mistaken in claiming that if the thesis of determinism is true, then we are all morally incapacitated. If this can be established, and the Pessimist's anxieties can be shown to be groundless, then there is no reason to accept the related claim which the Pessimist puts forward to the effect that if determinism is true, our reactive attitudes are never justified or appropriate. Strawson believes that the rationalistic arguments which he puts forward serve to discredit and refute Pessimism in just this way.

The rationalistic strategy, as I have noted, distinguishes between two different sorts of excusing considerations: specific and global considerations. Strawson maintains that the truth of the thesis of determinism does

---

11. According to Strawson, our reactive attitudes and retributive practices are intimately (i.e., naturally or "humanly") connected. In FR, however, Strawson has very little to say about the problem of punishment as it arises within the framework of his naturalistic account of responsibility (see FR, p. 22). More specifically, Strawson does not consider in any detail to what extent, or in what way, our retributive practices are a "given" of human nature. Nor does he explain the relationship between justificatory issues as they arise for our reactive attitudes and as they arise for our retributive practices. Suffice it to say that I believe that Strawson's position encounters a number of (further) difficulties in this area. These matters are explored and discussed in some detail in my "Hume on Responsibility and Punishment," *Canadian Journal of Philosophy* 20 (1990): 539–64 (esp. sec. 3).

not, as such, imply that either specific or global excusing considerations apply universally. I am concerned with Strawson's specific argument(s) purporting to show that the truth of the thesis of determinism cannot lead to the conclusion that global excusing considerations apply to everyone. Strawson states:

> The participant attitudes, and personal [and moral] reactive attitudes in general, tend to give place, and it is judged by the civilized *should* give place, to objective attitudes, just in so far as the agent is seen as excluded from ordinary adult human relationships by deep-rooted psychological abnormality—or simply by being a child. *But it cannot be a consequence of any thesis which is not itself self-contradictory that abnormality is the universal condition.*
>
> FR, p. 11; my emphasis[12]

This argument is crucial to the success of Strawson's rationalistic strategy. Strawson, that is, must establish, against the Pessimist, that determinism does not (or cannot) imply that everyone is "abnormal." Failing this, the rationalistic strategy would collapse. Nevertheless, the argument which Strawson puts forward is wholly inadequate. Throughout these crucial sections Strawson's argument turns (repeatedly) on a conflation or equivocation between being "abnormal" and being "incapacitated." Contrary to the general drift of Strawson's remarks, it is not abnormality, as such, which excuses but, rather, incapacity. Strawson appears to be aware of the difficulty: "Now it is certainly true that in the case of the abnormal, though not in the case of the normal, our adoption of the objective attitude is a consequence of our viewing the agent as *incapacitated* in some or all respects for ordinary inter-personal relationship" (FR, p. 12; Strawson's emphasis).[13] While it is incapacity that lies at the heart of our concerns in these circumstances, Strawson has, nevertheless, developed his reply to the Pessimist in terms of the language of "abnormality" (see esp. FR, pp. 8, 11, where Strawson places particular emphasis on this terminology). This terminology, as I will show, has considerable significance for Strawson's argument.

---

12. Strawson seems to be aware that these remarks are not altogether satisfactory. He continues: "Now this dismissal might seem altogether too facile; and so in a sense it is."

13. The inappropriate and misleading nature of Strawson's talk of "abnormality" in the context is revealed by its awkward coupling with references to children and those who are "morally underdeveloped." What is relevant here, clearly, is incapacity and not "abnormality."

If we replace Strawson's references to "the abnormal" and "abnormality" with references to "the incapacitated" and "incapacity," his reply to the Pessimist, quite simply, collapses. Obviously, it is not inconceivable or self-contradictory to suggest that there could be a world, or things might develop, such that everyone is or becomes incapacitated. Imagine, for example, the spread of some terrible disease or genetic mutation which affects the brain and thereby destroys our relevant capacities. Clearly, in this situation there is no correspondence or extensional equivalence between the "abnormal" and the "incapacitated." On the contrary, the "normal" person will be incapacitated and the "abnormal" person (if there is one) will have the requisite capacities. Given this, our reactive attitudes will be inappropriate in the normal case and appropriate in the abnormal case. These observations plainly indicate that it is misleading and mistaken to place any emphasis on considerations of "abnormality" and the like in this context. Strawson has identified the wrong grounds on which global excuses are founded.

In light of this, let us consider the Pessimist's position once again. The Pessimist, clearly, should not be understood as claiming that if determinism is true, we are all (psychologically) abnormal. Rather, the Pessimist claims only that if the thesis is true, then we are all morally incapacitated (and thus inappropriate objects of reactive attitudes). There is, I have pointed out, nothing self-contradictory about a thesis which suggests that incapacity is the universal condition. The relevant capacity, according to the (libertarian) Pessimist, is "free will" or "contra-causal freedom." Against this aspect of the (libertarian) Pessimist's position, Strawson repeats a charge often heard: that is, that libertarian notions of "free will" and "contra-causal freedom" involve "obscure and panicky metaphysics." The force of these remarks, in other words, is that (libertarian) Pessimists are insisting on a condition of responsibility "which cannot be coherently described."[14] I have considerable sympathy with these claims. Moreover, observations of this general nature certainly succeed in casting doubt on one interpretation of what the relevant capacities are supposed to be. It is far from obvious, however, that in itself this establishes that the truth of the thesis of determinism poses no threat to our moral capacities and hence to our reactive attitudes. On the contrary, no conclusion of this nature can be drawn until we have some alternative characterization of the relevant capacities in question. Strawson has suggested what these capacities do

14. Strawson, "Replies," p. 265.

not involve (i.e., free will, etc.), but he has little or nothing to say about what they do involve, or how they should be understood. The reason for this is that he thinks that he can circumvent this difficult and complicated issue by showing, simply, that no thesis can imply that we are all morally incapacitated (and hence determinism cannot pose a threat of this nature to our moral capacities and reactive attitudes). The specific argument that Strawson puts forward in this direction fails and, hence, as things stand, he has not established that it is impossible that we are all morally incapacitated.[15] Given this, we obviously need to identify and describe the nature of the capacities in question so that the Pessimist's claims (i.e., that the truth of the thesis of determinism would leave us all morally incapacitated, etc.) can be properly evaluated. In other words, without some (more plausible) alternative characterization of the nature of these moral capacities, we cannot say with any assurance whether the truth of determinism would or would not affect their functioning. While it may be that something of an appropriate nature can be said on behalf of the rationalistic strategy in this regard, we cannot find it in Strawson's remarks on this subject.[16] In short, while Strawson claims to have shown that determinism cannot (logically) imply that we are all morally incapacitated, he has failed to do so. He has, rather, succeeded only in repeating the standard objection that libertarian notions of "free will" and "contra-causal freedom" are obscure and unhelpful accounts of the capacities required of moral agents. In light of this, I think that we must conclude that Strawson's rationalistic reply to the

15. It is certainly true that were we to find ourselves in circumstances where everyone were morally incapacitated, and thus our reactive attitudes were never called for or in order, then, as Strawson suggests, in these circumstances we may well have an overwhelming sense of "human isolation" (FR, p. 11). Contrary to what is implied by Strawson's remarks (FR, pp. 13, 18), however, forward-looking considerations concerning "the gains and losses to human life, its enrichment or impoverishment" cannot serve to justify us in treating the incapacitated as if they were not incapacitated. In this respect I find myself in particular disagreement with Bennett. He states: "If we try to imagine our lives without reactive feelings we find ourselves . . . confronted by bleak desolation. We cannot be obliged to give up something whose loss would gravely worsen the human condition, *and so reactive feelings cannot be made impermissible by any facts*" (Bennett, p. 29; my emphasis). If the force of these remarks is that no facts of any sort can render our reactive attitudes altogether inappropriate or uncalled for, then Bennett is, I believe, clearly mistaken.

16. The sorts of (alternative) capacities that I am thinking of have been widely discussed in more recent literature. See, in particular, papers by Harry Frankfurt, Gary Watson, and Charles Taylor in Watson, ed. (n. 1 above); and also Daniel Dennett, *Elbow Room* (Oxford: Oxford University Press, 1984), esp. chaps. 2–5. All these authors, in different ways, emphasize our capacity to reflect upon our desires and restructure our will (i.e., those desires that lead to action) on this basis.

Pessimist is, as it stands, at best incomplete. No satisfactory reply to the Pessimist can avoid addressing itself to the question regarding the nature of the moral capacities required of individuals who are deemed appropriate objects of reactive attitudes.[17]

IV

Throughout this chapter my principal concern has been Strawson's naturalistic reply to the Pessimist.[18] Strawson, I point out, fails to distinguish between type- and token-naturalism. Token-naturalism is implausibly strong in both its nature and intent, and it serves only to discredit the naturalistic approach. The plausible and valuable element in the naturalistic approach is to be found in type-naturalism. Given his commitment to token-naturalism, we cannot naturalize responsibility along the lines that Strawson suggests. Nevertheless, when all vestiges of token-naturalism are removed, it is possible that we can construct a coherent and plausible (type) naturalistic framework within which some relevant rationalistic reply to the Pessimist may be developed. An approach of this nature does not encourage us to accept or reconcile ourselves to reactive attitudes (and their associated practices) irrespective of whether or not we have reason to repudiate them. On the contrary, this approach leaves our reactive attitudes where we want them: within the bounds of reason.

17. Throughout FR Strawson tends to assume that all Pessimists are libertarians and that they are, accordingly, motivated by libertarian metaphysical assumptions (FR, pp. 3, 20, 23–24, 25). It is not evident, however, that this needs to be the case. A Pessimist who accepts the two principal theses that Strawson is attacking (as described in Sec. I above) may also be what Strawson describes as a "moral skeptic": i.e., someone who believes that the attitudes and practices associated with moral responsibility are "inherently confused and that we can see this to be so if we consider the consequences either of the truth of determinism or its falsity" (FR, p. 1; cf. Ayer's position in "Free Will and Rationality"). Clearly, in dealing with the moral skeptic's claim that our reactive attitudes are never appropriate or called for, it will not suffice to argue that libertarian notions of "free will" are obscure and unhelpful. This is a point which the moral skeptic will readily concede.

18. It is worth emphasizing the point that in this chapter I have not been concerned with each and every (controversial) aspect of Strawson's discussion and approach. There remain, therefore, a number of interesting matters which I have not pursued in this context. Some critics of Strawson's may argue that there are (other) weaknesses or shortcomings of FR which require further attention and discussion. In contrast with this, those who are more sympathetic with Strawson's approach will no doubt argue that, criticism aside, there is more to be said for Strawson's approach than my criticisms suggest. I believe that there is some truth in both these views. Nevertheless, for our present purposes the important point to note is that both critic and sympathizer alike will have to take note of the specific objections which I have raised against Strawson's line(s) of argument.

4

Responsibility and the Condition of Moral Sense[*]

O wad some Pow'r the giftie gie us
To see oursels as ithers see us!

ROBERT BURNS

RECENT WORK IN contemporary compatibilist theory displays consider-able sophistication and subtlety when compared with the earlier theories of classical compatibilism. Two distinct lines of thought have proved espe-cially influential and illuminating. The first developed around the general hypothesis that moral sentiments or reactive attitudes are fundamental for understanding the nature and conditions of moral responsibility. The other important development is found in recent compatibilist accounts of rational self-control or reason responsiveness. Strictly speaking, these two lines of thought have developed independent of each other. However, in the past decade or so they have been fused together in several prominent statements of compatibilist theory. I will refer to theories that combine these two elements in this way as RS (Reason-Sentiment) theories. RS theories face a number of familiar difficulties that relate to each of their two components. Beyond this, they also face a distinct set of problems

* Versions of this chapter were read at the 25th Hume Society Conference (Stirling, Scotland; 1998), the Western Canadian Philosophical Association (University of British Columbia; 1998), the Inland Northwest Philosophical Conference (University of Idaho; 1999), the University of Calgary (2002), the University of Alberta (2003), the University of Victoria (2003), and the North Carolina Philosophical Society (Duke University; 2005). I am grateful to the audiences, and especially my commentators and co-speakers on these occasions: Pat Greenspan, Joe Campbell, and Stephen Scott. Thanks also to Kari Coleman, Owen Flanagan, John M. Fischer, Walter Glannon, Robert Gunnarsson, Ish Haji, Dennis McKerlie, Jan Narveson, Geoff Sayre-McCord, and David Widerker for helpful comments and discussion.

concerning how these two main components relate or should be *inte-grated*. My concerns in this chapter focus primarily on this set of problems.

According to one version of RS compatibilism, the role of moral sentiments is limited to explaining what is required for *holding* an agent responsible. In contrast with this, the role of reason responsiveness is to explain what moral capacities are required for an agent *to be responsible*, one who is a legitimate or fair target of our moral sentiments. More specifically, according to this view, moral sense is *not* required for rational self-control or reason responsiveness. There is, therefore, no requirement that the responsible agent has some capacity to feel moral sentiment. Contrary to this view, I argue that a responsible agent must be capable of *holding* herself and others responsible. Failing this, an agent's powers of rational self-control will be both limited and impaired. In so far as holding responsible requires moral sense, it follows that *being* responsible also requires moral sense. Moral sense is, therefore, a condition of responsible agency.

I

The most influential contemporary statement of the moral sentiment approach to issues of free will and moral responsibility is presented in P. F. Strawson's seminal paper "Freedom and Resentment."[1] The key idea in this chapter is that the nature and conditions of moral responsibility must be understood in terms of our reactive attitudes or moral sentiments. The attitudes and intentions of our fellow human beings, Strawson maintains, naturally and inescapably arouse reactive attitudes and feelings in us. Incompatibilist concerns about the implications of determinism can neither dislodge nor discredit our commitment to feelings and attitudes of this kind. Although our particular moral sentiments require some relevant justification, and issues of excuse and mitigation arise with respect to them, there is no general, external justification required for the whole framework of moral sentiments. This is a given of human nature. These observations about the natural operation of the human mind serve as a barrier to all systematic skeptical worries about the foundations of moral life.[2] These foundations are not based on a general rationale of some kind

---

1. P. F. Strawson, "Freedom and Resentment," reprinted in G. Watson, ed., *Free Will* (Oxford: Oxford University Press, 1982). Hereafter abbreviated as FR.

2. Strawson, *Skepticism and Naturalism* (London: Methuen, 1985), esp. pp. 38–39.

(e.g., a hypothesis about contra-causal freedom etc.) but rather depend on the natural workings of human feeling and emotion.

Strawson's approach distinguishes between two ways in which agents may be excused for their actions. The first are specific excuses, such as ignorance and accidents, and the second are exemptions, where the agent is judged to be morally incompetent. In the case of specific excusing considerations there is no suggestion that the agent is in any way an inappropriate object of moral sentiment. All that is claimed is that the particular conduct in question does not manifest any lack of due care or regard on the agent's part.[3] In contrast with this, when exempting considerations are applicable we are invited "to suspend our ordinary reactive attitudes toward the agent" on the ground that they are in some relevant respect abnormal or immature.[4] The account of exemptions is crucial to Strawson's approach because it serves to identify the boundary between responsible and non-responsible agents. That is, exemptions identify those individuals who are not moral agents or full members of the moral community as delineated by the legitimate scope of our moral sentiments. It is here, however, that critics have argued that Strawson's theory runs into fundamental difficulties.

Clearly any theory of the kind that Strawson is advancing must provide some plausible interpretation of moral capacity of a kind that allows us to make sense of exempting conditions. This is something that Strawson fails to provide, which opens the door for the incompatibilist to argue that the relevant capacity is some mode of libertarian free will or contra-causal freedom (this being what the "immature" and "abnormal" lack). As it stands, Strawson has no convincing line of reply to this criticism. What is needed, therefore, if Strawson's approach is to succeed, is some relevant compatibilist account of moral capacity.[5]

A related way of describing this general objection to Strawson's approach is to argue that his approach involves a fundamental confusion.

> . . . Strawson's theory may reasonably be said to give an account
> of what it is for agents to be held responsible, but there seems to

---

3. FR, 64–65.

4. FR, 64–67.

5. On this matter see my "Strawson's Way of Naturalizing Responsibility," *Ethics*, 102 (1992), 287–302.

be a difference between being *held* responsible and actually *being* responsible. Surely it is possible that one can be held responsible even though one in fact is not responsible, and conversely that one can be responsible even though one is actually not treated as a responsible agent. By understanding responsibility primarily in terms of our actual practices of adopting or not adopting certain attitudes towards agents, Strawson's theory risks blurring the difference between these two issues.[6]

The exact nature of this criticism needs careful interpretation. It is clear that Strawson wants to allow that in particular cases our reactive attitudes may fail to track moral responsibility (e.g., we feel a sentiment of blame because we have incorrect beliefs about the agent's intentions or state of mind). This is not where the objection lies. The force of the objection is that our established attitudes and practices may be *systematically* misplaced or misdirected. For example, the fact that a moral community actually *holds* juveniles or mentally incompetent individuals as responsible does not show that these individuals *are* responsible. The way in which our moral sentiments are directed in cases of this kind cannot, in itself, serve as a reliable guide to a standard of responsibility that is reflectively legitimate. What we need, therefore, is some independent account of moral capacity and the conditions of moral agency that can guide our moral sentiments.[7]

II

According to prominent versions of RS theory, these weaknesses in Strawson's approach can be eliminated by reason responsive or rational self-control theories, which serve as the basis of a more satisfactory account of moral capacity. That is to say, what the moral sentiment approach plainly needs is a more developed theory of the boundary between normal/abnormal and mature/immature as it concerns who is or is not an appropriate target of our reactive attitudes. Whereas Strawson's remarks on this subject are too thin and slight to do this job, reason responsiveness seems to

---

6. John Martin Fischer and Mark Ravizza, eds., *Perspectives on Moral Responsibility* (Ithaca: Cornell University Press, 1993), 18; their emphasis.

7. As I will explain further below, it is easy to slide from this observation to the mistaken view that moral sense has no role to play in accounting for these capacities and conditions.

provide exactly what we are looking for.[8] This aspect of RS theory has been worked out in detail in the recent and highly influential theory of John Fischer and Mark Ravizza. What sort of conditions must be satisfied for an agent to be an appropriate or fair target of reactive attitudes? According to Fischer and Ravizza a responsible agent is one who can in some suitable sense control his conduct. They refer to this as "the control condition" (RC, 13—14).[9] What is required is that the responsible agent must be able to both recognize and react to available reasons. In the case of reason recognition it is essential, on this account, that there is some pattern or regularity to the way that the agent recognizes reasons (e.g., it will not suffice that the agent is occasionally or intermittently able to recognize relevant reasons for action). On the other hand, it is not essential that the agent is regularly guided by reasons in this way. Reason reactivity is satisfied, they argue, when the agent's conduct shows that his conduct has on occasion been guided by his reasons.[10]

On the face of it, this account of reason responsiveness provides RS theory with a general interpretation of moral capacity of the kind that was missing from Strawson's discussion. The question that now arises, however, is whether there is more required of responsible agency than satisfying reason responsiveness. Fischer and Ravizza argue that there are further and distinct requirements to be met for the agent to be in control of her conduct. More specifically, the agent must not operate with reason responsive dispositions that have themselves been manipulated or implanted in such a way that she may be covertly controlled.[11] In other words, we must address concerns about the historical process by which the agent has acquired her reason responsive dispositions. In circumstances where implantation or manipulation of some kind has occurred

---

8. FR, 75–76.

9. John Martin Fischer and Mark Ravizza, *Responsibility and Control: A Theory of Moral Responsibility* (Cambridge: Cambridge University Press, 1998), 13–14. Hereafter abbreviated as RC.

10. Cp. R. J. Wallace, *Responsibility and the Moral Sentiments* (Cambridge, Mass.: Harvard University Press, 1994). Hereafter abbreviated as RMS. Wallace maintains that "rational self-control" requires that the agent is able "to grasp and apply moral reasons and to regulate [his] behaviour by the light of such reasons" (RMS, 86–87; cp. 156–61). Fischer and Ravizza take the same general view and provide a more detailed account of how this condition of rational self-control should be interpreted. These details, however, are not my concerns in this context.

11. See, e.g., RC, 108f; 197f; 230f.

the agent cannot be said to "own" the disposition that she is operating with. If illegitimate processes of this kind have occurred then responsible agency is compromised.

How, then, is "ownership" to be accounted for? Whether our reason responsive dispositions are owned or not will depend on the particular *history* involved in their acquisition. There are, according to this theory, three necessary steps required for ownership to take place. The first is that the agent (i.e., in the early stages of childhood) comes to see herself as an agent who produces "upshots" in the world.[12] When this stage is reached then the child is in a position to see herself as a "fair target of reactive attitudes as a result of how [she] exercises this agency in certain contexts."[13] Taken together, these two steps require that the responsible agent must have a certain view of herself as an agent and as a fair target of the reactive attitudes. Following Galen Strawson, Fischer and Ravizza describe this as committing themselves to a *subjectivist* approach to moral responsibility.[14] There remains the difficulty, however, that these first two steps in the process of "taking responsibility" may themselves be manipulated or covertly controlled. To deal with this problem a third step is necessary. The cluster of beliefs specified in the first two steps "must be based, in an appropriate way, on the individual's evidence."[15] This is intended to exclude is any case where there is direct implantation or manipulation of the agent's reason responsiveness. In other words, it is essential that the historical process by which an agent acquires their reason responsive dispositions and takes responsibility for them must come about in some *appropriate* way. What is "appropriate" does not exclude causal determinism but does exclude all forms of manipulation, implantation or process that permits covert control.[16]

It is clear, then, that on this account more than reason responsiveness is required for moral agency and responsibility. The responsible agent must be guided by reason responsive dispositions that have been produced by some "appropriate" historical process. The success of this appeal to history

---

12. RC, 208f.

13. RC, 211.

14. RC, 221–23; cp. Galen Strawson, *Freedom and Belief* (Oxford: Clarendon Press, 1986), esp. ch. 13.

15. RC, 238.

16. RC, 236.

and the process of "taking responsibility" must be judged in terms of whether or not we provided a principled basis for distinguishing between "appropriate" and "inappropriate" historical processes.[17] It is, however, at exactly this point that the argument runs dry. Fischer and Ravizza leave the relevant distinction unanalyzed and thereby ask the reader to accept that there is some intuitive distinction between cases whereby the acquisition of reason responsive dispositions is merely determined and cases where it is manipulated or covertly controlled in some way.[18] This is not, however, a distinction that incompatibilists will allow to serve as a boundary between responsible and non-responsible agency. The reason for this is that what fundamentally troubles incompatibilists about manipulation and implantation cases is not the matter of "ownership" as such, but that agents in these circumstances are operating with reason responsive dispositions that they have acquired through processes that they have *no control over*. From this point of view it is not enough that agents are reason responsive and have gone through an "appropriate" process of "taking responsibility." The fact remains that—just as in manipulation and implantation cases—even these "normal" agents have no (final or ultimate) control over the kinds of dispositions that guide their conduct. Unless compatibilists are able to show that an "appropriate" history serves to distinguish between agents who have control over their reason responsive dispositions and those who do not, it follows that appeals to history are irrelevant.[19]

III

In the previous section we reviewed the basic features of RS theory with particular reference to the way that Fischer and Ravizza have recently presented it. The conclusion that we reached was that although RS theories need to address the general problem of manipulation and implantation,

---

17. For more on this see my Critical Notice of *Responsibility and Control: A Theory of Moral Responsibility* in *Canadian Journal of Philosophy* 32 (2002), 587–606.

18. RC, 236.

19. There are, of course, "structural" or "time-slice" responses to this line of incompatibilist criticism. For example, it may be argued that some sense can be made of how an agent can secure control over the process of acquiring reason responsive dispositions by way of second-order, critical self-reflection. The fact remains, however, that even if this were possible (and there may be skepticism about this) any further process of this kind must, ultimately, be guided by reason responsive dispositions that are unchosen and not consented to. For more of this see my Critical Notice of *Responsibility and Control*, 601f.

appealing to history and the process of "taking responsibility" looks like an unpromising as a way of dealing with these concerns. For this reason I have expressed skepticism about the rationale that Fischer and Ravizza provide for taking a "historical" approach to RS theory. Having said this, it is important not to lose the baby with the bathwater when considering the importance of the "subjective" requirement that has been proposed for moral agency. The contrast between versions of RS theory offered by Fischer and Ravizza, on one hand, and Wallace, on the other, brings this out. Although Wallace's theory of rational self-control shares the same general features as the account of reason responsiveness offered by Fischer and Ravizza, Wallace does not commit himself to any further historical requirements relating to "ownership" issues. More specifically, Wallace's version of RS theory has nothing that corresponds to the "subjective" requirement that is involved in the first two stages of "taking responsibility," as described by Fischer and Ravizza. All that is required, on Wallace's account, is that the moral agent is capable of rational self-control. There is no further requirement that the agent is also capable of seeing herself as an agent who is a fair target of reactive attitudes or moral sentiments. While it is true, on Wallace's account, that an agent can be *held* responsible only when she is a target of these attitudes and sentiments, her *being* responsible is not a function of her possessing any capacity to hold herself responsible in these terms.[20] In contrast with this, Fischer and Ravizza are committed to the view that if the agent has no capacity for moral sense then she cannot be said to "own" her reason responsive dispositions, which will compromise the agent's responsibility for the conduct that flows from these dispositions.

The question that needs to be asked at this juncture is whether there is any *independent* rationale for the subjectivist requirement that the agent must be able to see herself as an appropriate target of moral

---

20. Strictly speaking, on Wallace's account all that is required for *holding* an agent responsible is that we *believe* that "such emotions would be warranted . . . despite the fact that we happen not to feel them" (RMS, 77). However, Wallace goes on to emphasize the point that it remains true that, without the relevant relationship to some reactive emotions, "blame would be rendered superficial" (RMS,78). Fischer and Ravizza argue, along similar lines as Wallace, that a morally responsible agent is "an apt candidate" for reactive attitudes but "need not be an *actual* recipient or target of any such attitudes" (RC, 7–8). The point that emerges out of all this is that although in *particular cases* we may be able to hold an agent responsible without any actual emotion or reactive attitude being involved, this cannot be the *general rule* or responsibility would be rendered "superficial." Holding agents responsible is not simply a matter of having factual beliefs of some kind (as Strawson argued).

sentiments—one that has nothing to do with "historical" concerns about "ownership." We may begin to answer this question by way of observing some problems that arise for RS theory when this subjective requirement is not met. It should be noted, in the first place, that there is a significant difference in the capacities required for holding and being responsible. Wallace makes clear that his understanding of the general capacity for rational self-control is "Kantian" in character.[21] In contrast with this, the "Strawsonian" role of moral sense—which has evident Humean roots— is limited to explaining what is involved in holding agents responsible. It is a striking fact, therefore, that the Strawsonian/Humean element of moral sense plays no role in Wallace's "Kantian" account of moral agency or rational self-control. This is indicative of another, related, problem in Wallace's RS theory. Because there is no requirement that responsible agents be capable of moral sense, it is entirely possible that we could encounter rational self-controllers who are responsible agents but who nevertheless have no capacity to *hold* themselves or others responsible.[22] In other words, on this theory a significant *asymmetry* may open up between those individuals who are responsible agents (legitimate targets of moral sentiment) and those agents who are able to hold themselves and others responsible. Membership in the moral community may divide and fail to overlap in respect of these two aspects of moral capacity. This is a puzzling result and it raises the question if asymmetrical theory of this kind is ever acceptable. Fischer and Ravizza, however, offer no principled reason for rejecting a theory on this basis. Nor do they take the view that reason responsiveness, as such, will be compromised in circumstances where an agent lacks moral sense or any capacity for reactive attitudes. Their reasons for insisting on the importance of the subjective requirement lie elsewhere.

IV

The proposal I want to consider is whether a capacity to hold oneself and others responsible is a required condition of being responsible. Stated in these general terms, we may call this a condition of *symmetry*: an agent

---

21. RMS, 12–15. Fischer and Ravizza are not committed to a "Kantian" view of agency.

22. Wallace explicitly allows that this can happen and cites the (fictional) example of "Mr. Spock of Star Trek fame" (RMS, 78n41). The fact that "Spock" is a fictional character is itself significant.

cannot be responsible unless she is also able to hold herself and others responsible. This condition takes a more specific form in RS theory, since it is committed to the more specific view that moral sense is the basis for holding agents responsible. In the case of RS theory, therefore, the condition of symmetry takes the following form:

> The responsible agent must be able to feel and understand moral sentiments or reactive attitudes.

Let us call this *the condition of moral sense*. It is possible to reject this condition without rejecting the condition of symmetry. This is possible, however, only if we do not interpret holding responsible in terms of moral sentiments. Among those who reject the condition of moral sense there are some who nevertheless accept the suggestion that holding an agent responsible involves reference to moral sense.[23] The specific difficulty of asymmetry will arise for those who are committed to this analysis of holding responsible (which is true of all RS theorists).

Why should we accept the condition of moral sense (i.e., if we do not do so on the basis of ownership and historical considerations)? It has recently been argued by Ishtiyaque Haji that an agent can "lack the capacity to hold oneself or others responsible without this lack in any way impinging freedom, epistemic, or authenticity requirements of responsibility."[24] The general assumption operating here is that moral sense is in no way required for rational self-control or reason responsiveness, as these are distinct issues. Contrary to this view, I will argue that there is a more intimate connection between moral sense and the kind of rational self-control that enables us to grasp and be guided by moral reasons. Agents who lack moral sense are missing something that is vitally important and that "normal" moral agents do and must possess. More specifically, when an agent lacks moral sense her *sensitivity* to moral considerations is diminished and her motivation to be guided by these considerations is impoverished and limited.

---

23. See, e.g., Ishtiyaque Haji, "The Emotional Depravity of Psychopaths and Culpability," *Legal Theory*, 9 (2003), 65–82; and cp. Derk Pereboom, *Living Without Free Will* (Cambridge: Cambridge University Press, 2001), xx–xxi. Haji endorses a Strawsonian (moral sense) view of holding responsible, whereas Pereboom rejects any view of this kind.

24. Haji, "The Emotional Depravity of Psychopaths and Culpability," 73. In this context, Haji is responding directly to an earlier (unpublished) version of this chapter, which was titled "Responsibility, Moral Sense and Symmetry."

To help us appreciate this point, consider the parallels between fear and reactive attitudes.[25] Take the case of "Jill," who is incapable of feeling or experiencing fear. It is not simply that she can control her fear, or "overcome" this emotion, it is that she cannot feel it in any circumstances or conditions. There is no question of her controlling or overcoming this emotion because it *never* arises in her. Clearly Jill is, in this respect, emotionally abnormal. Jill is, nevertheless, a highly intelligent person who can identify what conditions are *dangerous* and may *harm* her. Her intellectual abilities are such that she can describe objects and circumstances of this kind and discourse about them. Jill can also anticipate how normal human beings will react to these circumstances and objects, although she does not know what it is like for them to feel or experience fear or be moved by it. In this sense, Jill has an entirely "external" or "superficial" understanding of fear. Whereas fear, as we might say, *colors* the normal person's world, and draws attention and interest to dangerous or harmful objects and situation, this is not possible for Jill. Jill's world is monochromatic in this respect—lacking any emotional highlights to flag certain objects and situations. Since fear plays no role in Jill's life, she cannot be reached through this emotional route as it is completely closed off to her.

It is evident that Jill is not a full participant in normal human life in so far as we reason and engage with each other about dangerous and harmful situations and objects. Whereas normal human beings live in a world that is colored by emotional tones that give *salience* and *significance* to danger and harm, Jill lives in a black-and-white world that lacks these emotional tones. It would, of course, be a mistake to treat Jill as if she were psychotic or completely stupid and unable to recognize or converse with us *at all* about these matters. Clearly we can find points of common understanding and shared experience by which Jill can be (hopefully) motivated to avoid danger and harm, relying on channels that do not involve the emotional triggers of fear. It remains true, nevertheless, that we have every reason to recognize the significance of Jill's emotional abnormality and the limits that this places on her ability to recognize and respond to danger.[26] Jill's

---

25. This parallel is suggested by P. F. Strawson in his "Replies," in Zak van Straaten ed., *Philosophical Subjects* (Oxford: Oxford University Press, 1980), 265.

26. An even more extreme form of incapacity would be if Jill had no capacity for pain in the face of injury. A purely "intellectual" understanding of the fact of injury would leave her seriously impaired in her capacity to appreciate the significance of injury and be effectively motivated to respond to the threat of it.

emotional abnormality plainly has considerable *practical* significance for her in situations of this kind.

Consider now the parallel case of "Jack," who lacks all capacity for moral sense. Jack is, nevertheless, an intelligent person who *appears* to satisfy reason responsive requirements. That is to say, Jack can recognize and follow moral norms and he is able to anticipate the consequences of any failure to comply with these norms and standards. (Just as Jill is able to identify dangerous situations and avoid them.) The fact remains, however, that violations of these moral norms do not affect Jack in any emotional way. In this sense, Jack is morally *cold*. In these circumstances, an agent such as Jack (as we found in the parallel case with Jill's lack of fear) is not motivated to care about his moral qualities on the basis of his own or others' reactive attitudes or moral sentiments. He is unaffected by any consideration *of this kind*. More specifically, it is impossible for Jack to come to "internalize" the reactive attitudes that others may direct at him. It is not just—as may happen with a normal person—that Jack may not *accept* or *agree* with the reactive attitudes that are directed toward him. The problem is deeper than this. Jack cannot even potentially come to share reactive attitudes and feelings because he constitutionally lacks any emotional life of this kind.[27] To this extent, therefore, there is no question, for Jack, of accepting or rejecting the reactive attitudes that others direct at him. On this interpretation, it follows that Jack is incapable of any kind of "deep assessment" of himself and others.[28]

These observations make clear that in an important dimension Jack is not a *full participant* in (normal) moral life. There is a considerable sphere of moral experience and communication that is simply closed off to Jack. In our dealings with any individual of this kind it is both unreasonable and unfair to communicate and reason with him as if this incapacity were irrelevant to this person's ability to function as a moral agent. (Just as it would be unreasonable to treat Jill as if her incapacity for fear were irrelevant to the way she that responds to danger or harm.) At the same time, it is important not to exaggerate this problem (significant as it may be). Clearly Jack is an intelligent person and understands moral rules and expectations

---

27. One way of expressing this point is to say that Jack is not simply (systematically) *token* deprived of reactive attitudes but he is (constitutionally) *type* deprived.

28. The (useful) terminology "deep assessment" comes from Wallace. According to Wallace, blame is rendered superficial in any case where there is no recognizable connection with moral sentiments (RMS, 77–83; cp. 53f). See also my remarks in note 20 above.

and their associated sanctions. For this reason it would also be a mistake to assimilate Jack to other individuals who are wholly unable to participate in the moral community, such as animals or infants. Nevertheless, when it comes to the dimension of moral life that involves reactive attitudes, the most that Jack can do is "parrot" these responses or feign feelings of this kind. Just as Jill's world without fear left considerations of danger and harm without any emotional coloring, so too in Jack's world moral considerations lack any emotional coloring of the kind provided by moral sense. For this reason we must conclude that Jack's moral world—the way that he experiences it and is moved and directed within it—is *very* different from our own.

It is tempting to present Jack's lack of moral sense as a completely separate issue from his capacity for rational self-control. The situation, however, is not so simple as this. In the first place, Jack's moral development must also be fundamentally different from that of the normal person. This will plainly influence the way in which Jack learns to grasp and apply moral considerations. In ordinary moral development there is a close relationship between a child's evolving ability to understand moral norms and the child's ability to understand and internalize reactive attitudes when these norms have been violated.[29] Clearly Jack's moral development cannot evolve in this way and this must both limit and alter the way in which Jack eventually becomes able to grasp and be guided by moral considerations.

Apart from developmental issues (e.g., as they relate to moral education), it is important to recognize that Jack's "control" system, as it relates to moral considerations, is radically different from the normal person's. On the account given, Jack is able to guide and motivate his conduct with a view to "external" sanctions such as rewards and punishments. Related to this, Jack also has an "external" interest in not arousing negative moral sentiments, since this will obviously affect the way that others treat him. What Jack will lack, nevertheless, is an "internal" system of sanctions (or incentives) as associated with moral sentiments. The internal system operates in a quite different way than its "external" (rewards and punishments)

---

29. See, e.g., William Damon, *The Moral Child* (New York & London: Free Press, 1988), esp. ch 2. Damon observes that moral emotions, such as shame and guilt, "provide a natural base for the child's acquisition of moral values. As such, they both orient children towards moral events and motivate children to pay close attention to such events. These feelings provide the affective energy that motivate children's moral learning." (p. 28)

counterpart. More specifically, our experience of negative reactive attitudes is not simply a matter of wanting to avoid the unpleasant or painful consequences associated with them. In cases where we accept the response (e.g., blame) as appropriate or fair something much more complex is going on. In these cases, the agent finds the responses particularly troubling because she accepts or endorses the moral considerations and norms that serve as the basis of the adverse reactive attitudes. What this shows is that, for a normal moral agent, our capacity to experience and feel moral sentiments, towards ourselves and others, is intimately and inextricably connected with our understanding of the significance of the background moral claims and considerations.

To appreciate and understand moral considerations fully is precisely to be able to apply them to oneself and others and feel the appropriate way when violations occur. Failing this the agent just "does not really get it." They are responding to these claims and considerations in an entirely "external" manner. (Compare Jill's way of responding to danger and harm.) The agent's general capacity for rational self-control is, therefore, expressed and manifest *through moral sense*. Moral sense serves as a "feedback loop" through which the agent is confronted with the salience and significance of the moral considerations that she is presented with. Since Jack lacks all this psychological apparatus, it is very evident that Jack's capacity for rational self-control, in relation to moral life, is significantly impaired and compromised. What this general observation suggests is that it is possible to "over-intellectualize" not just what is involved in *holding* an agent responsible, but also what is involved in an agent *being* responsible (being capable of rational self-control as it relates to moral norms and expectations). Rational self-control is itself dependent upon and *integrated with* our capacity for moral sense.

V

Critics may argue that these observations about the relevance of moral sense for moral (normative) competence do not matter much. After all, as we have already pointed out, in the normal case, reason responsiveness evolves along side the development of moral sense, as these are not unrelated components of the moral personality. The distinction between the two capacities is, therefore, both empirically and conceptually unfounded. In reply to this line of criticism, the first thing to be said is that several philosophers have explicitly denied that there is any such interdependence between rational self-control and moral sense—either conceptually or empirically—of the kind that I have described.[30] The claims of the moral sense condition in this regard are, therefore, far from uncontroversial. Beyond this, the moral sense condition helps us to understand and interpret a particularly problematic set of cases associated with moral agency. The absence of moral sense, as such, does not make an individual a psychopath. Nevertheless, the absence of moral sense is an especially prominent feature of the psychopathic personality and the behavioral problems associated with it. Psychopathic personalities have, in particular, a pronounced lack of shame and remorse and this reflects wider emotional abnormalities.

What is especially puzzling and problematic about the case of the psychopath is precisely that these individuals appear "normal" and "mature" in respect of rational self-control (i.e., unlike animals, infants, psychotics etc.).[31] Several prominent proponents of RS theory have argued that, despite the façade of normative competence, the basis for exempting psychopaths still rests with the way in which their powers of rational self-control have been impaired.[32] These accounts, however, make no reference to the specific role that an incapacity for *moral sense* plays here. On the account that I have described, the difficulties that the psychopath faces in respect of rational self-control or reason responsiveness should be understood primarily in terms of the way in which their impaired moral sense limits and distorts their ability to recognize and react to moral reasons (i.e., as compared with a normal person who is capable of moral sense). For this reason, the account that I have provided is consistent with the general view advanced by Antony Duff that "a psychopath, although not intellectually

---

30. See note 23 above.

31. For further details on this see, e.g., Hervey Cleckley, *The Mask of Sanity*, 5th ed. (St. Louis: Mosby, 1976), esp. pp. 50–54. Cleckley makes the following observation: "Despite the extraordinary poor judgment demonstrated in behavior, in the actual living of his life, the psychopath characteristically demonstrates unimpaired (sometimes excellent) judgment in appraising theoretical situations." (p. 346) Cleckley also points out (pp. 340–41) that the psychopath can act in accordance with moral requirements and expectations, and often does—which makes it especially difficult to detect these individuals. What does distinguish the psychopath, on Cleckley's account, is that he has "absolutely no capacity to see himself as others see him." (p. 350)

32. See Wallace, RMS, 177–78; and compare John Deigh, "Empathy and Universalizability," *Ethics*, 105 (1995), 743–63, who argues for a related (Kantian) view on psychopathy. Fischer and Ravizza also argue that psychopaths should be understood in terms of a failure of the reason-responsive mechanism of some kind or other (RC, 78–80, 82–83).

incompetent, is unable properly to understand the 'nature and quality' of his acts, since he cannot grasp those emotional and moral aspects which are as much part of them as their empirical features."[33]

The puzzle with psychopaths is not simply that they are reason responsive and lack moral sense. It is that they have the "mask" or façade of moral understanding despite a lack of moral sense. In most cases where moral sense is absent it is accompanied by an *obvious* lack of moral understanding or normative competence. The psychopath is not obviously impaired in any systematic way that incapacitates them from understanding and following basic rules and anticipating the consequences of not following them.[34] Nevertheless, as I have argued, without moral sense, the way in which this agent becomes sensitive to moral considerations and is motivated to comply with them is very different from the normal, adult person. In particular, while the psychopath may well be motivated to avoid the unpleasant consequences of punishment and the negative treatment that may come with the reactive sentiments of others, this motivation is entirely "external" to the moral considerations that ground these attitudes and practices. What this agent cannot do, unlike his normal counterpart with moral sense, is come to view himself as a target of moral reactive attitudes that are not only unpleasant in themselves, but reflect the fact that he has "internalized" or accepted these reactions to his conduct.[35] An agent who is capable of internalizing or accepting reactive attitudes is capable not only of experiencing these emotions and the associated unpleasant feelings, but also of accepting the legitimacy and significance of the considerations that have produced these feelings (i.e., unlike the agent who has a merely "external" attitude to these sentiments or attitudes). It is this process—the interaction between recognizing and being guided by moral considerations and

---

33. Antony Duff, "Psychopathy and Moral Understanding," *American Philosophical Quarterly*, 3 (1977), 191–93. See also Michael S. Pritchard, *On Becoming Responsible* (Lawrence, Kan.: University Press of Kansas, 1991), 50–51, who defends Duff's general position. Duff and Pritchard maintain that moral understanding requires more than "intellectual" understanding. It also requires "practical understanding," or an ability to care about some moral values, which the psychopath is unable to do.

34. See Cleckley's remarks cited in note 31 above.

35. Keeping in mind that it is not simply that this does not happen in this or that specific case; it is *constitutionally* impossible for this to happen when an agent lacks moral sense as such. In the same way, there is a difference between an agent who fails to respond to this or that moral consideration and one who is constitutionally incapable of doing so.

understanding moral sentiments from the "inside"—that an agent without moral sense cannot benefit or draw from.[36]

The psychopath's way of dealing with negative reactive attitudes must always be "external" in character. Naturally these individuals will want to avoid punishment and the unwelcome treatment that comes with negative moral sentiments aroused in others. These individuals may also view these sanctions and the negative consequences that result from their conduct as both predictable and an acceptable part of the rules of society. What these individuals cannot do, however, is accept these reactions and sanctions in the *same way* as a normal person can. Whereas the person with moral sense is capable of accepting these responses in a way that involves coming to feel them from the inside or *sharing* these negative sentiments, this is simply not possible for the psychopath (or a person like Jack). He cannot, therefore, experience the grip and force of moral considerations through the channel of reactive sentiments themselves. Without an ability of this kind an agent's ability to recognize the salience and significance of moral claims, and to be motivated effectively by them, will be *radically* impaired. (The parallels with Jill's *practical* difficulties in respect of her inability to feel fear and the way that this limits and distorts her responses to danger and harm are obvious enough.)

The above discussion of the case of psychopaths shows that the condition of moral sense has concrete application to an important set of problem cases that we encounter in ordinary moral life.[37] Nevertheless, my concern in this context is not to provide an analysis or critique of the complex problem of psychopathy.[38] The interest of psychopaths, for our purposes, rests with the light that this sheds on what is required of normal moral agents whom we regard as fully responsible. For reasons that I have explained, these are agents for whom the functioning of moral sense is

---

36. As we noted with Jill, it is the interaction between recognizing danger and feeling fear from the "inside" that makes her incapable of responding to danger in the same way as a normal person. We "over-intellectualize" the *rationality* of a normal agent in dealing with danger if we represent her as being like Jill.

37. Robert Hare suggests that "the prevalence of psychopathy in our society is about the same as that of schizophrenia, a devastating mental disorder that brings heart-wrenching distress to patient and family alike" [*Without Conscience* (New York & London: Guilford, 1993), 2].

38. For a valuable discussion of this issue that is concerned with the general relevance of emotional incapacity and psychopathy see Walter Glannon, "Psychopathy and Responsibility," *Journal of Applied Philosophy*, 14 (1997), 263–75; and also Pat Greenspan, "Responsible Psychopaths," *Philosophical Psychology*, 16 (2003), 417–29.

directly relevant to the degree to which, and the way in which, their capacity for rational self-control effectively operates. Insofar as impaired moral sense limits or distorts their capacity for rational self-control, this incapacity will limit their ability to operate as full "participants" in the moral community. It is both unfair and unreasonable to treat these individuals who are incapacitated in these ways as if they are fully responsible. Similarly, it is crucial, for the purpose of moral education and understanding, that we carefully explore the intimate relationship between moral sense and rational self-control. In particular, we must avoid any false dichotomy between capacities required for *being* responsible (qua moral agency) and capacities required for *holding* agents responsible. The connection between being a moral agent and being able to hold ourselves and others responsible is much closer than this. Responsible agents must be capable of "deep assessment" in order to be able to effectively recognize and be motivated by moral considerations. Without "deep assessment" there is no "deep understanding" or "true appreciation" of moral considerations. This is what the condition of moral sense speaks to and demands.

VI

My central concern in this chapter has been to argue for the condition of moral sense. As we have noted, a number of philosophers have denied the validity of this condition. This includes several prominent compatibilists who endorse RS theory and accept that moral sense is essential for *holding* people responsible (i.e., for explaining the kind of "deep assessment" that is involved in viewing an agent as being responsible). The moral sense condition is also a condition of symmetry, as interpreted by any account that takes moral sense to be essential to holding an agent responsible. That is to say, symmetry requires that any responsible agent is also able to hold himself and others responsible. On the assumption that holding responsible requires moral sense, it follows that responsible agency also requires moral sense.[39]

---

39. In this chapter I have justified symmetry in terms of the particular demand of the condition of moral sense—taking moral sense to be essential for holding responsible. However, the argument for symmetry can be formulated in more general terms. The basic point is that any agent who is unable to hold himself responsible (i.e., effectively praise and blame himself and others) has a shallow and impoverished understanding of moral considerations. This incapacity affects the agent's ability both fully to understand and be motivated by moral considerations. Even a purely "intellectualist" account of what is involved in holding agents responsible should still, on this view, be committed to the general condition of symmetry.

Related to this point, the condition of moral sense imposes a "subjective" requirement on responsible agency. The responsible agent must be able to see herself as producing "upshots" in the world and as being an appropriate target of reactive sentiments. The basis on which I have defended this "subjective" requirement is, however, very different from the account suggested by Fischer and Ravizza. On their account, the importance of moral sense is that it plays a role in historical considerations as they relate to the issue of "ownership" of reason responsive dispositions. I have expressed doubts about the viability of this approach considered as a way of dealing with worries about implantation, manipulation, and covert control. The basis of my defense of the moral sense condition lies with the role that it plays in the agent's capacity for rational self-control or reason responsiveness. I have argued that when moral sense is impaired or the agent is incapacitated in this respect then this will directly affect the agent's ability to grasp and be motivated by moral considerations. Whereas the normal agent who is capable of moral sense will experience and understand reactive sentiments in a way that provides salience and significance to moral considerations, and also provides an internal and independent source of motivation (i.e., as distinct from "external" sanctions) for complying with these demands and expectations, the agent who lacks this general capacity will not be able to employ these resources to govern and guide her conduct. In these circumstances, the agent who lacks moral sense is neither fully responsible nor a full participant in the moral community. By way of analogy, I have suggested, agents who are incapacitated in this way are like individuals who lack any capacity to feel fear in the face of danger or harm. Their sensitivity to these considerations is radically and severely impaired and impoverished. The general point that emerges from this defense of the condition of moral sense is that it is important that we avoid "over-intellectualizing" what is involved in being responsible—not just what is involved in holding agents responsible.[40]

Although my reasons for accepting the condition of moral sense (viewed as a subjective requirement for responsible agency) are different from those provided by Fischer and Ravizza, I share their view that objections relating to manipulation and covert control must be addressed and that what has been said about reason responsive or rational self-control will not

---

40. Cp. Strawson, FR, 78. Strawson's remarks are not entirely clear on this (important) point and this may explain why some of those who follow him seek to combine a "Kantian" conception of moral agency with a Strawsonian account of holding responsible.

suffice to allay these concerns. It is my view, therefore, that any adequate compatibilist RS theory will need to find some independent way of dealing with (historical) worries of this kind.[41] That said, the observations we have made concerning the relevance of moral sense for moral agency are by no means without significance for the compatibilist position in its RS form. It is a familiar criticism of compatibilism that its account of responsibility is generally "superficial" and lacks "depth." It is, therefore, a particular aim of compatibilism to provide sufficient "depth" for its account of the conditions of responsible agency—and the reason responsive view has played a prominent role in all this. Related to this search for depth, as one prominent representative of the reason responsive approach has pointed out, is the fact that "complexity" matters.[42] By failing to recognize the important role that moral sense plays in relation to normative competence and rational self-control, compatibilists have failed to supply the necessary degree of both "depth" and "complexity" that is needed here. Put another way, responsibility is not simply a matter of *narrow depth* as conceived in "intellectualist" terms that ignore the role of emotion in moral life. It is also a matter of *width* as supplied by the interaction between reason and emotion as manifest and expressed in our capacity for moral sense.

This emotional dimension of responsible agency provides something more than an "atomistic" conception of rational competence that makes no reference to moral emotions and the social context in which they are acquired. It draws our attention to the fact that moral competence of the kind required for responsible agency develops in a social and emotional matrix that fosters and nourishes the general capacity to recognize and respond to moral considerations. No adequate theory of responsibility can ignore this important dimension of moral agency and the way that it evolves from childhood to adulthood.[43]

---

41. I discuss this problem in "History, Implantation and Hard Compatibilism" [presented at the Fifth European Conference for Analytic Philosophy; Lisbon, August 2005].

42. Daniel Dennett, *Elbow Room: The Varieties of Free Will Worth Wanting* (Oxford: Clarendon Press, 1984), 12. Although Dennett defends a version of reason responsive or rational self-control theory, he does not endorse any Strawsonian account of (holding) responsible—and therefore he is not an RS theorist.

43. The more general error here is the supposition that emotional incapacity is irrelevant to (intellectual) cognition. For an influential discussion of this general issue see, e.g., Antonio Damasio, *Descartes' Error: Emotion, Reason and the Human Brain* (London: Papermac, 1996). In the case of moral theory, the major source of this error is found in Plato and Kant (not Descartes).

I have discussed and defended the condition of moral sense almost entirely within a compatibilist framework. The reason for this should be clear. Contemporary compatibilist theory, following the lead of P. F. Strawson, has pursued the theme that moral sense is essential for holding agents responsible. On the other hand, Strawson's theory, as we have also noted, provided little detail in the way of an account of the capacities required to be a responsible agent (i.e., what is required to be a "normal adult"). Contemporary compatibilists have tried to plug this gap in Strawson's theory with an account of rational self-control that does not itself involve any reference to moral sense. I have argued that this is a mistake and that, where moral sense is lacking, rational self-control is seriously impaired and compromised. There is, however, no necessary connection between accepting the moral sense condition and being a compatibilist. That is to say, a libertarian incompatibilist might well agree that moral sense is an essential element in the kind of "deep assessment" involved in holding an agent responsible. The libertarian may also agree that the responsible agent must be reason responsive but will go on to insist that this capacity must include an ability to choose to act on his reasons in a sense that requires (categorically) open alternatives. Be this as it may, there is nothing about these specific commitments or the argument that I have presented for the moral sense condition, that does not also hold for the libertarian. That is to say, the responsible agent, on *any* interpretation, must be able to weigh and review moral considerations in light of a general capacity to hold himself and others responsible. Without this capacity this agent will have a *shallow understanding* of the moral considerations that are at stake and will fail to see the salience of these considerations or be motivated by them in the same way as a normal agent (whether she possesses libertarian free will or not). In so far as an ability to hold oneself responsible requires moral sense, it follows that even a libertarian agent will be significantly incapacitated without moral sense. From this we may conclude that although the condition of moral sense is especially significant for compatibilist RS theory, it is also a condition that is essential to any theory, including libertarian theory, that acknowledges moral sense as essential to holding agents responsible. Put more generally, no adequate theory that understands responsibility in terms of "deep assessment" and moral sense can deny that responsible agency (i.e., being responsible) also requires moral sense.

5

Moral Sense and the Foundations of Responsibility

It is a pity that talk of the moral sentiments has fallen out of favour. The phrase would be quite a good name for that network of human attitudes in acknowledging the character of which we find, I suggest, the only possibility of reconciling these disputants to each other.

P. F. STRAWSON, "Freedom and Resentment" (1962)

THROUGHOUT MUCH OF the first half of the twentieth century, the free will debate was largely concerned with the question of what kind of freedom was required for moral responsibility and whether the kind of freedom required was compatible with the thesis of determinism. This issue was itself addressed primarily with reference to the question of how freedom is related to alternative possibilities and what the relevant analysis of "could have done otherwise" comes to. The discussion of these topics made little advance on the basic strategies and positions already developed and defended on either side of the compatibilist/incompatibilist divide in the preceding two centuries. When P. F. Strawson's published his seminal article "Freedom and Resentment" in 1962 the dynamics of this debate were fundamentally altered. This is true both in respect of Strawson's general methodology, which demands a more empirically informed approach, and in terms of his core conceptual framework, which identifies a different set of considerations and issues at the heart of this debate. In particular, whereas the traditional or classical debate focused on the problem of (moral) freedom, Strawson directed his attention to the role of moral sentiments or "reactive attitudes" as the key to understanding and resolving the core problems lying at the heart of this debate. This essay is devoted to a critical assessment of Strawson's project and an analysis of the current debate concerning its prospects.

Strawson on Free Will and Reactive Attitudes

Strawson distinguishes two main camps in the free will dispute, labeling them "optimists" and "pessimists" respectively. (Hereafter I will use these terms with capitals, to indicate Strawson's more technical sense of these terms.) Optimists are compatibilists who hold that our attitudes and practices associated with moral responsibility would in no way be discredited or dislodged by the truth of the thesis of determinism. The Pessimist, by contrast, is the libertarian who holds that moral responsibility requires the falsity of determinism and the possession of some form of "contra-causal freedom" (P. F. Strawson 1962: 73, 74, 92). A third position distinguished by Strawson is that of the "moral sceptic," who holds that our "notions of moral guilt, of blame, of moral responsibility are inherently confused" whether determinism is true or false. Strawson's aim is to "reconcile" the Pessimist and Optimist positions (P. F. Strawson 1962: 72). Specifically, he aims to show that although the "Pessimist" is correct in holding that the Optimist's account of moral responsibility leaves out "something vital" (P. F. Strawson 1962: 73), what is needed to fill the gap in the Optimist's account is not any form of the "obscure and panicky metaphysics of libertarianism" (P. F. Strawson 1962: 93). Optimists are mistaken, Strawson maintains, in supposing that we can understand and justify our commitment to the attitudes and practices of moral responsibility simply in terms of a "one-eyed utilitarianism" that is exclusively concerned with the social benefits of these practices (P. F. Strawson 1962: 73, 92). Pessimists are mistaken in supposing that our commitment to these attitudes and practices rests on the assumption that determinism is false.

Granted that the foundations of moral responsibility do not, on Strawson's account, rest with either libertarian metaphysics or consequentialist considerations regarding the social benefits of these attitudes and practices, where are we to discover the relevant foundations for moral responsibility? Strawson's strategy is to take what may be described as a "naturalistic turn." Rather than asking directly, in the abstract, what *is* a responsible agent, Strawson suggests that we should consider in more detail, with more precision, what is involved in the attitudes that we take toward those who we regard as responsible agents. That is to say, what is involved in *holding* a person responsible? An approach of this kind depends less on a conceptual analysis of "freedom" and more on a descriptive psychology of human moral emotions. According to Strawson, our investigations in this area must begin with a basic fact about human beings: "the very great importance we attach to the attitudes and intentions towards other human beings, and the great extent to which our personal feelings and reactions depend upon, or involve, our beliefs about these attitudes and intentions" (P. F. Strawson 1962:, 75). In this way, the correct starting point is to be found in "that complicated web of attitudes and feelings which form moral life as we know it" (P. F. Strawson 1962: 91). When we proceed on this basis, we will place appropriate emphasis on the importance of (human) emotion in moral life and avoid the temptation—common to both Optimist and Pessimist strategies—to "overintellectualize" the free will debate (P. F. Strawson 1962: 91).

Two claims are fundamental to the Pessimist/skeptical view in the free will debate. The first is that if the thesis of determinism is true, then we have reason to reject and repudiate the attitudes and practices associated with moral responsibility on the general ground that they are unjustified or incoherent. The second claim is that if we do indeed have reason to suspend or abandon the attitudes and practices associated with moral responsibility, in light of these skeptical reflections, then we are, psychologically speaking, *capable* of doing this. Strawson's central arguments in "Freedom and Resentment" are directly targeted against these two main prongs of the Pessimist/skeptical position. I will distinguish the two basic arguments in question as Strawson's "rationalist" and "naturalist" arguments. The first aims to show that the truth of determinism would not, in itself, systematically discredit our reactive attitudes and feelings, as associated with moral responsibility. The second aims to show that even if, contrary to what Strawson supposes, we are persuaded by the skeptical challenge, it is psychologically impossible for us to entirely abandon or wholly suspend our reactive attitudes on the basis of a "general theoretical conviction" of this kind (P. F. Strawson 1962: 81, 82, 87). In other words, as Strawson argues elsewhere, our *natural* commitment to the reactive attitudes insulates them against any form of global skeptical challenge (P. F. Strawson 1985, ch. 2).

Both the rationalist and naturalist components of Strawson's efforts to refute the Pessimist are presented in the framework of his analysis of the rationale of excuses. The Pessimist/skeptic maintains that if determinism is true, excusing considerations will (somehow) apply to all human action or hold universally. Specifically, according to the Pessimist/skeptical view, if determinism is true then we must systematically withdraw and suspend our reactive attitudes—collapsing our commitment to the entire edifice of moral responsibility. Under what circumstances, Strawson asks, do we "modify" or "mollify" our reactive attitudes or withhold them altogether? There are, he suggests, two different categories of excusing consideration (P. F. Strawson 1962: 77–79). The first, which I will refer to as excuses in the strict or narrow sense, do not imply that the agent concerned is an inappropriate target of reactive attitudes, or someone of whom we cannot demand some relevant degree of good will or due regard (P. F. Strawson 1962: 77–78). In cases of this kind (e.g., accidents, ignorance), "the fact of injury [is] quite consistent with the agent's attitudes and intentions being just what they should be" (P. F. Strawson 1962: 78). The features that concern us relate to the proper interpretation of the action or injury (e.g., that it was accidental, unintentional, lacked any ill will). When we turn to the second category, what I will refer to as "exempting considerations," we are invited to withdraw or withhold entirely our reactive attitudes in respect of the agent. The exemption suggests that in some way the agent concerned is not an appropriate target of reactive attitudes and not someone of whom we can make the usual demand of good will. Agents of this kind are judged inappropriate targets of our reactive attitudes, and our associated retributive practices, because they are either psychologically abnormal or morally underdeveloped (e.g., mentally ill, immature).

This analysis of the rationale of excuses allows us to see more clearly, Strawson claims, what has gone wrong with the traditional free will debate. Granted that the issue of moral responsibility should be interpreted in terms of the conditions under which we view others as targets of reactive attitudes, would the truth of determinism "lead to the repudiation of all such attitudes"? (P. F. Strawson 1962: 80). Strawson answers, first, that the truth of determinism in no way serves (theoretically) to discredit our reactive attitudes in any systematic way. For this to be so, determinism would have to imply that one or other of the two basic forms of excusing considerations hold universally. There is, according to Strawson, no reason to believe that this is the case. Clearly determinism does not imply that every injurious action is done accidentally or unintentionally. Determinism does not imply that no one's conduct ever manifests ill will or fails to show proper regard for others. Nor does determinism imply that all agents are somehow "abnormal" or immature (P. F. Strawson 1962: 81). It follows from these observations that the truth of determinism in no way discredits or theoretically undermines our commitment to reactive attitudes of the kind involved in our ascriptions of responsibility. Contrary to what the Pessimist/skeptic maintains, therefore, the truth of determinism does not erode the necessary metaphysical foundations of our attitudes and practices associated with moral responsibility.

With this rationalistic argument in place, Strawson proceeds to support his critique of the Pessimist/skeptical position with his naturalist argument. Even if we had some theoretical reason to entirely abandon or suspend our reactive attitudes (e.g., as per the skeptical challenge), it would be psychologically impossible for us to do this. To do this would involve "adopting a thoroughgoing objectivity of attitude to others," which is something Strawson claims we are incapable of (P. F. Strawson 1962: 81–83; 1985, 39).

> To adopt the objective attitude to another human being is to see him, perhaps, as an object of social policy; as a subject for what, in a wide range of sense, might be called treatment; as something . . . to be managed or handled or cured or trained. . . . But it cannot include the range of feelings and attitudes which belong to involvement or participation with others in inter-personal human relationships . . .
>
> P. F. Strawson 1962: 79

Strawson allows that there are two circumstances in which the objective attitude is available to us. First, in circumstances where exempting conditions apply (e.g., mental illness), the objective attitude is, in fact, *required* of us, insofar as we are "civilized" (P. F. Strawson 1962: 81–82). There are also circumstances when the objective attitude may be adopted towards a "normal and mature" person simply because we want to use it as a refuge from "the strain of involvement" (P. F. Strawson 1962: 82). However, Strawson is careful to emphasize the limits of any policy of this kind. Although it is necessary to adopt the objective attitude towards those individuals who are "abnormal or immature," and although it is also possible to extend this attitude to some normal people on some occasions, a "sustained objectivity of inter-personal attitude, and the human isolation which that would entail, does not seem to be something of which human beings would be capable, even if some general truth [sc., determinism] were a theoretical ground for it" (P. F. Strawson 1962: 81). In other words, according to Strawson, the Pessimist/skeptic cannot *live* his skepticism—from a practical point of view skepticism of this kind is irrelevant (see, especially, P. F. Strawson 1985, 38–39). In the face of the skeptical challenge, Strawson's naturalistic riposte is to claim that "it is *useless* to ask whether it would not be rational for us to do what it is not in our nature to (be able to) do" (P. F. Strawson 1962: 87; emphasis in original). In this way, the skeptical challenge, based on worries about determinism, is not only groundless, it is also useless and irrelevant, because it has no potential practical or psychological traction in human nature and human life.

Beyond his rationalist and naturalist arguments, Strawson adds a third argument, which we may call his "pragmatic argument." Even if, contrary to the naturalistic observations that have been advanced, we were to suppose that we might be given a "god-like choice" concerning whether we should abandon or retain our (natural) commitment to the reactive attitudes, this choice, Strawson argues, must be decided in terms of the "gains and losses to human life, its enrichment or impoverishment" (P. F. Strawson 1962: 83). Clearly, on Strawson's account, any choice to abandon or altogether suspend our commitment to reactive attitudes would involve trying to live our lives from entirely within the "objective" stance— something that would imply total "human isolation" and a bleak, dehumanized existence (P. F. Strawson 1962: 81, 83, 89, 93). As Strawson presents it, any (notional) choice that we may be in a position to make concerning whether to continue to participate in a social community of human relationships, constituted and held together by our reactive attitudes, cannot and should not be decided with reference to a "theoretical" issue such as determinism. On the contrary, because our commitment to the reactive attitudes is, on this account, essential to our very humanity, no sane or sensible person would linger long over this question, even if it were to be presented to us.

Although Strawson's principal arguments are directed against the Pessimists skeptical view, he draws important conclusions from these arguments that make clear how his own compatibilist position diverges from that of the Optimist or classical compatibilism. The Optimist generally attempts to show that the truth of determinism does not prevent rewards and punishments from "regulating behavior in socially desirable ways" (P. F. Strawson 1962: 89):

> The picture painted by the optimist is painted in a style appropriate to a situation envisaged as wholly dominated by objectivity of attitude. The only operative notions involved in this picture are such as those of policy, treatment, control. But a thoroughgoing objectivity of attitude, excluding as it does the moral reactive attitudes,

excludes at the same time essential elements in the concepts of *moral* condemnation and *moral* responsibility.

P. F. Strawson 1962: 89; emphasis in original

The Pessimist is right, Strawson argues, to "recoil" at this picture of things but makes the mistake of assuming that "the gap in the optimist's account . . . can be filled only if some general metaphysical proposition [sc., indeterminism or contra-causal freedom] is repeatedly verified, verified in all cases where it is appropriate to attribute moral responsibility" (P. F. Strawson 1962: 92).

According to Strawson, in the final analysis, both the Optimist and the Pessimist are guilty of a shared misunderstanding:

> Both seek, in different ways, to over-intellectualize the facts. Inside the general structure or web of human attitudes and feelings of which I have been speaking, there is endless room for modification, redirection, criticism, and justification. But questions of justification are internal to the structure or relate to modifications internal to it. The existence of the general framework of attitudes is itself something we are given with the fact of human society. As a whole, it neither calls for, nor permits, an external "rational justification." Pessimists and optimists alike show themselves, in different ways, unable to accept this.

P. F. Strawson 1962: 91–92

It is, evidently, no part of Strawson's view to suggest that the reactive attitudes are altogether incapable of (rational) justification and criticism. On the contrary, Strawson's remarks explicitly make the point that "inside the general structure or web of human attitudes and feelings" there is a place and role for justification and criticism—this being an obvious corollary of his analysis and observations relating to the rationale of excusing and exempting conditions. The important point remains, however, that the basis of our general commitment or liability to the reactive attitudes is not itself something in need or capable of any form of theoretical or practical justification. These are emotional dispositions rooted in human nature at a deeper level than that provided by any (unconvincing and unnecessary) philosophical justifications.

Having identified the relevant lacunae in the Optimist's position, and the faulty alternative analysis provided by the Pessimist, Strawson

(1962: 93) goes on to conclude that "if we sufficiently, that is radically, modify the view of the optimist, his view is the right one." Reconciliation can in this way be achieved when we take note of the fact that our retributive practices "do not merely exploit our natures, they express them" (P. F. Strawson 1962: 93). When this core insight is fully appreciated, and the gap in the Optimist's position has been filled, there is no need to fall back into "the obscure and panicky metaphysics of libertarianism" (P. F. Strawson 1962: 93).

Assessing Strawson's Arguments

Having described the core arguments that feature in Strawson's strategy, we may now assess them for their strengths and weaknesses (see also Haji 2002; Kane 2005, ch. 10). Each of the three core arguments we have described—rationalist, naturalist, and pragmatic—encounter serious difficulties, if they are not fatally flawed. Let us consider, first, Strawson's rationalist argument. The key objective, for the success of this argument, is to show that, even if determinism is true, none of the standard excusing and exempting conditions can be generalized or said to hold universally (i.e., in virtue of the truth of this metaphysical thesis). Specifically, a crucial aspect of this argument involves showing that we have no reason to suppose, contrary to the Pessimist/skeptic, that exempting conditions apply to everyone if determinism is true. Critics, as well as some followers of Strawson, have found his argument unconvincing (see, e.g., Nagel 1986: 124–26; Watson 1987: 262–63; Russell 1992). According to Strawson (1962: 81),

> the participant attitude, and the personal reactive attitudes in general, tend to give place, and it is judged by the civilized should give place, to objective attitudes, just insofar as the agent is seen as excluded from ordinary adult human relationships by deep-rooted psychological abnormality—or simply by being a child. But it cannot be a consequence of any thesis which is not itself self-contradictory that abnormality is the universal condition.

The weakness in this argument is that it plainly equivocates between "abnormal" and "incapacitated." Contrary to what Strawson's language suggests, it is incapacity, and not abnormality, that serves as the relevant basis for exemptions. This leaves his anti-skeptical position open to a direct rejoinder from the Pessimist/skeptical camp.

The Pessimist/skeptic should not be understood as claiming that if determinism is true we are all abnormal. Rather, the Pessimist/skeptic claims only that if the thesis of determinism is true, then we are all incapacitated and, consequently, inappropriate targets of reactive attitudes. There is nothing self-contradictory about a thesis that suggests that incapacity is a universal condition. The relevant capacity, according to those Pessimists who accept libertarian metaphysics, is "free will" or "contracausal freedom" of some kind. P. F. Strawson (1962: 93), as we have noted, maintains that this view would commit us to "obscure and panicky metaphysics" and imposes upon us a condition of responsibility "which cannot be coherently described" (P. F. Strawson 1980: 265). Even if Strawson is right about this, his response does not show that the thesis of determinism poses no threat to our moral capacities and, hence, to our reactive attitudes as a whole. At most, all Strawson succeeds in doing is casting doubt on one interpretation of what the relevant capacities are supposed to be. What we require, however, in order to discredit the skeptical threat, is an account of what is involved or required of our moral capacities, such that we can say who is or is not exempted of responsibility (i.e., who is an appropriate target of reactive attitudes). Without some more plausible and detailed alternative characterization of the nature of moral capacity, we are in no position to give assurance that the truth of determinism is irrelevant to this issue. Although something of an appropriate nature can, perhaps, be said on behalf of the rationalist argument, we cannot find it in his own remarks on this subject (Russell 1992: 153–55). We may conclude, therefore, that Strawson's reply to the Pessimist/skeptic is, at best, incomplete.

What, then, can we say about Strawson's naturalistic argument? The difficulties Strawson faces here are, if anything, even more severe and fundamental. The key to Strawson's naturalistic response to the Pessimist/skeptical challenge is to claim that our commitment to the whole framework or web of the reactive attitudes does not require any kind of general rational justification and that no general "theoretical conviction" is capable of entirely dislodging this commitment. Nothing of this kind can lead us to repudiate all our reactive attitudes. Considered as a way of refuting or discrediting Pessimism and skepticism, Strawson's reply relies on two different forms or modes of naturalism, which Strawson fails to distinguish. Strawson's remarks suggest that he reads the Pessimist/skeptic as demanding some general rational justification for our liability or proneness to reactive attitudes. It may well be correct to claim, as Strawson does, that our liability to these emotions, as a type, is a natural fact about us that neither requires nor is capable of any rational (philo-sophical) justification. So considered, Strawson advances what I will call a "type-naturalist response" to the skeptical challenge. A response of this kind cannot, however, deal adequately with the Pessimist/skeptical threat properly understood.

The Pessimist/skeptic should be understood as claiming only that, given the truth of determinism, we are never justified in entertaining (any) tokens of reactive attitudes. In other words, however prone or liable to reactive attitudes we may be, in these circumstances, praising and blam-ing are never appropriate or legitimate. This form of skepticism—as it concerns tokens of reactive attitudes—is perfectly consistent with accept-ing Strawson's type-naturalism. Although we may be naturally prone or liable to these (moral) emotions, we are nevertheless capable of ceasing to feel or entertain these emotions if and when we judge, in the relevant circumstances, that these emotions are unjustified. The only naturalist reply to this (distinct) form of Pessimism/skepticism is to insist that no reasoning of any sort could ever lead us to cease entertaining or feeling emotions of this kind. Whatever considerations are brought to our atten-tion regarding our human predicament—whatever reason may suggest to us—we will nevertheless continue to experience and feel emotions of this kind (i.e., tokens of this type of emotion). This form of token-naturalism is, psychologically speaking, less plausible than its type-naturalist counter-part, because it is not evident that our (token) emotional response cannot be controlled by reason and reflection when we judge that these emotions are inappropriate and uncalled for. From another point of view, token-naturalist claims, even if they are accepted, would do nothing to refute or discredit the core Pessimist/skeptical objection and worry—which is that if determinism is true our reactive attitudes are never justified or legiti-mate. Even if it were true that we are, in some way, constitutionally incapa-ble of ceasing to entertain these emotions, this would not serve to address the relevant justificatory issue that is the focus of the Pessimist/skeptical challenge. Indeed, if our commitment to the fabric of responsibility rests, in the final analysis, on a *token*-naturalist psychology, this is more disturb-ing than simple skepticism—because it implies that attitudes and prac-tices that we recognize as reflectively unjust and inappropriate cannot be brought under the control of reason. A naturalism of this kind is as unat-tractive as it is implausible (Russell 1992, but see Nichols 2007).

Strawson's third core argument, his pragmatic argument, is likewise misguided and unconvincing. His type-naturalist claims about our natural liability or proneness to reactive attitudes does lend support to his claim that there is no question of us making some "godlike choice" about whether to retain or dispense with our general disposition to the participant stance (see, e.g., P. F. Strawson 1985: 31–38). Nevertheless, if we were given this godlike choice (i.e., relating to our commitment to this type of emotion), it does not follow we would be entitled to decide whether to entertain tokens of reactive attitudes on the basis of considerations relating to "the gains and losses of human life, its enrichment or impoverishment" (P. F. Strawson 1962: 83). On the contrary, should we be in a position to choose to retain this commitment—contrary to the type-naturalist hypothesis—we would still be constrained by the "internal" rationale of this commitment to suspend any and all tokens of reactive attitude where and when relevant excusing and exempting conditions apply. It follows from this that, if the Pessimist/skeptical challenge is well-founded, we cannot aim to justify *tokens* of reactive attitudes on the grounds that in their complete absence our lives would be somehow "impoverished" or "less human." If this were the case it would certainly be a bleak situation, but we cannot insulate ourselves from this (theoretical) possibility by simply setting aside the relevance of exempting considerations as they apply to the framework and coherence of the reactive attitudes (see, however, Nichols 2007, who finds more mileage in the pragmatic dimension of Strawson's strategy).

Exemptions, Moral Capacity, and Reflective Self-Control

The assessment of Strawson's "reconciling project" provided above makes clear that his approach encounters serious and substantial difficulties. It would be wrong, however, to conclude that no further headway can be made by following the tracks Strawson has laid down. On the contrary, a sympathetic reconstruction of Strawson's project, avoiding some of the weaknesses, and filling-in some missing elements, may still provide a plausible alternative to libertarian metaphysics, utilitarian-oriented compatibilism, and moral skepticism—each of which have their own difficulties and flaws. The relevant starting point for such a project rests with a more robust and plausible account of moral capacity. The absence of a detailed account of moral capacity, as we have seen, is a major weakness in Strawson's own contribution and, in particular, leaves his rationalist argument open to objection (Russell 1992; on similar difficulties relating to Hume's theory see Russell 1995, ch. 6). If a more adequate theory of moral capacity is available, then Strawson's approach can be provided with an account of exemptions that will serve his compatibilist objectives. An important and influential attempt to supply Strawson's with these elements has been provided by R. J. Wallace.

In *Responsibility and the Moral Sentiments,* Wallace defends a compatibilist position that combines two strands of philosophical thought, a Strawsonian account of holding people responsible and a Kantian theory of moral agency. Methodologically speaking, Wallace (1994: 5–6, 15) presents himself as offering a "normative interpretation" of the free will debate. In Wallace's account, it is crucial that we begin our investigations, as Strawson does, with a philosophically adequate description of what is involved in holding people responsible, because the conditions of responsibility must themselves be interpreted in terms of when it is *fair* for us to adopt the stance of holding an agent responsible (15–16). In other words, Wallace is skeptical of any effort to describe conditions of responsibility in the abstract without reference to what is involved in holding an agent responsible. His account of holding responsible has, in this sense, priority over his account of being responsible.

Wallace's discussion makes substantial contributions that fall on either side of the Strawsonian and Kantian elements mentioned above. On the side of his Strawsonian account of holding agents responsible, Wallace provides a different taxonomy of the reactive attitudes in relation to the moral emotions from that suggested by Strawson. Wallace uses this taxonomy of the reactive attitudes and moral emotions to carve out a distinct and different set of commitments on the issues of "objectivity," "naturalism," and "pessimism"—all issues where he diverges significantly from Strawson. On the other side of the divide, his Kantian theory of agency, Wallace presents an outline of a theory of "reflective self-control" that provides a principled, normative basis for exempting conditions, consistent with his basic compatibilist ambitions.

Let us begin with the key elements of Wallace's account of holding people responsible. To hold a person morally responsible is "to hold the person to moral expectations that one accepts" (Wallace 1994: 51). In this view, moral expectations are supported by moral reasons or justifications, and expectations of this nature constitute obligations (36, 63–64). Moreover, there is an essential linkage between holding someone to a (moral) expectation and being susceptible to (moral) reactive attitudes, such as resentment, indignation, and guilt. Susceptibility to these emotions is, Wallace maintains, "what constitutes holding someone to an expectation" (Wallace 1994: 21). This mutual dependence of emotion and expectation is what distinguishes the reactive attitudes (Wallace 1994: 21).[1] One notable advantage of this general account of what is involved in holding a person responsible, presented in terms of the essential relationship between expectations and reactive attitudes, is that it enables us to provide a theory of reactive attitudes that has some cognitive content, as opposed to a cruder, emotivist understanding of reactive attitudes or moral sentiments understood merely as raw feelings (Wallace 1994: 74–78; and see Russell 1995, ch. 6, as this issue relates to Hume's system..

Wallace's analysis, although it clearly provides the Strawsonian system with some precision and detail, comes at some cost. One of the more obvious difficulties (p. 209) is that if we accept this account of holding agents responsible, it follows that we are committed to a "narrow" view of responsibility that focuses exclusively on negative emotions (e.g., indignation, resentment, and guilt, as aroused in circumstances when expectations/obligation are judged to have been violated). Wallace (1994: 63–64, 71) attempts to explain away this worry about his "asymmetrical" treatment of responsibility in terms of what he claims is the absence of any particular "positive emotions" in relation to morally worthy actions. Suffice it to say that this is an oddity of Wallace's account that is not present in Strawson's own contribution. Another, and perhaps more fundamental, difficulty that Wallace considers is the objection that we may—and often do—hold people responsible without engaging any particular emotion toward the person concerned (Wallace 1994: 76, and also 23, 62). Wallace's reply to this objection is that although we must understand the stance of holding people responsible with reference to the relevant (moral) reactive attitudes, this does not require that "we actually feel the relevant emotion in all the cases in which it would be appropriate to do so" (Wallace 1994: 76). What his theory commits us to is a disjunctive requirement that in holding a person responsible we must either be susceptible to the reactive emotions or believe that it would be appropriate for one to feel the reactive emotions, when the relevant expectations are violated (Wallace 1994::23,

---

1. Wallace argues that not all reactive attitudes are moral reactive attitudes. It is only those reactive attitudes that involve moral expectations (obligations) backed by moral reasons that constitute the distinct class of moral reactive attitudes. There may, for example, be expectations based on etiquette that are also associated with reactive attitudes but lack any specific moral content. Wallace also argues that there are moral emotions other than moral reactive attitudes, such us shame, gratitude and admiration. Emotions of this kind cannot, he claims, be linked with (moral) expectations and reactive attitudes (Wallace 1994, 35–38).

62, 76). It follows from this that although feeling or engaged emotion is not required for holding a person responsible, some relevant connection with these emotions and feelings is still required (i.e., via the belief that they are appropriate).

Although Wallace is anxious to clear his theory of any emotivist or noncognitivist features, the essential connection between responsibility and the reactive attitudes remains fundamental to his account. Wallace (1994: 52) explains the importance of this connection—the foundations of moral responsibility in our emotions—in terms of the issue of "depth" (cp. Wolf 1990: 41). Without any reference to moral emotions and feelings of the kind Wallace has described, the force of moral judgments of blame and responsibility would be lost. True moral blame, he suggests, is a form of deep assessment that reflects or manifests an attitude toward the agent who has acted wrongly (Wallace 1994: 78). Any account that severs judgments of responsibility from the set of attitudes associated with them (i.e., the "distinctive syndrome" associated with moral assessment; see Wallace 1994: 24) would render blame "superficial" (Wallace 1994: 78). For this reason, Wallace insists that judgments of responsibility must reach beyond a mere description of what the agent has done (e.g., violating our moral expectations) and account for the condition of the judge who assigns blame (Wallace 1994: 81–83). It is the judge's stance that captures the attitudinal dimension that gives blame and our judgments concerned with moral responsibility their distinct force and depth. It is this feature of Wallace's position that explains why, on his account, our understanding of responsibility must begin with an adequate analysis of holding people responsible. However much Wallace's position diverges from Strawson's views in other respects, he remains faithful to this key feature.

Although the adjustments and modifications that Wallace makes to the Strawsonian side of his position are significant, his most important contribution rests with his Kantian account of moral agency and moral capacity. As we have noted, when we considered Strawson's rationalist argument, it is here that Strawson's position is at its weakest and most vulnerable. Wallace defends a theory of "reflective self-control" that is, as he presents it, a form of "practical freedom" of a recognizably Kantian kind (Wallace 1994: 12–15). To explain the nature and character of his conception of moral agency, Wallace distinguishes "two competing pictures of what it is to be a morally responsible agent" (86). The picture Wallace rejects is one that interprets "the apparent truism that moral responsibility involves a kind of control over one's action" in terms of possessing a causal power over a range of alternatives. In this picture, moral agency requires genuine alternatives—something that "invites an incompatibilist under-standing of responsibility, as requiring strong freedom of will" (Wallace 1994: 86). Another view of control over actions, however, is concerned with the possession of "normative competence." Normative competence should be understood in terms of (1) the power to grasp and apply moral reasons, and (2) the power to control or regulate behavior in light of such reasons (Wallace 1994: 86, 157). Agents who have these powers are capable of "reflective self-control." Although determinism may deprive us of gen-uine alternatives, it does not necessarily deprive us of the relevant powers of normative competence that Wallace has described. (Other influential compatibilist accounts of rational self-control are found in Dennett 1984; Wolf 1990; Fischer and Ravizza 1998.)

On Wallace's (1994: 15) normative interpretation, the "conditions of responsibility are to be construed as conditions that make it fair to adopt the stance of holding people responsible." In light of this, the relevant question to ask is: Would the truth of determinism make it unfair to hold someone responsible, where this is understood in terms of directing reac-tive attitudes at someone who has violated the relevant moral expecta-tions? Clearly, where ordinary excuses in the narrow sense apply we must withdraw or inhibit our reactive attitudes, because the point or force of excuses is to establish that "the agent did not really violate the moral obli-gations we accept after all" (Wallace 1994: 133, 147). In other words, where valid excuses hold, the agent has done nothing wrong and there is, in fact, no fault to be found in the quality of the agent's will (Wallace 1994:135). We may account for considerations of this kind, Wallace argues, without reference to alternative possibilities or the need for "strong freedom of will." What, then, about exempting conditions? In Wallace's normative competence picture, it is fair to hold an agent responsible so long as she possesses the relevant powers of "reflective self-control." In the case of children or the insane it would indeed be unfair to hold them responsible, given that they lack these capacities for reflective self-control. Again, how-ever, the relevant distinctions can be drawn here, Wallace argues, without relying on the metaphysics of indeterminism and (genuine) alternative possibilities (181). On this basis, Wallace concludes, a compatibilist view can be constructed and defended from within the constraints of the "nor-mative interpretation of the debate about responsibility."

Although Wallace's account of Kantian agency lends considerable sup-port to a broadly Strawsonian strategy, it remains vulnerable to a serious objection—one that Wallace anticipates but does not convincingly defuse. In Wallace's account, it is fair to hold a person responsible for doing wrong even though they may have been unable to exercise their powers of reflective self-control differently in the actual circumstances. All that is relevant to the question of the agent's responsibility, Wallace maintains, is that the agent possesses the relevant general powers (i.e., qua disposition) and in fact exercised those powers in such a way that the relevant expectations were violated (Wallace 1994: 161–62). The difficulty remains, however, that the mere possession of such powers does not give the agent control over *the way in which they are actually exercised* (on this see Kane 2002; see also Russell 2002, 244–45 concerning related difficulties for Dennett 1984). Although Wallace worries over this problem (Wallace 1994: 182–86, 196–214, 223), his position, in the end, reduces to his insistence that this further condition (i.e., that the agent can control how his powers are actually exercised) would simply "give the game away" to the incompatibilist (Wallace 1994: 223). What the Pessimist/skeptic needs here, and will not find in Wallace's discussion, is a convincing account of why it is fair to hold a person responsible for conduct that flows from powers that are exercised in ways over which they have no control. Without a more substantial reply to this objection, the Strawsonian strategy that Wallace pursues will not persuade its critics.

Holding and Being Responsible

Wallace, as we have noted, makes clear that his effort to reconstruct the moral sentiments approach to responsibility, along the lines advanced earlier by Strawson, falls into two component parts: Strawsonian and Kantian. This division of labor looks essential to the viability of the entire project, because the theory of "holding responsible," on one side, requires a theory of "responsible agency" on the other. This divide is, however, problematic from several points of view. It may be argued, for example, that insofar as Wallace's Kantian theory of agency is judged a success, it is no longer evident that we need a "normative interpretation of responsibility" that supposes that conditions of responsibility are to be construed as "conditions that make it fair to adopt the stance of *holding* people responsible" (Wallace 1994: 15; emphasis added). That is to say, if we can provide a full and complete account of being a responsible agent in terms of agents possessing powers of reflective self-control and being subject to relevant moral norms, why must we include any reference to the role of reactive attitudes or moral feelings in this context? Such elements may be judged as not only unnecessary, but also misplaced and misleading. Criticism along these general lines has been developed by Angela Smith in her recent article "On Being Responsible and Holding Responsible."

Smith (2007: 466, 472, 483) argues that Wallace's normative interpretation, and by implication all similar Strawsonian strategies, confuse two distinct sets of issues and conditions. Specifically, there is a distinction to be drawn between: (1) the conditions under which it is fair and appropriate to blame people, and (2) the conditions under which it is appropriate to judge them to be responsible and blameworthy (472). Smith's account of this matter turns on a related distinction between the agent being "at fault" or "culpable" and it being fair to blame the agent (see, e.g., Smith 2007: 466n5). Culpability or blameworthiness implies the agent is at fault and subject to (valid) criticism. It does not follow, however, from the fact that a person is at fault or culpable that "active blaming" is appropriate (Smith 2007: 473). Active blaming, as Smith understands it, "in some way goes beyond beliefs about a person's responsibility and culpability" (Smith 2007: 470). Smith grants that her terminology in this respect is potentially misleading if it is taken to imply that the "'active blamer' must actually *do* something to express her blame towards the person she blames" (Smith 2007: 477; emphasis in original). This is not necessary, because active blame may involve simply feeling resentment, indignation, or anger toward the agent, without expressing these emotions in any way. Nonetheless, although blaming presupposes culpability, culpability or fault does not, by itself, entail that blaming is appropriate (473n10; see the related discussion in Kutz 2000, ch. 2). This gap between conditions of culpability and appropriate blaming, Smith argues, shows that conditions of being responsible cannot be reduced to conditions of appropriate active blaming.

How, then, do we assess when it is appropriate to actively blame an agent for some fault or wrongdoing? The relevant variables here, according to Smith, include considerations such as (i) our own standing as possible or potential moral judges, (ii) the significance of the fault to which we are responding, and (iii) the nature of the agent's own response to the fault or conduct in question (Smith 2007: 478). In respect of all these issues, Smith claims, issues of culpability and appropriate blame come apart and may diverge. For example, I may regard myself as not standing in a relevantly close or intimate relationship with an agent to be in a position to actively blame him for a fault (e.g., treating his spouse in an inconsiderate manner), even though I may well judge the agent is at fault and culpable. Likewise, I may regard the fault or culpable conduct as too insignificant or unimportant to merit resentment or indignation without compromising the initial judgment that the agent is responsible for some wrongdoing. Finally, in some cases the agent's own response to her faults (e.g., her obvious remorse and guilt) may encourage the view that any active blame is uncalled for and inappropriate. Again, this conclusion may be reached without compromising our independent and distinct judgment regarding her responsibility or culpability for her actions. With respect to variables and considerations of these kinds, because they concern the conditions of when it is appropriate to actively blame a person, there "may be no single, definitive answer to this question, because the 'us' in question [i.e., qua moral judges] is made up of individuals who stand in a variety of different relations to the agent in question, and who therefore have different degrees of interest and concern for her attitudes and conduct" (Smith 2007: 471). The question of when an agent is culpable or actually at fault, by contrast, does not allow for this sort of variation and fragmentation in our answer. Smith takes for granted that, with respect to the question of whether the moral agent is or is not responsible, we must secure some unequivocal answer that is not available to us when we are considering the stance of the moral judge who must decide if active blame is called for or appropriate.

Wallace certainly provides some resources for a reply to Smith's line of criticism. The first point to be mentioned is that, on Wallace's account, "active blaming" not only need not involve doing something to express blame, it may not even require feeling or engaging our emotions at all. As already noted, it is part of Wallace's "disjunctive formulation" of holding someone to reactive emotions to allow this to include simply believing that it would be appropriate to feel these emotions (Wallace 1994: 23). Obviously, this qualification significantly closes the gap between what Smith describes as judgments about responsibility and actively blaming a person. At the same time, however, the connection between conditions of responsibility and holding a person to reactive attitudes must remain, for Wallace, because without this, judgments about responsibility or blameworthiness would be "rendered superficial" or "shallow." The aspect of "depth," which is essential to understanding what it is to be responsible, can be fully and completely appreciated only if we retain (some) reference to the attitudinal features found in the stance of the *judge* (Wallace 1994: 51, 77–83). The force of Wallace's normative interpretation, insofar as it insists on retaining this connection between being and holding responsible, is that any analysis that severs this connection, as Smith would have us do, leaves our understanding of what it is to be responsible incomplete and one-sided—lacking the needed and necessary psychological linkage between agent and judge.

Several features of the position that Smith takes on this issue are problematic. If we accept that conditions of being responsible and active blaming are to be distinguished in the manner Smith suggests then the following scenario would be entirely conceivable. We could find ourselves in a world where there are beings who are judged to be culpable, responsible agents but also no people who can be appropriately (actively) blamed. This would be a world in which blame had no place, even though it is populated by agents who are routinely judged to be responsible for their acts. It is not obvious that a world entirely drained of blame in this manner is one in which we could make adequate sense of responsible agency, or that we would be entitled to conclude that responsible agency was truly preserved. That is to say, in a world of this kind it is not obvious that the agents in question are really regarded as fully responsible for their actions. In Wallace's language, we may say a blameless world of this sort would be one in which judgments of responsibility lacked any "depth" or "force." Any account of responsibility given in these terms is, to this extent, itself incomplete and insubstantial. By severing our assessments of culpability and fault from their (natural) connections and associations with conditions of (active) blame we erode the very fabric of moral life, and strip away the evaluative significance and motivational traction of moral judgment.

In responding to Smith's criticisms of Wallace, I have suggested that Wallace's discussion provides us with some relevant materials for dealing with Smith's general objection. There is, however, another way of approaching the question of the relationship between being and holding responsible that indicates that Wallace's (related) split between Strawsonian and Kantian components runs into difficulties and problems that are similar to those that Smith's views encounter. Specifically, Wallace's hybrid model, lends itself to the theoretical possibility of a moral world where a gap (i.e., an asymmetry) opens up between those who are responsible agents and those who can hold agents responsible. Consider Wallace's example of Mr. Spock (of *Star Trek* fame) who, as Wallace describes him, is not susceptible of human emotion and is, consequently, incapable of reactive attitudes and/or of holding people responsible (Wallace 1994: 78n41). There is no reason, in principle, given Wallace's split between the Strawsonian and Kantian components of his analysis of responsibility, why an agent such as Mr. Spock may not be capable of "reflective self-control" (i.e., he is plainly "normatively competent" by Wallace's standards). At the same time, Mr. Spock is also, evidently, constitutionally incapable of holding himself or others responsible, because he lacks all capacity for reactive attitudes. For Wallace, there is no necessary or required connection between responsible agency and a capacity to feel or entertain reactive attitudes (i.e., between being a moral agent and being able hold oneself and others responsible). A world populated entirely by Mr. Spocks, such as the planet Vulcan (where Spock comes from), would be a world similar in kind to the world we have already envisioned when we considered Smith's views on the distinction between being responsible and active blame. A Vulcan world would be one in which, in Wallace's analysis, responsible agency (i.e., normative competence) would exist in circumstances where the responsible agents (i.e., the Vulcans) lack any capacity to hold agents responsible. Because there is, according to Wallace's analysis, no necessary connection between a capacity to hold agents responsible (i.e., by means of reactive attitudes) and responsible agency itself, this is, on his account, at least a coherent and conceivable possibility. What is significant about the Vulcan world, as described, is that it is indeed an imaginary world taken from science fiction, quite unlike any real, recognizable human world with moral life as we know it.[2]

In a Vulcan world, as I have described it, responsible agency operates effectively and unimpaired in the complete absence of any capacity for reactive attitudes or moral sentiments. It is, however, highly questionable if our moral capacities, as we actually find them, would be undamaged or fully effective without a capacity to (actively) hold ourselves and others responsible. In the complete absence of any capacity to see ourselves and others as objects of reactive attitudes our capacity for recognizing and responding to moral considerations would surely be impaired. One good reason for supposing this to be true is that our relevant moral emotions

---

2. On Smith's analysis some symmetry between being and holding responsible is preserved, in these circumstances, so long as we assume that Vulcan agents can judge when moral criticism is appropriate or called for (i.e., as distinct from any form of "active blaming"). For Wallace, in contrast, we can continue to view the Vulcan agents as genuinely responsible only if there are some (human) agents who are in a position to hold them responsible. In the absence of any (human) agents with reactive attitudes there would be no moral judges and, hence, no (deep) moral responsibility. Clearly, the difficulties that Smith and Wallace run into here are related but different.

give salience and significance to moral considerations and reasons. In the complete absence of any such emotional capacity, judgments of responsibility and their connection with moral considerations would lack the force and weight that we attach to them (via this mechanism). Agents such as Mr. Spock, and other Vulcans, would have a shallow and thin appreciation of moral reasons. Nor would they be motivated to recognize and respond to these reasons in the same way as (normal) human beings. If these general observations are correct, then it follows that for an agent to be responsible she must have a general capacity to hold herself and others responsible. There is, therefore, an intimate relationship between being and holding responsible as this concerns moral capacity. Considered from this point of view, we have reason to be skeptical about the suggestion that there could be a world in which there are agents who are responsible but who are, nevertheless, incapable of holding themselves and others responsible (Russell 2004).

History, Skepticism, and Pessimism: Hard Incompatibilism and Critical Compatibilism

Gary Watson, in his influential reflections on Strawson's "Freedom and Resentment" (Watson 1987), identifies the lack of a plausible theory of exempting conditions as a general failing in Strawson's contribution. We have already considered some features of this criticism and possible lines of reply, such as Wallace's sketch of our powers of reflective self-control or normative competence. There is, however, a more specific vein of criticism that Watson pursues that cuts deep to the heart of issues that divide compatibilists and incompatibilists. The central concern here is what Watson describes as "the historical dimension of the concept of responsibility" (Watson 1987: 281). In order to explain the nature of this problem, Watson describes in some detail the case of Robert Harris, who committed brutal murders in California in 1978. Watson presents a detailed description of the events of the murders themselves, with a view to generating a strong reactive (retributive) response in his readers. What was particularly disturbing about this case was the evidence of sadism and the complete lack of remorse. At the same time, there was no evidence of insanity or incapacity of any relevant kind (i.e., as described). Watson then switches the reader's attention to the historical background, detailing the horrors and extreme brutality of Harris's own childhood and adolescence. We are then invited to see Harris as victim, rather than a victimizer (Watson 1987: 275). The result of this switch in our attention and focus is not, Watson suggests, that it directly exempts Harris, but that it generates "ambivalence" in our response to him—emotional conflict is the product of these reflections (Watson 1987: 275). Watson goes on to suggest that cases such as this lead us to the general conclusion that, in the final analysis, we are not responsible for ourselves, because we are not the ultimate originators of our deeds (Watson 1987: 281–82). The upshot of these observations is that historical reflections of this kind make clear that "our ordinary practices are not as unproblematic as Strawson supposes" (Watson 1987: 283; also Nagel 1980; G. Strawson 1986, ch. 5; 1994; but contrast McKenna 1998; Nichols 2007).

Although Watson's own discussion stops short of endorsing a skeptical position, the general trajectory of his argument leads firmly in this direction. These sort of skeptical concerns about history suggest that it may not suffice to provide the Strawsonian strategy with an account of "reflective self-control" (i.e., along the lines of Wallace's approach). The incompatibilist or skeptical challenge may be pressed harder here by means of examples of implantation and manipulation. Counterexamples of this sort have been put forward, in one form or another, many times (see, e.g., Taylor 1963, 45–46; Dennett 1984; Pereboom 2007; and Pereboom 2011). Regarding the general strategies we are concerned with, the basic concern is that for any preferred compatibilist conception of moral capacity (e.g., some mode of reflective self-control) it is theoretically possible that an external manipulator could implant the preferred structure in the agent and covertly control his conduct by this means (for a detailed discussion of this sort of case, see Kane 1996: 64–69). The difficulty for any compatibilist account—including the Strawsonian strategy we are considering—is that they have no principled reason to conclude that these manipulated individuals are not responsible agents. Counterexamples of this kind, drawing on "historical" considerations, lead us back down a slippery slope into skepticism. This is not the context in which to try to address these specific difficulties and objections to the wider compatibilist project. However, suffice it to say, for now, that objections of this kind require compatibilists to look either for further historical conditions on responsibility (e.g., excluding agents with "abnormal" or "deviant" histories) or to provide some nonhistorical basis, consistent with compatibilist commitments, that can account for why manipulation and implantation (appear to) pose a threat to responsible agency. (For various strategies see, e.g., Fischer and Ravizza 1998, ch. 8; McKenna 2004; Russell 2010)

Let us grant, for the moment, that the skeptical challenge cannot be effectively repelled by the arguments and strategy advanced by Strawson and his followers; we are still left (qua skeptic) with a significant set of problems on Strawson's analysis. In recent years there have been several important efforts to deal with some of these issues relating to the question of whether skepticism about responsibility is, for human beings, livable and/or bearable (i.e., worth living). The general issue that we have to deal with here is how skepticism about moral responsibility relates to Strawson's account of the "objective attitude" and the question of "pessimism." It is Strawson's view, as we have noted, that skepticism about moral responsibility should be interpreted as the view that our reactive attitudes are never justified or appropriate and must be altogether abandoned or suspended. (Strawson, of course, does not accept that skepticism about contra-causal freedom or libertarian metaphysics itself justifies skepticism about moral responsibility.) It is also Strawson's view that a skepticism about responsibility, so interpreted, is psychologically impossible and, if possible, would be unbearably bleak and inhuman. The first of this pair of claims is part of his (strong) naturalism and the second is a feature of what he takes to be the linkage between skepticism and pessimism on this issue. We have already noted that even those who endorse Strawson's strategy of understanding responsibility in terms of our reactive attitudes need not accept his strong naturalist claim that it is psychologically impossible for us to live without the reactive attitudes. Wallace, for example, argues that our commitment to moral reactive attitudes and the associated system of moral expectations may be a cultural feature—one that other human cultures may not share with us (Wallace 1994: 3–2, 38–40, 64–65). To this extent, Strawson's strong naturalism does not seem essential to the wider position that he advances.

What about his views concerning the relationship between skepticism and pessimism in this sphere? It is certainly true, generally speaking, that skepticism about moral responsibility is widely associated with a pessimistic view of the human predicament (i.e., to the extent that responsibility is denied). Among Strawson's followers, however, there is some disagreement about the relationship between skepticism and pessimism. Some share Strawson's view that a life without any reactive attitudes would indeed be hopelessly bleak and humanly "impoverished" (see, e.g., Wolf 1981; Bennett 2008; and compare Smilansky 2001). Others, including Wallace, take a different view. Wallace, as we have noted, emphasizes the point that other forms of moral emotion may exist in the absence of reactive attitudes and it is a mistake (pace Strawson, Bennett et al.) to expand the class of reactive attitudes to include a wider range of emotions (e.g., reciprocal love) that are unconnected with expectations (Wallace 1994: 27; but see also P. F. Strawson 1962: 79). From this perspective there is no obvious or necessary linkage between a life entirely devoid of reactive attitudes, properly delineated, and Strawson's bleak description of living exclusively from the "objective stance," with the "human isolation" that this would imply (P. F. Strawson 1962: 81).

Whereas Wallace is persuaded by Strawson's broad anti-skeptical strategy, others who are not have more directly challenged his effort to present skepticism about moral responsibility as implying a deeply bleak view about our predicament in such a world. Among those who have challenged the simple connection between skepticism about responsibility and pessimism, Derk Pereboom (1995, 2001, 2007) has been especially influential (see also Honderich 2002, ch. 10; Sommers 2007). In several different contributions Pereboom has argued that skeptical worries about the ultimate source of conduct and character cannot be convincingly addressed by either compatibilist or libertarian theories of freedom and, for this reason, moral responsibility (i.e., understood in terms of "basic desert") cannot be rescued from the various skeptical arguments that discredit it (Pereboom 2007:, 86, 119, 123). Although much of Pereboom's attention is devoted to these skeptical arguments, in support of his "hard incompatibilist" position, it is his efforts to vindicate some form of (qualified) optimism consistent with his skepticism that is relevant to our present concerns. Whereas on the orthodox view that Strawson describes, skepticism about moral responsibility implies that a wide range of concerns and values attached to responsibility would be eroded, if not erased, Pereboom argues that this slide into pessimism is (grossly) exaggerated and largely unfounded.

Pereboom (2007: 116–18) discusses a wide range of features of human life that may be thought to be threatened by skepticism about moral responsibility, including our sense of self-worth and our having meaning and purpose in life. It is, however, Pereboom's effort to find room for personal relations and a robust emotional life, consistent with his "hard incompatibilism," where he most clearly diverges from Strawson. Pereboom grants that "the objective attitude," as Strawson describes it, would be bleak and depressing. He denies, nevertheless, that our emotional lives would be impoverished in the way that Strawson suggests if we embrace skepticism or hard incompatibilism. He argues, in the first place, that only some forms of reactive attitude would be threatened by skepticism about moral responsibility. There are, he says, reactive attitudes that either would "survive" or have "analogues" that would be "sufficient to sustain good [personal] relationships" (Pereboom 1995: 269; 2007: 119). Moreover, many of those that do not survive or have no "analogues," we would be better off without (e.g., certain kinds of anger and resentment). With this general position in view, Pereboom runs through a variety of personal emotions, such as forgiveness, gratitude, mature love, regret, and forms of "moral sadness," that would persist or even thrive in the face of skepticism about moral (p. 218) responsibility in the sense of "basic desert" (Pereboom 1995: 269–71; 2001: 199–207; 2007: 118–22). (See also Pereboom 2011 for further discussion of all of these topics.) Granted these alternative modes of reactive attitudes and personal emotions can survive and persist in the manner that Pereboom suggests, then skepticism about moral responsibility can be presented as being a potential source of genuine *optimism*—not a dreaded "difficult truth" that we must face up to (see also Watson 1987: 284–86; Sommers 2007).

The various responses to Strawson that we have reviewed have challenged the way in which he suggests that skepticism about responsibility implies pessimism of some significant kind (e.g., despair, anxiety) about the human predicament. This is certainly a view that Pereboom, Honderich, and Sommers, among others, have questioned. By way of conclusion, however, I would like to raise some questions and doubts in the opposite direction. Let us assume that some version of Strawson's and Wallace's project of vindicating moral responsibility in terms of holding agents responsible on the basis of reactive attitudes can be defended (subject to further refinements and elaboration). Where does this leave us with respect to the optimism/pessimism duality that Strawson has drawn our attention to? A seemingly natural corollary of the suggestion that skepticism implies pessimism is that anti-skepticism (i.e., leaving responsibility in its place) must vindicate optimism—the view that with respect to the issue of moral responsibility we have no basis for finding the human predicament "difficult" or "depressing." Strawson's language—like the language of most compatibilism in general—encourages this "sunny" view (for an especially optimistic version of compatibilism as triumphing over the "gloom-leaders" of pessimism, see Dennett 1984: 7). It is worth mentioning, therefore, that there is another view that may be taken on this issue, one that regards the general vindication of moral responsibility along Strawsonian lines as a basis for a (moderate) pessimism about the human predicament.

The view I am describing has itself two core components. The first is a compatibilist theory of moral responsibility that builds on the work of Strawson, Wallace, and others (i.e., subject to further refinements). Among the relevant points of disagreement that will arise on this side of things, is whether or not we need a "revisionary" account—which will, in turn, depend on what we take our "ordinary intuitions" to be on this subject (see, e.g., Vargas 2007 and Vargas 2011). On the other side, where this view clearly diverges from most orthodox forms of compatibilism, it is argued that incompatibilist worries and concerns about ultimacy and sourcehood are well-founded and cannot simply be dismissed as illusory, confused, or groundless (as is argued, for example, by Dennett 1984, ch. 1; for criticism of this, see Russell 2002). At the same time, this view—let us call it "critical compatibilism"—does not accept the incompatibilist or skeptical view that these pessimistic concerns about the impossibility of ultimacy for human agents licenses skepticism about moral responsibility itself. On the contrary, the key contention of critical compatibilism, so described, is that pessimistic reflections about the impossibility of ultimate agency and sourcehood are rooted in the thought that it is because we are morally responsible agents that these reflections on the limitations of agency (rooted in human finitude) present themselves as especially "difficult" or "hard truths" to deal with and accept. With respect to the source of these pessimistic features of critical compatibilism, two concerns are particularly significant. They are that responsible agency persists and endures in the face of both fatalism and moral luck (Russell 2000, 2002, 2008). The mistake of the incompatibilist and skeptic, from the perspective of critical compatibilism, is that it takes these features to discredit and undermine responsible agency, whereas it is the persistence of responsible agency in the face of these conditions that is the real and appropriate basis for pessimistic concern. Likewise, it is the mistake of complacent (optimistic) compatibilism, to try to conceal or minimize these difficult and problematic truths about the human predicament from us.

Interpreted this way, critical compatibilism, in its key claims, takes a position that is the opposite of Pereboom's "hard incompatibilism."[3] The hard incompatibilist is a skeptic about moral responsibility but denies that

---

3. Both hard incompatibilism and critical compatibilism may be described as nonstandard views, in that they reject the simple skepticism-pessimism (or anti-skepticism–optimism) linkage, as is generally assumed in the relevant literature (e.g., P. F. Strawson 1962). One of the more interesting features of Pereboom's contributions is that he challenges this orthodoxy.

this has the bleak and depressing implications that Strawson and others have attributed to it. The critical compatibilist, by contrast, rejects skepticism about moral responsibility but insists, contrary to the complacent compatibilist, that genuine and legitimate sources of pessimistic concern survive in these circumstances and conditions. For the critical compatibilist, reflection on our human predicament with respect to agency and moral responsibility is not a comforting source or basis for complacent optimism. Defeating the skeptical threat with respect to moral responsibility still leaves us having to deal with the deeper issues relating to human finitude and our associated limitations in this sphere (Russell 2002, 2008, 2017).

Concluding Remarks

In this chapter, my primary concern has been to explore and describe the significance of P. F. Strawson's attempt to rebut the skeptical challenge to moral responsibility. Strawson's strategy, as we have noted, tries to chart a middle course between what he takes to be "the panicky metaphysics of libertarianism," on one side, and myopic, utilitarian-oriented compatibilism on the other. The strategy that Strawson pursues is, in important respects, a return to the traditional insights of the moral sense school—most notably, the views of David Hume and Adam Smith. (On the Hume-Strawson relationship, see Russell 1995, ch. 5.) At the same time, Strawson's method of turning away from narrow issues of conceptual analysis relating to the "logic" of freedom, constitutes a genuine and radical break with the standard literature and debate that dominated much of the twentieth-century discussion. Whether one is persuaded by Strawson's general strategy in "Freedom and Resentment" or not, it is fair to say that all those who currently work in this area must find a way through or around the arguments and issues that he has presented us with. The framework of the debate now includes the skeptical/naturalist and optimist/pessimist dualisms that Strawson introduced as key elements of his analysis. All parties in this debate must now locate their own positions with reference to this framework and take a clear stand on the basic points and issues that Strawson's contribution has brought to the fore.

BIBLIOGRAPHY

Bennett, Jonathan. 2008. "Accountability (II)." In McKenna and Russell 2008: 47–68. (A revised version of "Accountability" in van Straaten 1980.)

Dennett, Daniel. 1984. *Elbow Room: The Varieties of Free Will Worth Wanting.* Oxford: Clarendon Press.

Fischer, John, and Mark Ravizza. 1998. *Responsibility and Control.* Cambridge: Cambridge University Press.

Fischer, John, Robert Kane, Derk Pereboom, and Manuel Vargas. 2007. *Four Views on Free Will.* Oxford: Blackwell.

Haji, Ishtiyaque. 2002. "Compatibilist Views of Freedom and Responsibility." In Kane 2002: 202–28.

Honderich, Ted. 2002. *How Free Are You? The Determinism Problem.* 2nd ed. Oxford University Press.

Kane, Robert. 1996. *The Significance of Free Will.* Oxford: Oxford University Press.

———, ed. 2002. *The Oxford Handbook of Free Will.* Oxford & New York: Oxford University Press.

———. 2005. *A Contemporary Introduction to Free Will.* Oxford: Oxford University Press.

———. 2011. *The Oxford Handbook of Free Will.* 2nd ed. Oxford & New York: Oxford University Press.

Kutz, Christopher. 2000. *Complicity: Ethics and Law for a Collective Age.* Cambridge: Cambridge University Press.

McKenna, Michael. 1998. "The Limits of Evil and the Role of Moral Address." *Journal of Ethics* 2: 123–42. (Reprinted in McKenna and Russell 2008: 201–18.)

———. 2004. "Responsibility and Globally Manipulated Agents." *Philosophical Topics* 32: 169–92.

McKenna, Michael, and Paul Russell, eds. 2008. *Free Will and Reactive Attitudes: Perspectives on P. F. Strawson's "Freedom and Resentment."* Farnham: Ashgate.

Nagel, Thomas. 1980. "Moral Luck." *Proceedings of the Aristotelian Society* (1976). Reprinted in Watson, ed., 1982, *Free Will.* Oxford: Oxford University Press: 174–86.

———. 1986. *The View from Nowhere.* Oxford & New York: Oxford University Press.

Nichols, Shaun. 2007. "After Incompatibilism: A Naturalistic Defence of the Reactive Attitudes." *Philosophical Perspectives* 21: 405–28.

Pereboom, Derk. 1995. "Determinism *Al Dente*." *Nous* 29: 21–45. Reprinted in Derk Pereboom, ed. *Free Will.* Indianapolis: Hackett: 242–72.

———. 2001. *Living Without Free Will.* Cambridge: Cambridge University Press.

———. 2007. "Hard Incompatibilism." In Fischer, Kane, Pereboom and Vargas 2007: 85–125.

———. 2011. "Free Will Skepticism and Meaning in Life." In Kane 2011.

Russell, Paul. 1992. "Strawson's Way of Naturalizing Responsibility." *Ethics* 102: 287–302. (Reprinted in McKenna and Russell 2008: 143–56.)

———. 1995. *Freedom and Moral Sentiment: Hume's Way of Naturalizing Responsibility.* Oxford & New York: Oxford University Press.

———. 2000. "Compatibilist Fatalism." In Ton van den Beld, ed., *Moral Responsibility and Ontology.* Dordrecht: Kluwer.

———. 2002. "Pessimists, Pollyannas, and the New Compatibilism." In Kane 2002: 229–56.

———. 2004. "Responsibility and the Condition of Moral Sense." *Philosophical Topics* 32: 287–305.

———. 2008. "Free Will, Art and Morality." *Journal of Ethics* 12: 307–25

———. 2010. "Selective Hard Compatibilism." In *Action, Ethics and Responsibility: Topics in Contemporary Philosophy.* Eds., Joseph Campbell, Michael O'Rourke and Harry Silverstein. Cambridge, MA: MIT Press.

———. 2017. "Free Will Pessimism." *Oxford Studies in Agency and Responsibility*, Vol. 4. D. Shoemaker, ed. Oxford University Press: 93–120.

Smilansky, Saul. 2001. "Free Will: From Nature to Illusion." *Proceedings of the Aristotelian Society* 101: 71–95. (Reprinted in McKenna and Russell 2008: 235–53.)

Smith, Angie. 2007. "On Being Responsible and Holding Responsible." *The Journal of Ethics* 11: 465–84.

Sommers, Tamler. 2007. "The Objective Attitude." *Philosophical Quarterly* 57: 321–41.

Strawson, Galen. 1986. *Freedom and Belief.* Oxford: Oxford University Press.

———. 1994. "The Impossibility of Moral Responsibility." *Philosophical Studies* 75: 5–24. Reprinted in Watson 2003: 212–28.

Strawson, P. F. 1962. "Freedom and Resentment." *Proceedings of the British Academy* 48: 1–25. Reprinted in Watson 2003: 72–93. (References are to Watson 2003.)

———. 1980. "P. F. Strawson Replies (to Ayer and Bennett)." In van Stratten 1980: 260–66.

———. 1985. *Skepticism and Naturalism: Some Varieties.* London: Methuen.

Taylor, Richard. 1963. *Metaphysics.* Englewood Cliffs, NJ: Prentice-Hall.

van Straaten, Zak, ed. 1980. *Philosophical Subjects: Essays Presented to P. F. Strawson.* Oxford: Oxford University Press.

Vargas, Manuel. 2007. "Revisionism." In Fischer, Kane, Pereboom and Vargas 2007: 126–65.

———. 2011. "Revisionist Accounts of Free Will: Origins, Varieties, and Challenges." In Kane 2011: 457–74.

Wallace, R. J. 1994. *Responsibility and the Moral Sentiments.* Cambridge, MA: Harvard University Press.

Watson, Gary. 1987. "Responsibility and the Limits of Evil: Variations on a Strawsonian Theme." In Schoeman 1987: 256–86.

———. ed. 2003. *Free Will.* 2nd ed. Oxford: Oxford University Press.

Williams, Bernard. 1986. *Ethics and the Limits of Philosophy*. London: Fontana.

Wolf, Susan. 1981. "The Importance of Free Will." *Mind* 90: 386–405. Reprinted in McKenna and Russell 2008: 69–83.

———. 1990. *Freedom Within Reason*. Oxford and New York: Oxford University Press.

6

*Responsibility, Naturalism, and "The Morality System"**

> *Theory typically uses the assumption that we probably*
> *have too many ethical ideas.... Our major problem now*
> *is actually that we have not too many but too few, and we*
> *need to cherish as many as we can.*
>
> BERNARD WILLIAMS, *Ethics and the Limits of Philosophy*

LYING AT THE heart of P. F. Strawson's core strategy in "Freedom and Resentment" is his effort to direct his naturalist claims and observations not only against the philosophical extravagance of a general skepticism about moral responsibility but also against all nonskeptical attempts to provide responsibility with some form of external rational justification (Strawson 1962: 23). According to Strawson, efforts of this kind not only are misguided and unconvincing in themselves, but also when they fail they encourage a general skepticism about moral responsibility. The alternative strategy that Strawson pursues is one that places the foundations of responsibility on our natural, universal emotional propensities and dispositions relating to moral sentiments or reactive attitudes. This naturalistic turn invites us to focus our attention on familiar facts about human moral psychology, and to drop our focus on the analysis of the concept of "freedom" as a way of dealing with the threat of determinism. Beyond these general features, however, the details of Strawson's strategy become both

* I am grateful to David Shoemaker and other participants at the New Orleans Workshop on Agency and Responsibility (November 2011) for their very helpful comments and criticism. Versions of this chapter were also presented at a Workshop on Moral Agency, Deliberative Awareness, and Conscious Control (Erasmus University, Rotterdam, October 2010) and at the University of Arizona (February 2012). Thanks also to those who were present on those occasions for their comments and suggestions, and especially to Michael McKenna, David Shoemaker, Maureen Sie, and Andras Szigeti.

complex and layered. As a consequence of this, interpretations and assessments of his arguments differ greatly. There is, nevertheless, a general consensus among both followers and critics alike that there are significant strands in Strawson's specific naturalistic arguments that are implausible and unconvincing and that some "retreat" from the original strong naturalist program that he advanced is required.

In this chapter I take up two closely related issues arising out of this overall problem. First, I want to consider if the right way to amend and modify the naturalistic program is to adopt a "narrow" construal of our moral reactive attitudes along the lines proposed by R. Jay Wallace, one of Strawson's most prominent followers on this subject. The narrower approach, as I will explain, involves a substantial retreat from Strawson's original naturalistic program and has significant implications for Strawson's core claim that our commitment to responsibility requires no external rational justification. The second issue that will be addressed is whether or not we should interpret moral responsibility entirely within the confines of what Bernard Williams has described as "the morality system" (Williams 1985: ch.1). The narrow construal of responsibility requires that we understand moral responsibility within the conceptual resources provided by the morality system, making notions of obligation, wrongness, and blame essential to the analysis of moral responsibility. There is, therefore, an intimate connection between these two issues. With respect to both these issues I will argue that the narrow approach, while it has legitimate criticisms to make of Strawson's original strategy, nevertheless takes us in the wrong direction and involves an unacceptable distortion and truncation of moral responsibility.

1. Two Modes of Naturalism

Strawson's naturalistic account of moral responsibility insists that a proper understanding of this matter must begin with a description of what is involved in *holding* a person responsible. The key to his analysis is the role that reactive attitudes play in this sphere, where this is understood in terms of our natural emotional responses to the attitudes and intentions that we manifest to each other. Strawson's naturalistic strategy, as based on this general observation, has two aspects or dimensions that need to be carefully distinguished—although this is not done in his own presentation. There is, in the first place, a strong form of naturalistic argument that involves the claim that even if we had some theoretical reason to abandon entirely or altogether suspend our reactive attitudes (e.g., as required by skeptical arguments based on considerations of determinism), it would be psychologically impossible for us to do this (Strawson 1962: 9–12, 18). A systematic repudiation of all reactive attitudes of this kind, he argues, would result in "a thoroughgoing objectivity of attitude" to others, with the resulting loss of all our inter-personal relations (Strawson 1962: 12–13). While the objective attitude may be appropriate when we are dealing with the abnormal and incapacitated, and may even on occasion be available to us when dealing with normal adults, we cannot "do this for long, or altogether" (Strawson 1962: 9–10). Armed with these claims, Strawson suggests an easy way to deal with the skeptic. No matter what theoretical arguments may be presented, our human nature is such that we will continue to feel or entertain *tokens* of reactive attitude. According to this view, skeptical arguments will inevitably fail to dislodge or wholly eradicate these attitudes and responses. Let us call this strong line of reply token-naturalism, since it turns on the claim that our tokens of reactive attitudes cannot be systematically eliminated or abandoned whatever (philosophical) arguments may be advanced against them.

Most philosophers have found Strawson's token-naturalism too strong and unconvincing. There are two basic objections to be made against it.[1] First, the psychological claim that it makes is doubtful in point of fact. It is not at all obvious that we are constitutionally incapable of entirely ceasing to entertain tokens of reactive attitude should we be persuaded that they are systematically unjustified. Moreover, even if the psychological claims were true, this does nothing to remove or discredit the objections put forward by the skeptic, since these claims do not address the justificatory issue that concerns us. It would, in fact, be disturbing to discover that we will naturally continue to entertain tokens of reactive attitude in face of well-founded grounds for discrediting these emotional responses to others.

While Strawson's token-naturalism may be judged too strong, there is a weaker form of naturalism that is more convincing and has attracted greater interest. What is crucial to naturalism, on this account, is that we are all *liable* or *disposed* to reactive attitudes. It is from within the framework of this weaker form of naturalism that Strawson develops his general rationale of excuses and exemptions. While we may all have a natural

---

1. For a more detailed development of this analysis of Strawson's naturalism see Russell (1992).

liability to reactive attitudes, particular tokens can be discredited by reference to excuses and exemptions. Excuses operate by way of showing that the agent's conduct was consistent with the underlying general demand for "some degree of goodwill or regard" (Strawson 1962: 7). In cases of this kind, involving an accident, ignorance, and other such factors, the conduct in question does not manifest any ill-will or malicious intent, even if some injury has occurred. With respect to exemptions, however, we are asked to view the individual as an altogether inappropriate target of our reactive attitudes on the general ground that we are dealing with someone for whom we cannot make the moral demand due to an abnormality or incapacity of some relevant kind. Strawson employs this two-level account of excuses and exemptions to show that the thesis of determinism fails to engage any of these recognized considerations and cannot, therefore, constitute a basis for systematically discrediting all our reactive attitudes associated with moral responsibility.

This weaker naturalist approach may be described as a form of *type-naturalism*, where this is understood in terms of our natural disposition to reactive attitudes (just as we have a natural liability to love, fear, joy, and other basic emotions). What is crucial, however, is that unlike token-naturalism, type-naturalism offers no easy way of discrediting the skeptic. On the contrary, it is essential, on this approach, that a plausible account of excusing and exempting conditions is provided consistent with compatibilist commitments. At this level, concerning our natural liability to reactive attitudes, we must still engage in arguments that counter the skeptical challenge. At the same time, type-naturalism does insist on the "internal" nature of these replies to the skeptic (Strawson 1962: 23). While it is possible that our token reactive attitudes could be systematically discredited from within, there remains no need or possibility of providing an external, rational justification of a more general kind for our (natural) propensity to these emotions (any more than we need to do this for our similar liability to love, fear, etc.). Although justificatory issues remain with us, and cannot be evaded by way of token-naturalist claims, these justificatory requirements do not take the form of a demand for general or external rational justifications.

2. *Reactive Attitudes and Narrow Responsibility*

Having established a distinction between token- and type-naturalism, let us now consider Wallace's amended account of the Strawsonian project, as developed on the basis of his narrow construal of the reactive attitudes. Wallace's compatibilist account weaves together two distinct strands of thought. The first is a broadly Strawsonian description of holding people responsible, interpreted in terms of our reactive attitudes (Wallace 1994: 8–12). The other strand is his Kantian theory of reflective self-control or moral agency (1994: 12–15). Taken together, these two strands constitute what Wallace calls his "normative interpretation" of responsibility, which maintains that the correct way to understand what it is to be a morally responsible agent is by way of describing those conditions under which it is *fair* to hold an agent responsible (1994: 5, 15, 64). Our stance of holding a person responsible must itself be understood in terms of the mutual dependence between expectations and reactive attitudes (Wallace 1994: 20–25). To hold someone to an expectation, or a demand of some kind, is to be susceptible to reactive attitudes when the expectation is violated (Wallace 1994: 21). We are susceptible to a reactive attitude if we either feel this emotion or believe that it would be appropriate to feel it in these circumstances (Wallace 1994: 23, 62). While these moves are generally consistent with Strawson's original approach, Wallace aims to substantially modify and amend this approach by providing a narrower and more fine-grained account of moral reactive attitudes.

According to Wallace, Strawson's account of reactive attitudes is too "inclusive" and needs to be refined into several different categories relating the various emotions we are concerned with (Wallace 1994: 25–40). On Wallace's analysis we need to draw two overlapping distinctions (Wallace 1994: 33). The first is between moral and nonmoral reactive attitudes. Both forms of reactive attitudes depend on their reciprocal relationship with a system of expectations. In the case of moral reactive attitudes the relevant set of expectations are justified with reference to moral reasons, and the expectations they justify are obligations (Wallace 1994: 35–36). However, not all expectations are backed by moral reasons, as we find in the case of etiquette, where a breach may generate resentment even though no distinctive moral claim has been violated (Wallace 1994: 36–37). According to Wallace, the central cases of reactive attitudes are the emotions of resentment, indignation, and guilt (Wallace 1994: 29–30), which are all negative in character. This is a feature of our reactive attitudes, he suggests, that explains their "special connection to the negative responses of blame and moral sanction" (Wallace 1994: 62, 71).

Wallace draws out several significant points from this narrow account of the reactive attitudes. The first is that reactive attitudes are not coextensive with the emotions we feel towards people with whom we have interpersonal relationships, since reactive attitudes must be identified with reference to their "constitutive connections with expectations" (Wallace 1994: 31). There are many interpersonal emotions we may experience—such as attachment, friendship, sympathy, love, and so on—that cannot be counted as reactive attitudes since they do not have any relevant connection with expectations. It follows from this that we must reject Strawson's claim that a life without reactive attitudes would commit us to an (impossible) universal adoption of the "objective attitude." People may continue to entertain various other forms of interpersonal emotions and relations even in the *complete absence* of reactive attitudes narrowly conceived. Moreover, against Strawson, Wallace argues that even if some form of interpersonal relations are an inescapable feature of human life, it does not follow that the reactive attitudes are "similarly inevitable" (Wallace 1994: 31). This point leads Wallace to his second distinction relating to his account of the reactive attitudes.

We also need to draw a distinction, Wallace says, between moral reactive attitudes and other kinds of moral sentiment. Not all moral sentiments take the form of moral reactive attitudes, with some identifiable tie to expectations and obligations. Among the examples of nonreactive moral sentiments Wallace cites are shame, gratitude, and admiration; all of which involve different kinds of "modalities of moral value" (Wallace 1994: 37–38). This distinction allows us to acknowledge that there are other cultures with forms of ethical life that do not have any commitment to reactive attitudes but may have other kinds of moral sentiment, as we find in shame cultures (Wallace 1994: 31, 37–40). Evidently, then, on Wallace's narrow interpretation of reactive attitudes, Strawson's naturalism is excessive not only at the token level, but also at the type level, since it is entirely conceivable that there are cultures where members are not subject or liable to reactive attitudes at all. For Wallace, abandoning naturalism at both the token and type levels is a price well worth paying, as it is the only way to avoid an overly inclusive account of reactive attitudes and a false dichotomy between the reactive attitudes and the objective attitude. The narrow construal, Wallace maintains, is more faithful to the relevant psychological and sociological facts and also permits us to identify more accurately the justificatory issues that arise with respect to issues of moral responsibility.

Wallace is well aware that his narrow construal of the reactive attitudes commits him to an interpretation of moral responsibility understood entirely in terms of the conceptual resources of "the morality system."[2] The morality system is understood as a particular form of ethical life, associated with our modern, Western, Christian culture. Its central normative concepts are obligation and blame, along with related notions of wrongness and voluntariness. These are all the same key elements that feature in Wallace's narrow construal of moral responsibility. The narrow account renders moral responsibility, so interpreted, as a local and contingent cultural achievement, involving a legalistic, neo-Kantian view of morality. Understanding moral responsibility in narrow terms presents its adherents with their own set of difficulties. Some of these difficulties are anticipated in Wallace's discussion.

3. The Costs of Going Narrow

One of the most obvious costs of analyzing moral responsibility in terms of a narrow interpretation of our reactive attitudes is that it commits us to an "asymmetrical" account with respect to "worthy and unworthy actions" (Wallace 1994: 71). Since our moral reactive attitudes are, on the narrow interpretation, aroused only when expectations that we endorse are violated, it follows that any moral sentiments we experience that are positive responses to other "modalities of moral value" are not strictly reactive attitudes—and so no part of moral responsibility. While we may feel gratitude or admiration for a morally worthy act, the moral emotions involved are not to be accounted for in terms of the specific structure of beliefs about the violation of moral obligations (Wallace 1994: 37–38). Wallace is unapologetic about this asymmetrical feature of the narrow view on the ground that it accounts for the "special connection" that exists between holding people responsible and our retributive practices involving blame and punishment (Wallace 1994: 71). Beyond this, Wallace also claims that holding a person responsible for a worthy action "does not seem presumptively connected to any positive emotion in particular" (Wallace 1994: 71).

Wallace's defense of the asymmetrical features of the narrow account of moral responsibility is unconvincing for several reasons. First, while we may agree that there is a close connection between moral reactive attitudes and our retributive practices, this does not imply that we need to interpret our reactive attitudes as *exclusively* negative in character, and as *always* connected with blame and moral sanctions. If we allow that there are reactive attitudes of a positive kind, based on beliefs concerning worthy actions and

---

2. Wallace 1994: 39–40, 64–66; and Williams 1985: esp. ch. 10.

admirable character traits, then these too may be connected with positive retributive dispositions such as praise and rewards. Second, it is not obvious that our emotional resources with respect to our responses to morally worthy actions and traits are any more impoverished or limited than in the case of our negative reactive attitudes. As Wallace's own observations suggest, we not only have "thin" ethical concepts such as approval and praise (correlates to disapproval and blame), but we also have many "thicker" concepts, including gratitude and admiration. Finally, and most importantly, any asymmetrical account of the kind advanced by the narrow view inevitably truncates and distorts our experience of moral life and the various ways in which our reactive attitudes are grounded and directed. A one-sided view that is exclusively concerned with negative reactive attitudes, focusing entirely on their connection with blame and retribution, offers us an impoverished and unbalanced interpretation of responsibility and fails to properly accommodate the constructive role of reactive attitudes in endorsing and supporting morally worthy or admirable actions and traits.

Another objection to the narrow interpretation, which Wallace also anticipates and tries to fend off, is that it presents an account of moral responsibility that has a "local" bias toward (our own) modern, Western Christianized culture—i.e., toward "the morality system." It follows from the narrow account that the ancient Greeks and shame cultures, among others, have practices that are at best "analogous" to ours, based as they are on different moral beliefs with distinct patterns of moral response (Wallace 1994: 65–66) Considered in terms of the narrow interpretation, these alien forms of ethical life do not share *our* understanding of moral responsibility, not simply in the sense that they have a *different* understanding but rather that they have *no commitment* to moral responsibility (since their ethical responses cannot be understood in terms of the narrow account of reactive attitudes). This view of things renders moral reactive attitudes and moral responsibility as both local and contingent, and thereby places a conceptual barrier between ourselves (modern, Western, etc.) and alien forms of ethical life that are removed from us in historical time and geographical space. From one point of view this narrow account *oversimplifies* our own (modern) attitudes and practices, which are not perfectly or purely represented by "the morality system" and evidently involve dimensions of holding people responsible that cannot be compressed into the narrow and rigid framework provided. From another point of view, it denies us the *critical* apparatus and resources to question and challenge the way we (moderns) have (locally) arranged and structured our own attitudes and practices relating to responsibility. When we are confronted with other cultures and forms of ethical life outside "the morality system" they must, according to the narrow account, be set aside as—by definition—no longer possessing *any* conception of responsibility. Even if it is granted that we moderns are straightforwardly committed to "the morality system" and its narrow construal of responsibility, this still puts unnecessary and excessive (conceptual) distance between ourselves and these alternative forms of ethical life. More specifically, it erects a conceptual barrier to any genuine critical exchange and confrontation on the subject or question of responsibility itself—since there is, on this account, no shared or common ethical life with respect to the attitudes and practices that are actually constitutive of moral responsibility.[3]

Finally, there is a further objection to the narrow construal of moral responsibility, which raises difficulties that Wallace does not anticipate or directly address. Granted that moral responsibility narrowly interpreted in terms of the concepts provided by the morality system is both local and contingent, it follows that we must reject Strawson's original claims concerning our *type*-naturalist commitments to the reactive attitudes. If this is the case, then a fundamental plank of Strawson's original naturalistic strategy must be abandoned: namely, the claim that we do not need and cannot provide any external rational justification for moral responsibility. If we accept the narrow construal, then there is no natural, universal liability to reactive attitudes and they do not serve as a natural foundation for all recognizably human forms of ethical life. Since the framework of moral responsibility is erected around culturally local forms of moral emotion, confrontations with other cultures and forms of ethical life will place us in the position of needing external rational justification for the entire framework of moral responsibility so conceived. Internal justifications, provided in terms of a rationale of excuses and exemptions, will not serve this purpose even if it is successful in fending off the (internal) skeptical challenge based on worries about determinism. To this extent, the skeptical threat remains with us not just at the token level but also at the type level. Nor is it an option to retreat back to other "analogous" forms of moral emotion

---

3. Clearly confrontation between ethical cultures that are removed from each other in historical time or geographical space may be, as Williams observes, either "notional" or "real" (Williams 1985: ch. 9). Be this as it may, historical sensitivity about the contingency of our own "local" commitments naturally puts pressure on reflective confidence in our own attitudes and practices. To this extent our *awareness* of other modes and forms of ethical life, less attached to the rigidities of "the morality system," may bring us to question whether our confidence in "our *modern* concept of responsibility" is altogether well-founded.

since, if the narrow account is correct, this will not secure or preserve responsibility properly understood. The crucial point remains that if we embrace the narrow construal then, contrary to Strawson's core original view, we are faced with the task of providing the whole edifice of moral responsibility with an external rational justification.

4. Type-Naturalism and Broad Responsibility

Whatever difficulties may be found for the narrow construal of moral responsibility, it is important to begin with a full appreciation of Wallace's critique of the original Strawsonian strategy, much of which is justified. There are four particular features of Wallace's critique that should be endorsed as clearly justified.

(1) Token-naturalism is, as we have noted, psychologically implausible and fails, in any case, to discredit the justificatory issues advanced by the skeptical challenge (e.g., as based on worries about the implications of determinism).

(2) We do require a more fine-grained and less inclusive account of the reactive attitudes. In particular, it is essential that we exclude interpersonal emotions that lack any relevant cognitive element containing ethical content, as in the case of emotions such as love, sympathy, friendly feeling, and so on.

(3) It is also essential that any plausible naturalistic strategy is one that is historically or genealogically sensitive, displaying an awareness of the considerable variation in human ethical life and the range of moral emotions this may involve. In particular, we must avoid any crude form of naturalism that projects *our* (local) sentiments onto (alien) others.

(4) Finally, it is entirely correct to argue, as Wallace does, that we need a theory of moral capacity to provide the basis for an account of exemptions, in order to answer the (internal) skeptical challenge that determinism would somehow render us all morally incapacitated and thus inappropriate targets of reactive attitudes. This last issue is, however, not itself part of the revised Strawsonian analysis of *holding* people responsible and is not, therefore, a matter for our present concern.[4]

---

4. I have argued elsewhere that there is a more intimate relationship between our capacity for holding agents responsible and our capacity for reflective self-control than (Kantian) theories such as Wallace's acknowledge. See, in particular, Russell 2004 and Russell 2011.

Our concerns rest with the issues arising out of the first three items on the list above. In the case of all three of these items, I will argue, Wallace's narrow-view construal of responsibility involves a series of unnecessary and misleading oppositions. It is possible for us to avoid the weaknesses identified in Strawson's original strategy without collapsing into the excessively narrow view of moral responsibility that reflects the meager resources of "the morality system."

We may begin by noting that we can readily reject token-naturalism without rejecting type-naturalism. If we adopt this approach then, it is true, we will be denied the sort of easy way with skepticism that token-naturalism encourages. Moreover, as already explained, the type-naturalist approach, building on our natural liability to reactive attitudes, still leaves us needing a theory of excuses and exemptions that is consistent with compatibilist commitments, if we are to defeat the skeptical challenge. Although the skeptical effort to discredit all tokens of reactive attitudes is one that we must take seriously, if we accept type-naturalism, we do not need any external rational justification for reactive attitudes (i.e., justification at the foundational level). Whether this further claim is acceptable or not will depend on whether we accept the narrow construal of our reactive attitudes. Clearly if we go narrow, then type-naturalism and the associated claim regarding the dispensability of external rational justifications must be dropped. The resolution of this issue depends, therefore, on our interpretation of reactive attitudes.

As I have argued, although we do need a narrower account of our reactive attitudes, we need to make sure we do not go too narrow, as otherwise we will generate some of the difficulties that have already been noted. Wallace's narrow view places considerable and appropriate emphasis on the "propositional content" involved in the beliefs that serve to delineate our reactive attitudes (Wallace 1994: 11,19,74).[5] The narrow view would restrict the contents in question to the limited range provided by the conceptual resources of "the morality system." It is these limits that result in the problems of asymmetry and localism, as we have described them. We need to find, therefore, a *middle path* that avoids the inclusiveness of Strawson,

---

5. Wallace claims that Strawson's account of reactive attitudes does not manage to clearly connect them with any propositional content (1994: 39). This charge seems unfair to Strawson since he is careful to ground reactive attitudes in our beliefs about the attitudes and intentions of other human beings and "the very great importance" that we attach to them (Strawson 1962: 5).

on one side, and the excessively narrow approach of Wallace on the other. To put ourselves back on the right track we may turn again to Bernard Williams's critique of "the morality system."

The narrow view, as we have seen, presents ethical considerations in highly restricted terms, specifically with reference to obligation and blame, which is appropriate when obligations are violated. Williams identifies these features as central to the morality system (Williams 1985: ch. 10). This tendency to reduce and simplify is also manifest in ethical theory, a philosophical project which is itself intimately linked to the assumptions and prejudices of the morality system (Williams 1985: ch. 1). One aim of ethical theory is to provide an account of morality that will provide an exact boundary between ethical and nonethical considerations. This is done primarily by reducing the diversity of ethical (and nonethical) considerations, with a view to identifying a narrow and strict range of ethical considerations that may serve as moral reasons available to all rational agents—the universal constituency. The most notable features of moral theory are its simplicity, reductionism, and systemization of our ethical concepts and claims. Williams's critique of the morality system involves challenging and rejecting these assumptions. In the first place, while our ethical considerations certainly include obligations, under some interpretation, they extend well beyond this. The scope of the ethical relates more broadly to "the demands, needs, claims, desires, and, generally, the lives of other people, and it is helpful to preserve this conception in what we are prepared to call an ethical consideration" (Williams 1985: 12; see also 1985: 153, where Williams mentions our need to share a social world in relation to these various ethical considerations). What is required, from this perspective, is an account of ethical considerations that also includes forward-looking concerns relating to welfarism and utilitarianism, as well as ethical considerations that relate to our ideals and self-conceptions that mark out actions that fail the standards and boundaries that we may set for ourselves (e.g., considerations of what we regard as demeaning, base, dishonorable, etc.). When we interpret ethical considerations in this *broader* manner we find that these interests are plural and varied in their nature and secure no sharp boundary between ethical and nonethical considerations. Vagueness, conflict, and diversity—contrary to the demands of "theory" and the prejudices of "the morality system"—are of the essence of human ethical life.

Our own ethical reactive attitudes must be understood in these broader and vaguer terms. One of the implications that Williams draws from this is that we should be skeptical of the effort to understand reactive attitudes in the reductive, thin language of binary judgments: approval and disapproval, guilt and innocence, and so on (Williams 1985: 37, 177, 192). If we reconfigure our ethical reactive attitudes in terms of a broader construal of the ethical considerations that ground them and serve as their propositional content, then we may acquire a very different understanding of the scope and content of moral responsibility, as based upon these emotions. Our ethical qualities are manifest in the "deliberative priority" and "importance" that we give to ethical considerations as expressed in our conduct and character. So interpreted, ethical reactive attitudes may be construed as *reactive ethical value,* where this is understood as emotional responses to the weight and value given by an agent or person to ethical considerations widely conceived (i.e., in terms of our human needs, interests, welfare, claims, and the requirements of social cooperation). Ethical reactive attitudes involve coming to see a person in a certain ethical "light" based on these lower-order evaluations of their ethical qualities. Clearly we have varied and diverse ethical norms and standards that serve as the relevant basis for evaluating an agent's ethical qualities understood in these terms. These evaluations of agents based on their ethical qualities serve to generate or arouse a myriad of ethical reactive attitudes which may be either "positive" or "negative" in nature. As Williams argues, our ethical and emotional language here is not at all "thin" (e.g., praise and blame etc.) but "thick" and varied, involving notions such as "being creepy," or a "cad," and so on—all of which are responses loaded with ethical significance. Different cultures and different forms of ethical life will not only have different lower-order ethical norms, but also deploy a different or variable set of ethical reactive attitudes (reflecting their variable propositional content).

The significance of this criticism of "the morality system," along with the style of ethical theory associated with it, for our understanding of ethical reactive attitudes should be clear. The revised account is broad enough to accommodate positive ethical reactive attitudes (e.g., gratitude, admiration, etc.) as well as "alien" reactive attitudes (e.g., shame) all under the umbrella of those ethical considerations that serve to ground or justify them. This avoids the costs of going too narrow, by way of relying on the limited and restricted resources of the morality system. The broader construal is, nevertheless, controlled and focused enough to exclude elements that do not relate at all to ethical considerations and ethical qualities (e.g., friendly feeling, sympathy, romantic love, etc. do not count as ethical reactive attitudes because they are not reactive to *ethical* qualities as such). On this analysis, we should not be surprised or disappointed to find that there is no sharp or clear boundary between ethical reactive attitudes and other emotional responses to qualities and features of those with whom we are dealing. No such sharp boundary should be expected if we want an accurate understanding of the nature of ethical life and the way in which it "bleeds" into human life in general.[6]

Taking this broader approach to ethical reactive attitudes has other significant advantages as well. It avoids, for example, the "legalism" of the narrow account, which turns moral responsibility into a model of legal responsibility—eliminating the more nuanced and complex set of responses we have outside legal contexts. We also avoid the failings of what Williams refers to as "progressivism," the assumption that we moderns alone have access to a full and complete concept of moral responsibility and are "better off" than those who lack our own understanding.[7] It is Williams's view not only that we should be open to the possibility that we might learn from the ancients but also that this is in fact our situation. Learning from the ancients is possible—and desirable—precisely because we *share* a concept of moral responsibility with them, however differently we may interpret various key elements associated with it (Williams 1993: 55).

For our present purposes, our concern is not to present a worked-out alternative to the narrow model of reactive attitudes—not the least because, for reasons given, this may itself be a problematic ambition driven by the aims of "ethical theory." What is important, however, is to insist on finding some middle ground that can accommodate ethical reactive attitudes broadly conceived without expanding this set to include interpersonal emotions that have no relevant ethical content (i.e., which do not involve our emotional reactions to a person's ethical qualities). Wallace's own observations suggest that this can readily be done, since he allows "analogous" forms of responsibility and also speaks of "responsibility for worthy acts" (Wallace 1994: 38–40, 64–66, 71). To see, in a particular case, how this middle ground between an excessively narrow and overly inclusive view may be found, let us consider *shame*. Shame may be based on standards and norms that have no ethical content, as in the case of concern about one's physical appearance (e.g., my frail constitution) or economic status

6. This is, of course, a recurrent theme throughout Williams's writings.

7. Williams 1985: 32 n. 2; and, more generally, Williams 1993: esp. ch. 1. Williams's view is, of course, the opposite of this, since he holds that we would be better off without the morality system (Williams 1985: 174), just as we don't need ethical theory and should abandon its aims (Williams 1985: 17, 74).

(e.g., my family's poverty). In other cases, however, the relevant standards and norms may move into the territory of our ethical qualities and characteristics, such as feeling shame about being lazy or being vulgar. Whether a response is an ethical reactive attitude or not will depend on the *nature* of the quality or consideration it is a *reaction to*. There are, moreover, clear cases of ethical shame that cannot be analyzed or understood in terms of the apparatus of obligation and doing wrong. We may, for example, feel ashamed of failing to live up to our own ethical ideals and standards, even when we are well aware that we have not failed to comply with any obligations and cannot be blamed for our conduct. An example of this is provided in Joseph Conrad's *Lord Jim,* where Jim is ashamed of himself because he fails to act heroically and is, therefore, disappointed in himself in these ethical terms but not in terms of any recognizable requirements of "the morality system."[8] The general point here is that there is a wide range of ethical reactive attitudes lying outside the theoretical schema of the narrow interpretation that, nevertheless, do not collapse into an overly "inclusive" set of interpersonal emotions lacking any relevant ethical content. Some cases of shame will be cases of ethical reactive attitudes and others will not. What will settle this issue will be the specific content and target of what we are ashamed of. Moreover, the fact that there are no sharp or precise boundaries to draw here is a failing only if we assume the prejudices of the morality system and the forms of "theorizing" associated with it.

We have noted that it is essential that the naturalist approach to moral responsibility should be sensitive to historical and cultural variations with regard to our understanding of moral responsibility and the specific and various forms which our ethical reactive attitudes may take. It should be pointed out that Strawson is himself alive to these concerns. Speaking of our increased "historical and anthropological awareness of the great variety of forms which these human attitudes may take at different times and in different cultures," Strawson says:

> This makes one rightly chary of claiming as essential features of the concept of morality in general, forms of these attitudes which may have a local and temporary prominence. No doubt to some extent my own descriptions of human attitudes have reflected local and

---

8. For an illuminating discussion of this example see Doris 2002: 160–4.

temporary features of our own culture. But an awareness of variety of forms should not prevent us from acknowledging also that in the absence of *any* forms of these attitudes it is doubtful whether *we* should have anything that we could find intelligible as a system of human relationships, as human society.

1962: 24–25, *Strawson's emphasis*

It may be argued, along the lines of Wallace's criticisms of Strawson's claims about the objective attitude, that Strawson's remarks in this passage run together two distinct issues. One claim is that we could not recognize a society as truly human without any ethical reactive attitudes. Clearly this need not be the case, so long as we do not overly expand the class of ethical reactive attitudes to include all interpersonal emotions. Nevertheless, the general point that Strawson is primarily concerned to make in this context still stands: namely, without *some form* of ethical reactive attitudes we could not recognize or find intelligible a system of human relationships that would qualify as a *human ethical life*. In other words, an ethical life devoid of all forms of ethical reactive attitudes is not recognizable or intelligible *to us* as a form of *human* ethical life.

It should be clear, in light of Strawson's observations, that we do not need to choose between naturalism and genealogy, where this is understood in terms of sensitivity to historical and cultural variation and diversity. On the broad construal, ethical norms and the ethical considerations to which they give weight, may vary greatly from one culture and historical period to another. With these variations we will also find variations in the particular forms of ethical reactive attitudes that are adopted and endorsed. One form these ethical reactive attitudes may take is the narrow form encouraged by the morality system—which makes obligation and blame its central features. While this form of ethical reactive attitude may be local and contingent, it does not follow that ethical reactive attitudes *broadly construed* are local and contingent, unless we take the local form to be the sole legitimate representative form of moral responsibility. Since the broad construal neither interprets ethical reactive attitudes nor moral responsibility in these restrictive terms, it is able to acknowledge that the ancient Greeks, among others, have ethical reactive attitudes that are recognizably continuous with our own conception of moral responsibility. This can be done without in any way denying that there are significant differences between their culture and our own with regard to the attitudes and practices involved (e.g., with respect to issues of voluntariness and intention). The irony about this situation is that it is the narrow construal, which rejects (type) naturalism, which cannot accommodate genealogical sensitivity to cultural and historical variation. Given that the narrow construal insists that moral responsibility be understood in terms of the concepts of the morality system, and that this interpretation alone constitutes genuine or real moral responsibility, it is compelled to exclude all other understandings (i.e., as based on a broader construal of ethical reactive attitudes) as falling outside the parameters of moral responsibility. It is, therefore, the narrow construal that is insensitive to genealogical variation and diversity as it arises within the framework of moral responsibility. For reasons that have been explained, this is not simply a verbal issue, as it involves and encourages a truncated and distorted understanding of moral responsibility and the way in which it is naturally rooted in human ethical life.

It has been shown that "asymmetry" and "localism" are unnecessary and unacceptable costs of the narrow approach. What, then, about the further issue relating to type-naturalism and external rational justifications? If we adopt the broad construal then no external rational justification of our liability to ethical reactive attitudes is required, where ambitions of this kind involve what Strawson describes as the tendency to "over-intellectualize the facts" concerning the natural foundations of moral responsibility (Strawson 1962: 23). In contrast with this, the narrow construal needs to provide some relevant external rational justification since, *per hypothesis,* it is a local (modern, Western) achievement. Clearly the broad view can accept that the *local forms* of ethical reactive attitudes (e.g., as based on the requirements of the morality system) may come and go. Considered from this perspective, the morality system and its associated narrow interpretation of moral responsibility may be judged vulnerable to extinction for several related reasons. First, as already argued, it suggests a truncated and distorted account of our own ethical concerns (i.e., even from a modern, Western perspective). Second, it generates (unnecessary) problems of asymmetry and localism as we have described them. Third, the narrow account is also especially vulnerable to internal skeptical collapse due to worries about determinism. (Although Wallace believes these internal skeptical objections can be defeated, not all those who endorse the morality system believe this can be done, much less done on the basis of compatibilist commitments.) It follows from all this that there is a real prospect of this *local* form of ethical reactive attitudes collapsing under both internal and external skeptical pressure. What does not follow from

this, however, on the broad construal, is the total collapse of moral responsibility in any recognizable form. We may still have available other forms
of ethical reactive attitudes that are not similarly vulnerable in any of these
dimensions. Clearly it would be a mistake, therefore, to present the collapse of the local form of moral responsibility associated with the morality
system as putting us in the predicament of having to adopt some form of
utilitarian, forward-looking approach that has no place for ethical reactive
attitudes *of any kind*. Alternative forms of reactive attitudes remain available and viable within the structure of ethical life that is still recognizably
human and intelligible to us.[9]

The question we must now turn to is what is the relationship between
skepticism and type-naturalism as understood on the broad approach?
Skepticism may take the form of aiming to discredit *local* understandings of our ethical reactive attitudes. This does not, as has been argued,
show that all forms of ethical reactive attitude are thereby discredited or
that moral responsibility, as such, cannot be vindicated. It remains true,
nevertheless, that whatever local forms our ethical reactive attitudes may
take, they (all) remain vulnerable, in principle, to internal, global skeptical challenge at the *token* level. That is to say, our commitment at the type
level, even on a broad construal, does not secure any general immunity
from potential global skepticism with respect to *all* tokens of our ethical reactive attitudes.[10] The crucial point that needs to be emphasized,
however, is that even in these circumstances, the skeptic remains committed to ethical reactive attitudes at the *type* level (unless, of course, the
capacity to feel and experience ethical reactive attitudes is itself damaged).
In other words, although the skeptic may systematically disengage from
all *tokens* of ethical reactive attitude from "the inside," she cannot abandon the propensity or liability to these attitudes. That is a project that,
from one point of view, would require radical intervention with her own
nature (e.g., by way of genetic engineering or medical surgery) and, from

---

9. Wallace refers to the utilitarian approach as "the economy of threats" model (Wallace 1994:
54–61). It is crucial to his critique of this model that it lacks "depth," where depth is provided
by the "attitudinal" features of blame and retribution (Wallace 1994: 56, 75). On a broader
construal, however, "depth" can be found in other forms of ethical reactive attitude, such as
shame and anger—a point that Wallace comes close to endorsing in some passages. See,
e.g., Wallace 1994: 89.

10. This may well be regarded as highly unlikely or even incredible—but it is not inconceivable. Imagine, for example, the spread of some terrible disease or genetic mutation that

another point of view, would place her outside the recognizable human ethical community.[11]

We have already noted that whereas the narrow construal would place the ancient Greeks (and other shame cultures) outside the framework and fabric of moral responsibility, the broad construal does not. What, then, about the skeptic? In contrast with individuals who are engaged participants in forms of ethical life involving ethical reactive attitudes, the skeptic has systematically disengaged from all such participation or involvement. Disengagement of this kind requires (internal) doubts about the justification for *any* proposed tokens of ethical reactive attitude. So described, the skeptic cannot evade the challenge of providing some account of the excusing and exempting considerations that apply universally in such a manner that all *tokens* of ethical reactive attitude are discredited. If the skeptic fails or refuses to provide any such rationale for her (disengaged) stance then her skeptical stance has not been vindicated or justified. Contrast the skeptic with another distinct character, whom we may call the "Vulcan."[12] Vulcans are understood to be entirely rational but incapable of human emotion. As such, Vulcans may rationally understand (human) ethical norms but are incapable of feeling or entertaining ethical reactive attitudes (or similar moral emotions with an attitudinal aspect). Vulcans have, in other words, no type-naturalist commitments with regard to ethical reactive attitudes. It is, for this reason, a mistake to assimilate the skeptic to a Vulcan, as plainly the skeptic is not a Vulcan. The Vulcan faces no skeptical problem with respect to ethical reactive attitudes. They have no token commitment because they have no type commitment to this range of (ethical) emotion. For the (human) skeptic, however, the skeptical challenge is *real* because their type propensities require something to be said with respect to disengaging all tokens of these reactions to the ethical qualities of others in their community. In this way, both the skeptic and the anti-skeptic, in contrast with the Vulcan, can accept Strawson's type-naturalism and dispense with the search

---

affected us all by damaging our most basic and universal moral capacities in such a manner that exemptions applied universally (however broadly interpreted).

11. An individual who lacks any *type* commitment to ethical reactive attitudes would not be recognizably human, not because she is a systematic skeptic with respect to these attitudes but because the skeptical issue *does not arise for her* with respect to these attitudes, since she is constitutionally incapable of experiencing or entertaining such attitudes.

12. Vulcans are aliens from the planet Vulcan, as described in *Star Trek*. The character of Mr. Spock was half Vulcan and half human. Wallace refers to this example in a related context at Wallace 1994: 78 n.41. See also Russell 2011: esp. 212–14.

for external rational justifications. What divides them is the issue of whether or not a theory of excuses and exemptions can handle relevant internal skeptical worries (e.g., as based on the implications of determinism).

5. *Against the Narrow Construal of Moral Responsibility*

It has been argued that the narrow construal of reactive attitudes and its associated account of moral responsibility has unacceptable costs. While it is true that there are significant failings in Strawson's original naturalistic project that need to be addressed and corrected (e.g., we should reject token-naturalism), we should retain the core feature of type-naturalism. In order to do this we need to provide a *broader* account of ethical reactive attitudes that extends beyond the constraints and limits of "the morality system" and its conceptual structures. It is only by taking this route that the difficulties we have described relating to "asymmetry" and "localism," as well as the fruitless and misguided search for external rational justifications, can be avoided. We may summarize the significance of these observations in the following points.

(1) The narrow construal of moral responsibility, as developed on the basis of the morality system, both distorts and truncates our understanding of human ethical life as it relates to moral responsibility. In particular, it makes it impossible to accommodate both positive ethical reactive attitudes and alien ethical reactive attitudes as they may arise from outside our (modern, Western) culture. Even our own *local* understanding of moral responsibility is not fully or adequately captured by this narrow construal.

(2) It is the broad construal, along with its commitment to type-naturalism, which is able to accommodate genealogical sensitivity to historical and cultural variation in relation to our understanding of moral responsibility. The narrow construal excludes all alternative forms that do not fall into the constraints imposed by "the morality system" as mere analogues or prototypes of moral responsibility. As such, the narrow construal constitutes a form of conceptual imperialism with regard to (real, true) moral responsibility and also commits us to an implausible "progressivism" concerning our own (modern, Western) views. In contrast with this, the broad approach recognizes the variation in modes and forms of ethical reactive attitude within a wider understanding and appreciation of the emotional fabric of moral responsibility.

(3) Type-naturalism, as understood on the broad construal, provides no easy way of dealing with a potential internal skeptical challenge (i.e., in contrast with the aims of token-naturalism). Even allowing for our natural liability to ethical reactive attitudes, on a broad construal, we must still formulate some relevant schema of excuses and exemptions. From this perspective it is always conceivable that a systematic or global skepticism could be generated from "the inside" (i.e., extending to all our token ethical reactive attitudes). This possibility does not, however, license a search for external rational justifications, since our liability or propensity to such emotions is natural and not rationally grounded. The skeptic remains committed to ethical reactive attitudes at this level, even if she has entirely abandoned or disengaged any commitment to tokens of these attitudes (in light of internal skeptical pressures of some kind).

(4) Much of the motivation behind Wallace's narrow construal of the reactive attitudes is to find a satisfactory compatibilist account of moral responsibility consistent with the core requirements and constraints of the morality system. From this perspective the internal skeptical challenge is especially acute, since it is targeted on the notions of wrongness, blame, desert, and retribution that are central to moral responsibility as the morality system interprets it. It is evident, however, that the broad construal of ethical reactive attitudes, along the lines that has been sketched, significantly *deflates* these (internal) skeptical pressures. The reason for this is that a broader and more liberal conception of ethical reactive attitudes does not place such heavy weight or emphasis on the very elements of the morality system that have proved especially vulnerable to skeptical criticism (i.e., desert, blame, etc., along with their apparent dependence on ultimate or absolute agency). Even if—contrary to what Wallace argues—it proves impossible to vindicate this local interpretation of moral responsibility, as understood on the narrow construal, it does not follow, given a broad interpretation of ethical reactive attitudes, that global skepticism results. All that follows from the success of the skeptical challenge, so described, is that the *local* understanding of moral responsibility encouraged by the morality system cannot survive critical reflection.[13]

---

13. It is true, of course, that many skeptics about moral responsibility are concerned to discredit the local conceptions of moral responsibility associated with the morality system. However, for reasons that have been discussed, skepticism of this kind does not in itself constitute global skepticism—since it does not discredit, and may not even aim to discredit, alternative forms of ethical reactive attitudes. Having said this, it is important to note that many skeptical projects of this kind either explicitly or tacitly endorse the narrow construal

In sum, we may contrast the relative strengths and weaknesses of the broad and narrow accounts in these terms. The narrow construal not only generates a partial and incomplete account of moral responsibility but also leaves the entire edifice of moral responsibility, so understood, vulnerable to both internal and external skeptical threat. The broad construal not only avoids the significant difficulties that the narrow construal encounters (e.g., asymmetry) but also provides for the complexity, variation and nuance that we find in this sphere. Moreover, the broad construal, by moving away from the rigidities and (peculiar) demands of the morality system, deflates the internal skeptical threat and eliminates all worries relating to the misguided ambition of providing a satisfactory external rational justification. These are fundamental points relating to moral responsibility and the defects of the morality system that the discussions of both Strawson and Williams converge on.

REFERENCES

Doris, John (2002). *Lack of Character: Personality and Moral Behavior* (Cambridge & New York: Cambridge University Press).

Russell, Paul (1992). "Strawson's Way of Naturalizing Responsibility." *Ethics* 102. 2: 287–302.

———(2004). "Responsibility and the Condition of Moral Sense." *Philosophical Topics*, 32, 1; 2, 287–305.

———(2011). "Moral Sense and the Foundations of Responsibility." In *Free Will*, 2nd ed., ed. Robert Kane (New York: Oxford University Press): 199–220.

Strawson, P. F. (1962). "Freedom and Resentment." Reprinted in P. F. Strawson, *Freedom and Resentment and Other Essays* (London, New York and Oxford: Methuen, 1974).

Wallace, R. Jay (1994). *Responsibility and the Moral Sentiments* (Cambridge, MA: Harvard University Press).

Williams, Bernard (1985). *Ethics and the Limits of Philosophy* (London: Fontana).

———(1993). *Shame and Necessity* (Berkeley, CA: University of California Press).

---

and its assumption that alternative accounts of ethical reactive attitudes somehow fail the standard of *real or genuine* forms of moral responsibility. When this assumption is made, the critique of our local conception of moral responsibility framed in terms of the requirements of the morality system is (mistakenly) *inflated* into a form of *global* skepticism about moral responsibility. Suffice it to say that much of the contemporary free will debate, along with its associated worries about the skeptical threat, proceeds on this assumption of the narrow construal and the morality system.

PART III

Practical Reason, Art, and Manipulation

7

*Practical Reason and Motivational Skepticism**

IN HER INFLUENTIAL and challenging paper "Skepticism about Practical Reason" Christine Korsgaard sets out to refute an important strand of Humean skepticism as it concerns a Kantian understanding of practical reason.[1] Korsgaard distinguishes two components of skepticism about practical reason. The first, which she refers to as content skepticism, argues that reason cannot of itself provide any "substantive guidance to choice and action" (Korsgaard, 1986, 311). In its classical formulation, as stated by Hume, it is argued that reason cannot determine our ends. Our ends are determined by our desires, and reason is limited to the role of identifying the relevant means to these ends. The second component, which Korsgaard calls motivational skepticism, suggests doubt about the scope of reason as a motive. The claim here, as Korsgaard interprets Hume's view on this matter, is that "all reasoning that has motivational influence must start from a passion, that being the only possible source of motivation" (SPR, 314).[2] Korsgaard's fundamental objective in "Skepticism about Practical Reason" is to show that motivational skepticism must always be based on content skepticism. In other words, according to Korsgaard, motivational skepticism has no independent force. In

* I am grateful to Don Brown, James Kelleher. and the participants in the *Moralische Motivation* Conference (Marburg 2004) for their very helpful comments and discussion.

1. Hereafter abbreviated as SPR, with page references to Korsgaard (1996).

2. Hume expresses the basic idea behind the distinction between content and motivational skepticism in a passage of his *Treatise* where he criticizes Samuel Clarke's ethical rationalism. The relevant passage begins: "These two particulars are evidently distinct. 'Tis one thing to know virtue, and another to conform the will to it" (Hume, 2000, 3.1.1.22).

this chapter I argue that Korsgaard's attempt to discredit motivational skepticism is unsuccessful.

I

Korsgaard's approach to this problem turns on a fundamental distinction between "internalist" and "externalist" moral theories. According to internalist theories the knowledge (or acceptance) of a moral judgment implies the existence of a motive. In contrast with this, externalist theories hold that "a conjunction of moral comprehension and total unmotivatedness is perfectly possible: knowledge is one thing and motivation another" (SPR, 315).[3] The obvious worry about externalist theories is that they allow for a gap between recognizing reasons and responding to them. That is to say, there is, on the externalist account, no requirement on practical reasons that they are actually capable of motivating the agent. Clearly, however, unless reasons provide motivation they cannot prompt or explain any action. As Korsgaard points out, where there is doubt about whether a given consideration is able to motivate an agent, there will be doubt about "whether the consideration has the force of a practical reason" (SPR, 317).

Hume's motivational skepticism takes the form of the objection that even if content skepticism can be answered (e.g., by way of identifying some relevant moral principles that serve as measures of right and wrong) we would still be left with external reasons that cannot motivate the agent. Whereas a Humean theory of practical reasons locates their motivational source in our passions and desires, the Kantian theory imposes no such limitation on the sources of motivation. According to the Kantian theory, the operations of reason can, by themselves, provide us with practical conclusions that carry their own motivational force. Humean motivation skepticism questions how this can be done.

Korsgaard maintains that Humean skeptical doubts about the motivational source of pure practical reasons do not present any genuine difficulty for the Kantian theory, independent and distinct from Humean content skepticism. On the contrary, the doubts raised, she maintains, are a product of confusion about what "internalism" actually requires. Korsgaard agrees that it is a requirement on practical reasons that they be capable of motivating us. However, it does not follow from this, contrary to

---

3. Cp. Korsgaard's account of externalism with the passage from Hume cited in note 2 above.

what Hume and his followers suppose, that if a consideration fails to motivate the agent then it cannot be (for her) a reason for action. To explain
this point Korsgaard describes the "internalism requirement" in the following terms: "Practical-reason claims, if they are really to present us with
reasons for action, must be capable of motivating *rational* persons" (SPR,
317, my emphasis). When the internalism requirement is interpreted this
way, Korsgaard argues, it is evident that it does not require "that rational
considerations always succeed in motivating us" (SPR, 321).

Hume grants that passions and actions may be described as (indirectly) "irrational" in so far as they are founded either on false beliefs
about the existence of objects or false beliefs about causal relations in
respect of choosing some relevant means to our end.[4] Korsgaard argues,
however, that there is another possibility that Hume has overlooked. An
agent may fail to choose "obviously sufficient and readily available means
to [her] end" (SPR, 318). In these circumstances the agent fails to respond
appropriately to a reason she recognizes. This is a case of what Korsgaard
calls "true irrationality." The important point here is that true irrationality, where an agent is not motivated by her reasons, can occur even when
the reasons involved are instrumental reasons, which are concerned with
taking an action recognized as the relevant means to our end as given by
desire.

> Even the skeptic about practical reason admits that human beings
> can be motivated by the consideration that a given action is a means
> to a desired end. But it is not enough, to explain this fact, that
> human beings can engage in causal reasoning. It is perfectly possi-
> ble to imagine a sort of being who could engage in causal reasoning
> and who could, therefore, engage in reasoning that would point out
> the means to her ends, but who was not motivated by it.
>
> SPR, *319*

It is a weakness in Hume's position, Korsgaard maintains, that he cannot
account for "true irrationality." According to Hume, when we are not motivated to pursue the means to a given end, this shows that we do not in fact
desire this end, or that we desire something else more. We are, in other
words, always motivated to take what we believe to be the relevant means

---

4. Hume, (2000, 2.3.3.6).

to our end. Korsgaard argues that this way of understanding the internalism requirement clearly "malfunctions" (SPR, 318).

The internalism requirement does not imply, Korsgaard argues, that nothing can interfere with "motivational transmission" whereby our practical reasons "set the body in motion" (SPR, 320). On the contrary, a number of different things can interfere with the motivational influence of some rational consideration. When interruptions of this kind occur, generally we are able to provide some explanation for the failure beyond the fact that the person in question is simply practically irrational. More specifically, we can, in principle, say something about how this person's "motivational path" was blocked. This involves citing specific a psychological mechanism that explains why the failure has occurred. Among the various kinds of explanation that Korsgaard refers to are rage, grief, and physical and mental illness. Nevertheless, however we may explain failures of this kind, the fact that reasons sometimes fail to motivate us is not itself inconsistent with the internalist requirement that reasons must be capable of motivating us in so far as we are rational.

It is, of course, true that if content skepticism is correct, then we have no reasons for action that extend beyond the limits of our existing passions and desires. But if pure practical reasons do exist, then we must allow for the possibility that agents may fail to be motivated by them simply because they are "truly irrational." Indeed, as we have already noted, this observation applies to instrumental reasons no less than to pure practical reasons. There is, therefore, no basis for motive skepticism if it is grounded merely on the observation that agents are not always motivated by considerations that are presented to them as "reasons for action." It is mere confusion to suppose that since reasons must be capable of motivating us, considerations that fail to motivate us cannot be reasons for action.[5]

It is evident that Korsgaard's way of interpreting the internalism requirement renders the relationship between reasons and motivation conditional in character. More specifically, on Korsgaard's account, a reason for action is capable of motivating an agent only if the agent actually "listens

---

5. If I understand Korsgaard correctly, this constitutes the gist of her objection to Bernard Williams' position in "Internal and External Reasons." Korsgaard takes Williams to slide, illegitimately, from the (correct) internalist claim that reasons for action must be capable of providing motivation, to the (incorrect) claim that considerations that fail to motivate cannot be reasons for action. The background assumption, making this slide look plausible, is that only our existent ends and desires (i.e., the agent's "subjective motivational set") can provide any source of motivation. (I return to Korsgaard's reply to Williams further below.)

to reason" and is rationally disposed (SPR, 324). Rationality, she points out, is not a condition that we are always in. The disposition to be rational is necessary if reasons are to be able to motivate us. (Much as a rational disposition is necessary if good arguments are to lead us to belief in their conclusions.) We do not, however, need any (further) "special psychological mechanism" to explain the linkage between reasons and motivation—the condition of rationality already does this work for us.[6]

II

The question that arises from Korsgaard's discussion is whether she has effectively discredited motivational skepticism, understood as a distinct and independent concern from that of content skepticism. I believe that Korsgaard has not accomplished this task. To see why this is so, consider again Korsgaard's account of cases where agents fail to respond to rational considerations. Korsgaard, as we have noted, acknowledges that it will not do to explain such cases by saying simply that the person concerned is "irrational." The force of the internalism requirement, as she notes, is psychological, and it places a "psychological demand" on ethical theories (SPR, 329). When the motivational influence of a rational consideration is interfered with, and the "transmission of motivation" does not occur, it is perfectly in order to say something about the way in which the psychological mechanism involved has been disrupted (e.g., by grief, rage, illness, etc.). At the same time, however, Korsgaard suggests that it is a mistake to seek out a "special psychological mechanism" of any kind in circumstances where an agent effectively responds to her reasons (i.e., when she is motivationally guided by them). There is, therefore, on this account, an asymmetry in respect of providing an explanation when it comes to cases where our reasons succeed or fail to "transmit motivational influence." Although it is possible to identify some relevant "psychological mechanism" when failure occurs, there is no corresponding "psychological mechanism" required to explain why an agent is successfully motivated

---

6. It is worth noting that on the Humean account the relationship between reasons and motivation is also conditional, but in a different way. The Humean view suggests that a reason for action is conditional on having some relevant desire. We have no reason for action where our existing desires are not engaged. Since on this account reasons for action are always based on existing desire, there is no difficulty in explaining the linkage between reasons and motivation. Where motivation based on desire is absent, so too, on this view, are reasons for action.

by her reasons. The standing condition of rationality provides sufficient explanation for the fact that the (rational) agent is motivated by her reasons for action.[7]

What argument does Korsgaard offer in defense of this asymmetry? In defense of this view Korsgaard leans heavily on an analogy between theoretical and practical reason. It would, she argues, clearly be "odd" to demand "the intervention of special psychological mechanisms" to convince human reasoners that the conclusion of sound arguments are true (SPR, 316; cp. 320). A rational person is not only capable of performing logical and inductive operations, but is also "appropriately convinced by them" (SPR, 320). If we are rational we believe the conclusion of a sound argument. In the same way, if we are rational we will be motivated by our practical reasons. It is true, of course, that we will not always be motivated by our reasons just as we may not always believe the conclusion of a good argument (i.e., because we are not always rational). However, it does not follow from this that we require any "special psychological mechanism" to explain either how sound arguments convince or to explain how (pure) practical reasons motivate. Just as we do not require any special psychological mechanism to bridge a gap between being presented with a good argument and believing its conclusion, so too we do not need any special psychological mechanism to bridge a gap between being presented with good reasons and being motivated by them.

Does this analogy between theoretical and practical reason serve to discredit motivational skepticism? This analogy is at its weakest at the very point where motivational skepticism finds pure practical reason particularly problematic. That is to say, in the case of practical reasons, what we are concerned with, as Korsgaard points out, is the generation of "motivational force" which is capable of "setting the body in motion." As described, this is a (natural) effect of pure practical reasons. It is this power or capacity that the motivational skeptic finds it difficult to account for. Although Korsgaard speaks metaphorically of being "moved" or "driven" to belief, belief involves no movement of any kind (much less voluntary action). Moreover, whereas beliefs are a matter of how we view and interpret the

---

7. The asymmetry in Korsgaard's position reflects her (Kantian) view that the right approach to ethics is to assume that our "investigations into what it is to be a rational person . . . will have psychological conclusions" (SPR, 334 n. 17). She contrasts this approach with the (Hobbesean) view that we take the psychological facts as given, and then derive our ethics from them.

world, practical reasons are directed at making change in the world. In other words, practical reasons do work in the world in a way that beliefs, as such, do not. It is this specific feature of practical reasons that we are trying to account for.

In the case of pure practical reasons, the motivational skeptic is asking for some model or theory that explains how motivation is produced. We are told that changes of a particular kind in the world—voluntary actions—are brought about by the activity of pure practical reason (just as beliefs are produced by the activity of theoretical reason). We are also told that the agent's desires and established inclination are not the source of this power to move the agent. Reason by itself brings about change of this particular kind. Nevertheless, whatever the content of our reasons may be, we need to know how it is possible that reason alone can move agents in this way. Motivational skepticism is nothing more than the demand that defenders of pure practical reasons provide some explanation of the (natural) process involved.

What may encourage Korsgaard's view that there is no real difficulty here is the suggestion that a person must be motivated by her practical reasons in so far as she is rational (i.e., as stipulated by the internalism requirement). Be this as it may, however, the question remains about how it is that the operations of pure practical reason are able to move the agent (i.e., without the appearance of "occult" causation). It is here that we require some psychological bridge building, if we are to explain how motivation is generated whereby reasons result in action. The Humean theory identifies the source of motivation as being located with some relevant passions or desires. Since reasons always attach to existent desires and inclinations of some kind, it is possible, on this theory, to explain how our reasons carry motivational force. When we are presented with pure practical reasons, however, the situation is not so clear. Without any motivational source in existent inclination and desire, we are asked to accept that pure practical reasons nevertheless carry motivational power in virtue of their rational "authority." When the Kantian theorist is challenged to explain how this is possible, the relevant reply, Korsgaard argues, is to say simply that rational agents, in so far as they are rational, must be motivated by their reasons (i.e., just as rational beings must believe the conclusion of a good argument). The concern that drives Humean skepticism about motivation is that this is not any kind of an answer to the problem posed. More specifically, Korsgaard does not tell us how pure practical reasons actually provide motivation; what she tells us is only what is required to be a rational agent (namely, that they must be motivated by their reasons). No source of motivation has been identified or described except the standing condition of rationality itself.[8]

It is clear, I believe, that the analogy that Korsgaard aims to draw between theoretical and practical reason does not serve to relieve the Kantian position of the burden of explaining how pure practical reasons actually generate "motivational force" (for rational agents). It may be suggested, however, that Korsgaard has something to say on this issue that goes beyond the theoretical/practical reason analogy. In the closing sections of her paper Korsgaard criticizes the (Humean) arguments advanced by Bernard Williams in his influential paper "Internal and External Reasons" (Williams, 1981). Williams argues that for a reason to be capable of motivating an agent it must do this on the basis of the agent's existent "subjective motivational set." Motivation, in other words, cannot be created *ex nihilo*; it must draw on some source already present in the agent's psychological disposition. Williams concludes from this that pure practical reasons cannot exist, since in the nature of things they are disconnected from the agent's subjective motivational set as constituted by her given ends and desires. The mistake here, according to Korsgaard, is the (undefended) assumption that the agent's "subjective motivational set contains only ends and desires"—as clearly that would eliminate all practical reasoning except the means/ends variety (SPR, 328). Contrary to this view, Korsgaard argues, all we need to suppose, consistent with the existence of pure practical reasons, is that a capacity to be motivated by considerations stemming from pure practical reason belongs to the subjective motivational set of every rational being. This is, moreover, consistent with the fact that people sometimes fail to be motivated by reasons of this kind because of "interference" in the "transmission of motivational force" (i.e., people are not always rational).

Does this reply to Williams serve to explain how the operations of pure practical reason carry "motivational force"? It is evident, I think, that no relevant answer has been given to this problem. When Korsgaard's argument is boiled down, it comes to this: If pure practical reasons exist (i.e.,

---

8. There is some parallel between this form of explanatory evasion and Hobbes's description of the kind of explanation provided by the scholastics: "Nay for the cause of understanding also, they say the thing Understood sendeth forth intelligible species, that is an intelligible being seen; which coming into the Understanding, makes us Understand" (Hobbes, 1994, 1, 5).

granted that content skepticism is unfounded) then, in so far as an agent is rational, she will be motivated by reasons of this kind. If the agent is not so motivated, this is not evidence that these reasons do not exist or are not "valid" for the agent, but only that in the circumstances the agent is not rationally disposed (i.e., she is not "listening to reason"). While we can provide some explanation for failures of this kind, Korsgaard maintains, there is no need to say anything more about how it is that motivational force is generated in the case of those agents who are responsive to reason.

What is lost here is any (plausible) theory concerning the source of motivation as provided by pure practical reason. That is to say, we have no account of how it is that reasons of this kind are capable of "setting the human body in motion." The work that practical reasons of this kind are supposed to do in the world remains a metaphysical mystery. What the Humean is looking for, and cannot find in Korsgaard's discussion, is how it is that pure practical reason acquires causal traction in the world. Even if it is true that rational agents must be motivated by their (pure) practical reasons, insofar as they are rational, we are left entirely in the dark about the source of motivation and how it gets "transmitted" into action.[9]

Those of a Kantian disposition may still be unconvinced on the ground that what we are looking for is a (crude) psychological theory of practical reason—one that aims to reduce human rationality to a system of hydraulics. I want to show that our concerns are not in any way inappropriate or illegitimate by describing a parallel example, where similar issues and problems present themselves. Consider the relationship between flames, flammable things, and burning. There are circumstances where a flame is applied to a flammable object and, for some reason, it fails to ignite and make it burn. We may, in these circumstances, investigate what has interrupted the (normal) process of ignition and burning. The sort of explanations that we are searching for will refer to specific conditions, such as that the object was wet or damp, and so on. On the other hand, we may also be interested to know how it is that flames, when applied to flammable

---

9. There is a striking difference between Korsgaard's approach and Kant's in respect of this issue. That is, for Kant it is a fundamental problem to explain how the *causality* of pure practical reason can be accounted for. He deals with this problem primarily through his (infamous) distinction between phenomenal and noumenal causality. According to Kant, when we consider human beings from an empirical (phenomenal) perspective there is no available source of motivation provided by pure practical reason. Contemporary Kantians, including Korsgaard, have generally abandoned this approach. The problem, however, as I have argued, plainly remains with us.

objects, (successfully) ignite them and cause them to burn. What we are looking for, in this case, is some theory that describes the relevant general "mechanism" involved. One such theory is that flames are hot or contain heat, and that this accounts for the process involved. Assume, for our present purposes, that this suggestion (i.e., that flames contain heat, etc.) is adequate. Suppose now that it is claimed that there exist flames that are cold or without heat, but that they are, nevertheless, capable of igniting flammable objects and causing them to burn. When we ask how this is possible we are told: "Flames, including 'cold flames,' must ignite flammable objects, otherwise those things are not flammable. It is true, of course, that in some circumstances flames fail to produce ignition and burning—but that does not show that they are not flames. In cases like this, where flames fail to ignite and burn, we will be able to say something about why the failure has occurred (e.g., the object is wet or damp, etc.). Beyond this, however, we do not need to provide any general theory about how flames manage to make flammable objects ignite and burn—except to remember that when this fails to happen the object is not flammable."

It is evident, I think, that this way of responding to the problem comes across as evasive. Korsgaard's way of handling skepticism about motivation, however, seems to have the same general form. The problem posed is certainly structurally similar. The Humean has a general theory about how reasons are able to provide and "transmit" motive force. The explanation, on their account, is that our reasons derive their motive force from our passions and desires, and this is how reasons are capable of moving us. When a consideration fails to draw on any of existing passions or desires then it cannot motivate the agent and so it cannot be a practical reason. Korsgaard wants to show that the scope of our practical reasons need not be limited in this way. The operations of reason may be able to yield conclusions that do not depend on our existing ends and desires (i.e., contrary to content skepticism). Granted this is the case, reasons of this kind will motivate us in so far as we are rational. However, when we ask how this is done—noting the parallel between (cold) flames and pure practical reasons—we are told simply that if reasons of this kind exist then they must be able to motivate rational agents, otherwise the individual in question is not rational. As in the first case, concerning flames, this seems little more than explanatory evasion. The motivation skeptic has not been given any (relevant) answer to the issue that concerns him.

It is possible, I believe, to identify more precisely where Korsgaard's answer to the motivational skeptic goes wrong. Let us return to the point where we entered this discussion. Hume's motivational skepticism, I suggested, takes the form that even if content skepticism can be answered (i.e., under some interpretation pure practical reasons exist) we would still be left with external reasons that are incapable of providing motivation. Korsgaard maintains that this is impossible. The basis of her confidence, it seems, is that she accepts the internalism requirement as a constraint on all practical reasons. That is to say, according to her position, nothing counts as a practical reason unless it is capable of motivating rational persons. It does indeed follow from this that if pure practical reasons exist they necessarily motivate persons in so far as they are rational (SPR, 320). However, the trouble with this reply to the motivational skeptic is that it simply begs the question. The answer provided is driven by observations about the logic of "reasons" based on the assumption that the internalism requirement holds for pure practical reasons. This rules out the very possibility of pure practical reasons being external reasons. That is to say, on Korsgaard's account, pure practical reasons must be capable of motivating rational persons or else they cannot be reasons. Here, again, we find that what is offered is not any (psychological) account of the source of motivation but the (logical) claim that if pure practical reasons are incapable of providing motivation they cannot be reasons (i.e., given the constraints imposed by the internalism requirement).

Humeans are, of course, internalists in so far as there is, on their account, an "internal" relation between reasons and motivation because our reasons are based upon our existing desires and inclinations. What the motivational skeptic finds missing in Korsgaard's account, therefore, is any counterpart to desires that can explain how it is that pure practical reasons are capable of providing motivation. From the perspective of the motivational skeptic, we cannot simply assume that the internalism requirement holds with respect to pure practical reasons until some (psychological) account of the internal relation between reasons and motivation is provided. To assume that the internalism requirement holds for pure practical reasons is simply to beg the question as to whether or not reasons of this kind carry any motivation.[10]

---

10. Faced with these difficulties the motivational skeptic may turn-the-tables on Korsgaard: Since we are unable to identify any plausible source of motivation for pure practical reasons they cannot *exist*—assuming, that is, that all reasons must be capable of providing motivation. (Similarly, if we assume that flames must be capable of burning and there is no intelligible theory about how "cold flames" can do this, it follows that "cold flames" cannot exist—i.e., are not really "flames.")

III

Let me conclude this chapter by describing the significance of my criticisms of Korsgaard's answer to motivation skepticism. Nothing that I have said shows that Humean ethics is correct and/or that Kantian ethics is mistaken. My aims and objectives are much more limited than this. What has been shown is that Korsgaard's attempt to discredit Humean skeptical doubts as they regard motivation and practical reason does not succeed. While Korsgaard is committed to an internalism requirement that has "psychological force," she offers an account of motivation by pure practical reason that lacks any psychological substance. That is to say, as I have argued, on analysis, Korsgaard has no theory of motivation at all in so far as it concerns pure practical reason. What Korsgaard aims to do is to show that the demand for some general psychological theory of this kind (i.e., in terms of "special psychological mechanisms") is in some way misguided or illegitimate. Nothing she says, however, shows this to be the case. Even when we set aside content skepticism, the puzzle about motivation by pure practical reason remains. In itself, this does not show that the (alternative) Humean view of practical reason is correct. Nor does it show that no adequate Kantian answer can be found. What it does show is that skepticism about motivation is a real, distinct problem and that Korsgaard has failed to provide any convincing answer to it.[11]

Our analysis and discussion of Korsgaard's argument shows that when we sever the link between reasons and desires we encounter a problem about whether the internalism requirement holds for pure practical reasons. Granted that the internalism requirement, as Korsgaard suggests, is a psychological demand on our ethical theories, what is needed is a richer moral psychology. If Kantian ethical theory is to find some way to explain motivation, as it concerns pure practical reason, it needs to say more about this problem. Certainly it cannot evade it on the basis of the assumption that pure practical reasons must be capable of motivating rational persons.

---

11. In a later paper "The Normativity of Instrumental Reason" (Korsgaard, 1997) claims that in "Skepticism about Practical Reason" she may "give the impression" that she attempts to account for the power of pure practical reason to motivate simply by *stipulating* "that in so far as we are rational we must be motivated by the (alleged) principles of reason, and in this way meet the internalism requirement" (219, n. 11). It is my contention in this paper that her argument against motivational skepticism does indeed turn on a stipulation of this kind and that there is no other argument on offer (or, if there is, we need to look beyond "Skepticism about Practical Reason").

Any assumption of this kind simply begs the question against the motivational skeptic.

BIBLIOGRAPHY

Hobbes, Thomas (1994): *Leviathan*. Edwin, Curley (ed.), Indianapolis.

Hume, David (2000): *A Treatise of Human Nature*. Norton, David and Norton, Mary (eds.), Oxford.

Korsgaard, Christine (1986): "Skepticism about Practical Reason," in *Journal of Philosophy*, 83, 5–25; reprinted in Korsgaard, Christine (1996): *Creating the Kingdom of Ends*, Cambridge, 311–34. Quoted as SPR.

Korsgaard, Christine (1997): "The Normativity of Instrumental Reason," in Cullity, Garrett and Gaut, Berys (eds.): *Ethics and Practical Reason*, Oxford, 215–54.

Williams, Bernard (1981): "Internal and External Reasons," in Williams, Bernard (1981): *Moral Luck*, Cambridge, 101–113.

8

Free Will, Art, and Morality

> *It is certainly not the least charm of a theory that it is refut-*
> *able; it is precisely thereby that it attracts subtler minds.*
> *It seems that the hundred-times-refuted theory of "free*
> *will" owes its persistence to this charm alone; again and*
> *again someone comes along who feels he is strong enough*
> *to refute it.*
>
> NIETZSCHE, *Beyond Good and Evil*[1]

PHILOSOPHICAL DISCUSSIONS OF the free will problem, as generally presented, tend to focus narrowly on worries relating to moral responsibility.
It is clear, nevertheless, that the issue of free will, as it concerns the way in
which human action and activities are embedded in the natural order of
events, is of broader interest than this. More specifically, all of us aspire to
be something more than simply *moral* agents. We want freedom because
we also value a certain conception of ourselves as agents who secure and
bring into existence values *other* than moral values by means of the exercise of our own agency. Perhaps nothing manifests this concern more evidently than artistic activity—although this is by no means the only other
area of human activity that we care about or that is relevant to concerns
about human freedom. Through artistic activities of various kinds we create valuable and worthwhile things and events by means of our agency.
Moreover, activities of this kind serve as the basis of evaluations of agents
(i.e., artists) and their works (i.e., performances and creations). For this
reason, the problem of "free will" is directly involved here.

One general form incompatibilist worries take is that we do not want to
be "mere cogs" in the natural order of events. The specter of "mechanism"
threatens to undermine our sense that we can and do "truly contribute"

---

1. Nietzsche (1966, p. 18).

to *culture* and can thereby "make a difference" through our own creative and deliberate activities (e.g., the activity of writing this chapter). Worries of this kind are of interest for at least two related reasons. First, as I have indicated, they reveal the *wider* character of the problem of free will (i.e., as it concerns the significance and value we place on human agency beyond the sphere of morality). Second, getting clear about issues of free will in the arts, and other non-moral areas of human activity, may help us better understand to what extent morality encounters *unique* and *distinct* problems in relation to free will.

The discussion in this essay begins with some observations regarding a number of structural similarities between art and morality as it involves human agency. On the basis of these observations we may ask whether or not incompatibilist worries about free will are relevant to both art and morality. One approach is to claim that libertarian free will is essential to our evaluations of merit and desert in both spheres. The other, is to claim that free will is required only in the sphere of morality—and that to this extent the art/morality analogy breaks down. I argue that both these incompatibilist approaches encounter significant problems and difficulties (and that incompatibilists have paid insufficient attention to these issues). At the same time, I also argue that although the analogy between art and morality may be welcomed by compatibilists, this analogy does not pave the way for an easy or facile optimism on this subject. On the contrary, while the art/morality analogy may lend support to compatibilism it also serves to show that some worries of incompatibilism relating to the role of luck in human life cannot be easily set aside and deny compatibilism any basis for complacent optimism on this subject.

Human Agency and the Art/Morality Analogy

Human beings evaluate the activities and actions of their fellows in a wide variety of areas: arts, professions, athletics and morality—to name a few of the most obvious examples. We also evaluate other personal qualities such as looks, intelligence, strength and so on.[2] In general, evaluation

---

2. The relationship between personal qualities of these kinds and agency is both complex and subtle. For example, our voluntary actions may manifest various natural traits (e.g., intelligence) that are involuntarily acquired. At the same time, the natural traits we have (e.g., beauty, strength) may be acquired through our own voluntary actions and activities. There is no simple line of demarcation to be drawn here. I return to this point further below.

and assessment are inescapable and essential features of human life—
however varied the individual (cultural) forms of such evaluation and its
modes may be. From the point of view of agency and agent evaluation
there exists a certain common or shared structure to these modes of evaluation. This structure falls into three important and distinct dimensions.

(a) Ability, Opportunity and Effort:

Any of the basic human activities we have described (art, athletics,
morality, etc.) require some relevant general capacity to participate.[3]
With regard to this it is important to keep in mind that abilities and
opportunities vary in ways that do not depend solely on the agent. For
example, to become good at the piano, or at football (soccer), requires
an ability (talent) and an opportunity to develop and train whatever ability or talent we have. Whether talent, education, or training is available
or not largely depends on factors over which the agent has little or no
control. At the same time, it is also clear that the agent has a role to
play by way of motivation, effort, discipline, application, or "will." These
are factors intrinsic to the agent that involve *developing* their talents or
taking advantage of their abilities (e.g., being good at the piano is not a
matter of *pure luck*—unlike, say, being born with beautiful green eyes).
In sum, in activities of this kind we find that there are both "internal"
and "external" factors at play and that they interconnect with each other
in complex ways.

(b) Performance and Achievement:

Our various human activities or exercise of agency may result in a "performance," or produce created artifacts or events. In the arts this may take
the form of playing an instrument, painting a picture, writing a novel and
so forth. (In other spheres it may take the form of playing a game, ful-
filling a professional role, or taking on some "civic" role of some kind).
These performances and products vary in both *content* and *significance*. We
may classify them as "moral," "artistic," "professional," "recreational," or
as "serious" or "trivial." The particular kind of activities or performances

---

3. It is worth noting at the outset that moral abilities or capacities are sometimes given a
misleading "all-or-nothing" characterization. A notable example of this is the much-debated
ability "to have done otherwise." The fact is, however, that moral abilities such as sympathy,
imagination, attention, discrimination and so on, may vary greatly from person to person
(and may vary for any single person over time). This parallels what we find with abilities
required for other activities (e.g., art, athletics, etc.).

we pursue and bring about through our agency will vary depending on our available opportunities, abilities, and talents. For this reason what activities we in fact pursue, and the specific form they take, will generally be a function of variables that we are *presented with*. Furthermore, these are conditions that will either constrain or foster *achievement*.

(c) Assessment and Evaluation:

Just as the kinds of activity and performance vary, so too does the *level* (degree, quality, etc.) of achievement. That is to say, in relation to the sorts of activities being described (art, athletics, etc.), we may say that they have been done well or done poorly. Moreover, with all activities of these kinds certain *standards* of evaluation are generally *constitutive* of the practices and activities involved (e.g., the very notion of "being able to play the piano" or "paint a picture" presupposes some relevant standard of achievement or competence). In this way, for these forms of human life and activity we find that our achievement and performances will inevitably be assessed (i.e., insofar as we undertake the activity or involve ourselves in it). Considered from the spectator perspective, we may also say that such activities invite us to take up an "evaluative stance" toward the agent and the performance.[4]

A further feature of our evaluations and assessments is the way in which these are generally accompanied by some associated system of rewards and punishments. Once again, these features of our evaluative stance may take various forms, ranging from (expressed) approval/disapproval, to prizes and awards, promotions or demotions, humiliation and ridicule, titles and honors, and—in the more weighty cases—legal sanctions such as prison, corporal, or even capital punishment. In all these cases, the system of retributive attitudes and practices vary in strength and degree, depending on the nature of the activity involved. Agents in these circumstances are liable to either positive or negative responses by others, and these are fundamental to motivating agents to improve their performance and avoid failures of any kind.

---

4. It is a mistake to suppose that morality is different from all other activities because it is somehow "inescapable" for human beings. First, not all humans are capable of this form of activity. Second, depending on how activities are categorized and described, others may be just as "inescapable" (e.g., athletics in some relevant mode or form). Third, even if morality was unique and distinct in terms of being in some sense "inescapable" for human agents, this by itself would not properly account for the *significance* we attach to this mode of activity.

Another distinction that needs to be considered, within the dimension of evaluation and assessment, is that between evaluation of agents and their activity. More specifically, praise and criticism is not limited to the external performance (product, creation, etc.). It goes down deeper to the qualities of the *agent* considered as the *source* of the performance. Great performances and achievements secure rewards and prizes, criticism and condemnation, for the *person* who produces them. It is the *agent* who receives whatever retributive response is called forth by her activities or performance. This is obvious and familiar in the arts. We distinguish between praising the pianist and the performance, the painter and the painting, the playwright (actors, directors, etc.) and the play (performance). It is clear, nevertheless, that praise of the former kind depends on praise of the latter kind.[5]

Given this three-dimensional analysis of the framework of human agency it is evident that issues of *fairness* arise in respect of such activities and that this is not unique to artistic or moral evaluation. Among the most general questions we may ask are these:

(a) Is the standard of evaluation the right or correct standard?
(b) Has this standard been properly applied to the agent and/or the performance?
(c) Are the conditions and circumstances of evaluation and assessment fair and reasonable?[6]

In both moral and non-moral areas of human activity—including the arts and athletics—the agents involved may be unfairly treated in any of these respects. Where there is some failure of this kind, the agent may receive punishments, blame, criticism, contempt, ridicule, or damage to

---

5. There are, of course, further complexities here. For example, we may give a negative evaluation of a particular work or performance but refrain from condemning the agent on this basis. This gap has a parallel in morality, where we may condemn a particular action, but judge it out of character and (on some accounts) an inappropriate basis for condemning the agent. Perhaps this is most obvious in athletics, where great players may often have bad games.

6. Take, for example, the evaluation of piano performances. We may want to ensure (a) that the judges know what qualities should be looking for; (b) that each performer is accurately and consistently evaluated with reference to this standard (no bias is involved, etc.); and (c) each performer is placed in appropriate conditions (e.g., in terms of piano, hall, etc.).

self-esteem that is unjust or unfair. Nevertheless, we assume in all these interrelated spheres of human activity that insofar as the agent has the relevant ability and performs the relevant activity the issue of assessment and evaluation naturally arises and presents itself to us.

Creativity, Merit, and Luck: The Case of Mozart

Although the relevance of free will for art and artistic activity has been neglected it has not been entirely overlooked. More specifically, it has been argued by some prominent and distinguished incompatibilists, most notably Robert Kane, that in the absence of free will, understood in terms of a lack of *origination* or *ultimacy*, our artistic activity and achievement would be impoverished in two especially significant respects. First, without free will, it is claimed, "genuine creativity" would be compromised.[7] In this regard, Kane quotes Karl Popper:

> [Physical determinism] ... destroys, in particular, the idea of creativity. It reduces to a complete illusion the idea that in preparing this lecture I have used my brain to create *something new*. There was no more in it, according to physical determinism, than that certain parts of my body put down black marks on white paper.[8]

The general worry here is that "novelty" and "genuine creativity" presuppose a metaphysical picture of things whereby the *source* of performances or artistic objects must in some required way *transcend* the antecedent conditions from which they arise. That is to say, they must be *original* in the sense that they cannot be (fully) explained or accounted for by the circumstances or conditions in which they come into being. They are in this sense *pure creations* (i.e., on analogy with a God-like creation of the universe). The second and related worry is that in the absence of free will there would be no "true desert for one's achievements."[9] According to Kane, if there are circumstances that completely determine and explain

---

7. Kane (1996, pp. 81f).

8. Kane (1996, p. 81); citing Popper (1972, p. 222). In a similar vein, J. Melvin Woody argues that a "framework of deductive proof [associated with the deterministic hypothesis] rules out genuine novelty by requiring us to suppose that each moment is already implicit in its predecessors" (Woody 1998, pp. 241, 235).

9. Kane (1996, pp. 82f).

our creative and artistic activities, then "the outcome would be a matter of *luck*" (my emphasis) and the agent would be denied all sense of "accomplishment." This sense of "accomplishment" and the associated requirements of "true desert" demand what Kane describes as the "kind of sole authorship" or "underived origination that many ordinary persons believe they want when they want free will."[10]

Let us consider these two (incompatibilist) claims about the importance of free will in relation to artistic activity with reference to the life and work of Wolfgang Amadeus Mozart. The details of Mozart's life are generally well known. He was born with enormous natural gift and talent, both for performance (on the piano and other instruments) and composing. His father, Leopold, was himself a musician of ability and talent and he was in a position to teach and develop his son's natural gift. Mozart was born into circumstances in mid-eighteenth-century Salzburg and Vienna that further supported this process. Apart from anything else, his circumstances were such that he was provided with sufficient motivation and encouragement that enabled him to develop the necessary discipline and desire needed to realize his potential and achieve what he did. Let us assume that these external/internal causal factors were such that his performances and compositions were *determined*. By this I mean that Mozart's compositions and performances can be fully, causally explained in terms of the background conditions and circumstances into which he was born. (For our present purposes it does not matter that the specific case is considered historically accurate—it may be treated as a hypothetical example.)

With this example in mind, let us return to the two basic incompatibilist worries described in the previous section. First, does this hypothesis about Mozart discredit the "creativity," "originality" or "novelty" of his work—either his performances or his compositions? The answer to this question is that it does not. To suggest otherwise, is to misjudge or misrepresent the relevant *basis* on which such assessments must be made. To judge whether or not Mozart's works are "original," "fresh," etc., we must *compare them to other works*. It is the performance/composition by Mozart as compared with other (earlier) works that serves as the relevant basis for any judgment of this kind (i.e., is it "new," "original," etc?).[11]

---

10. Kane (1996, p. 79).

11. Similarly, if we want to know if a runner has run the *fastest*, we must look to other performances. For this purpose it is irrelevant to ask if the runner had free will. In this sense we may say that *originality*, like being the fastest, is a *comparative* issue.

Even if there exist deterministic causal paths leading to the emergence of Mozart's works (e.g., as per the account sketched above), none of this would serve to show that the works concerned are not "creative," "original" or "new contributions" to the evolution of Western music. Clearly, the presence or absence of libertarian free will cannot decide *this* issue one way or the other. Indeed, from the point of view of our everyday common-sense discussion and consideration of issues of creativity and originality, any attempt to turn to the metaphysical issue of free will and determinism in order to decide matters of this kind would be regarded as (conversationally) odd or peculiar. This is indicative of the fact that there has been a failure to understand what is actually at issue in these circumstances.

The conclusion we may draw from the above observations is that the issue of free will is of no relevance to our assessments of creativity and originality. However, even if this point is granted, the incompatibilist may still argue that worries about our judgments about merit and "true desert" remain with us. That is to say, given our hypothesis about determinism, and the lack of ultimate origination, we still must change our assessment or judgment concerning Mozart's desert qua artist/composer. Because his *work* is judged "original," "creative," "great," etc., we may naturally assume that praise of him—the agent who produced this work—must also be appropriate or in order. In fact, however, the incompatibilist continues, although if the deterministic story is true of Mozart, then all praise of him (the artist or person) must be regarded as *shallow* or *superficial* and any rewards and honors cannot be truly deserved.[12] According to incompatibilists, such as Kane, if the deterministic story that has been told about Mozart's life is true, then Mozart was simply *lucky*—the fortunate causal vehicle for forces and factors that worked their way *through him* but do not *begin with him*. If Mozart was nothing more than a *causal intermediary* in the natural flow of events, initiating no new series through his agency, then all merit drains away and recedes back along the (infinite) causal chain. In consequence of this, as there is no real originating agent, all real merit or desert simply *evaporates*.[13]

---

12. In relation to this compare Thomas Reid's observations on Cato: "What was, by an ancient author, said of Cato, might indeed be said of him. *He was good because he could not be otherwise.* But this saying, if understood literally and strictly, is not the praise of Cato, but of his constitution, which was no more the work of Cato, than his existence" (Reid 1969, p. 261).

13. As a biographical aside, I note that although Mozart was recognized as a great genius by many—including some of his more gifted contemporaries (e.g., Haydn)—Mozart nevertheless encountered others who belittled his achievements and were reluctant to recognize

On the free will model, Mozart would be the "real creator," a "true originator" a "genuine source" of his compositions and performances. In these circumstances our praise and esteem would be *deep* because Mozart's creations *arise* from and *begin* with his *agency*. Deep responsibility for works of art, on this view, requires some form of ultimate origination of this general kind. Without this, musical gift and its associated achievements would become much like good looks; just a matter of good fortune. Nothing about what was done or achieved would really reflect on the artist as an *agent* who "truly brought this work into the world," when it (categorically) might not have been.[14]

Are these incompatibilist worries about the implications of determinism as applied to artistic merit well-founded? Is praise, criticism, admiration, and the like, rendered *shallow* when applied to individuals such as Mozart, insofar as we view them in a deterministic light? It is worth noting that this way of extending compatibilists' worries beyond the bounds of morality into the sphere of art presents the incompatibilist with a slippery-slope problem. That is to say, it is not clear why these concerns as applied to art and artistic achievement, should not also apply to other areas of human activity, such as athletics. The same general argument seems to hold equally in this sphere (however trivial as it may be considered). Take the case of Pele—perhaps the most gifted football (soccer) player of all time.[15] Clearly luck played a significant role in his career, in ways that are similar to the account provided of Mozart's life. Pele was born with enormous natural athletic ability. Moreover, he was born in Brazil, a country with a great football tradition that was able to provide him with coaches and trainers who spotted and developed his talent and potential. Let us suppose, therefore, a deterministic story of a similar kind can be told about his career and all his athletic achievements. (Again, all that is needed for

---

their true merit. (Famously, Mozart died in poverty without any proper recognition of this event.) No doubt, this reflects the fickle nature of public and professional reputations, not to mention the role of resentment in the face of a gift of this magnitude. While there is much to be said about this (unhappy) side of Mozart's life, and how it relates to issues of merit, appreciation, and reputation, I will not discuss these details.

14. Once again, the example of God's original act of creation would serve as a relevant model, where creation is understood as *creation ex nihilo* or as the act of an "unmoved mover." Suffice it to say, how we account for *pure* acts of creativity on the libertarian model is not so clear. This seems especially true of recent "soft libertarian" theories, such as Kane's. For present purposes, however, I will set these concerns aside.

15. I realize this is controversial. For example, a good case can also be made for George Best, and perhaps others (I will leave it to readers to find their own preferred example).

this is the *hypothesis*—which relies on the actual case only insofar as it lends itself to describing this example.) The incompatibilist, who is committed to the view that free will worries apply to the case of Mozart, has no *principled* basis on which to refuse to extend these worries to the case of Pele (as described). To do this, however, seems to force abstract and obscure philosophical concerns into a self-evidently inappropriate context. Indeed, this seems a clear case of excessive "over-intellectualizing" of an otherwise straightforward example of a great football player who deserves recognition for his various achievements.[16] Nothing about the deterministic story serves to discredit or alter the basis of our praise and admiration for Pele, much less to show that he was not (really) talented or not (really) skilled or that he did not perform or achieve (truly) great things on the football pitch. The presence or absence of either determinism or free will, in this context, seems entirely irrelevant to these sorts of considerations and assessments. Indeed, typically, these sorts of concerns are never even *contemplated*.[17] Moreover, even if one were to introduce and present these (abstract) philosophical worries to the world of football—taking the veil off our usual philosophical innocence in relation to this matter—there is no reason to suppose our assessment of Pele as a great footballer would be altered or affected at all. On the contrary, our judgments about Pele's achievements and merits as a player have nothing to do with such questions. It is fair to say that from the perspective of the ordinary person worries of this kind—at least in this context (athletics)—would be regarded as peculiar and wholly out of place.

The conclusion that we have reached with regard to the Pele example presents an obvious difficulty for the incompatibilist who claims that free will is required for "true desert" in the sphere of art (e.g., as per our Mozart example). Although there are obvious differences between the arts and athletics, in terms of the kinds of activities involved, with respect to human agency and the evaluation of agents and their performances, there is no clear or obvious difference that would justify claiming free will is needed in one sphere but not the other. Even if we grant that one sphere of activity is more important or significant than the other—and not everyone

---

16. Compare P.F. Strawson (2003, pp. 91–92).

17. Of course, coaches, fans, and players may have considerable interest in knowing what sort of conditions give rise to great players. Significantly, however, no one in these roles supposes that because some such conditions may be identified this discredits their (independent) assessments of great players.

would concede in a simple or unqualified form—this still does not serve to show that free will is needed for the one but not the other. The relative importance and value that we attach to the activity is not a relevant basis upon which to rest the relevance or boundary of free will.[18]

It is important to note, with respect to both the Mozart and Pele examples, we have described, that it is simply wrong to suppose that the "true desert" or "merit" of the agent in question is a simple or direct function of the *effort of will* involved in becoming a great player or artist. On the contrary, to a considerable extent the agent's *lack* of (required) effort may actually serve as the relevant *basis* of our praise and esteem for the player or artist. In circumstances of this kind, it is often said with reference to the great player or artist, that their performance or achievement was "effortless," and this is intended as praise and evidence that they *deserve* it. Clearly there are further complexities here that need to be noted, such as that our effortless performance may itself be the product of considerable application, effort and discipline in the past. This need not, however, be the case. While it is certainly unlikely that any great achievement is possible without some appropriate degree of application and effort, the fact remains that similar efforts and levels of application lead to very different achievements and judgments about merit. Judgments about merit are not, therefore, simply a matter of judging the quality or degree of effort coming from the agent. On the contrary, no amount of effort, simply by itself, secures achievement or generates any measure of merit or desert.[19]

---

18. One further reason for rejecting this strategy is that the significance itself may depend, not on the arts/athletics divide, as such, but on the significance of the *token activity or performance*. For example, a football player's performance in the World Cup may be judged of much *greater importance* than someone playing the piano at a family gathering. There is no reason to suppose *significance* tracks the (simple) art/athletics divide; or that the occasion or level within each sphere is irrelevant to assessing the significance and value of the specific performance and the merit of the agent involved. Moreover, the divide between athletics and art is not always so clear or sharp (consider, for example, dance or ice-skating). Similar observations may be made with respect to any suggested divide between morality and other forms of human activity.

19. Every teacher is familiar with the situation of a student who applies herself but achieves little to nothing in the face of another who makes little or no effort and still achieves a great deal. It is a bad and irresponsible teacher who grades work with a view solely to effort, while ignoring the disparity in the actual *quality* of the performance or paper. Nor does it help to say that the student who wrote a bad *paper*, but tried, is a good *student*, and the student who wrote the good paper, without any effort, is nevertheless a *bad student*. This involves the wrong-headed view that the good/bad student distinction simply tracks effort but not ability and actual achievement.

In light of these observations, we may conclude that incompatibilist worries that determinism, or the supposition that agents lack libertarian free will, must somehow eliminate the possibility of creativity or originality, or discredit our attributions of praise and blame (i.e., render them "shallow"), are without foundation. In the case of "creativity" and "originality," our judgments about this are made with reference to other (earlier) works and their features and qualities. The presence or absence of deterministic paths bears no relevance on these matters. In the case of "true desert" or "genuine merit," the claim that an artist is undeserving in circumstances of determinism is similarly mistaken. We may have little or no knowledge (and give little or no thought to) the conditions that account for an artist having ability, and being in a position to develop and cultivate his talents. Despite this, we can still be in a position to make sound judgments about who has made significant achievements and performances and is truly deserving of praise or criticism. This reflects the fact that our judgments about who is "truly deserving" of praise are based on conditions *entirely independent* of metaphysical issues of free will and determinism. Moreover as have noted, if we take a different stand on this issue in relation to art and artistic activity, we are liable to find ourselves on a slippery slope that commits us to the (wholly implausible) conclusion that even mundane activities, such as athletics, require that we evaluate agents and their performances in light of the presence or absence of free will. Given these observations, we may conclude that incompatibilism, in relation to art and artistic activity, lacks any credible support and is at odds with all our established attitudes and practices in ordinary life.

Transcending Luck: Morality, Incompatibilism, and Absolute Fairness

The general conclusion we have reached is that the case for incompatibilism with respect to *artistic* achievement and merit is unconvincing. This conclusion has significant implications for incompatibilism with respect to morality. On one hand, incompatibilists may retreat to the citadel of morality and insist that there is a *boundary* to be drawn between morality and other spheres of human agency and activity (art, athletics, etc.) with respect to free will considered as a necessary condition of genuine agency and desert. Although there exist some structural similarity and parallels between the framework of human agency in morality and art, this general analogy does not hold with regard to the relevance or irrelevance of *free will*. Morality is, these incompatibilists will argue, *different* from art in this regard.

In contrast with this, other incompatibilists (e.g., Kane) may refuse to retreat and argue, instead, contrary to the conclusion reached above, that the analogy does hold and so the case for the relevance of free will to artistic achievement and merit must and can be provided with further defense. However, for reasons that we have considered, this approach must eventually confront the issue of whether *any boundary* needs to be drawn between morality and art, on one side, and more mundane activities such as athletics on the other. The general problem that surfaces here is whether the incompatibilist is going to endorse the view that *all* achievement and merit, insofar as it concerns human agency and activities, requires free will. If not, some *alternative boundary* will need to be identified that places morality and art in some privileged position (in contrast with more mundane activities). If some boundary of this kind is to be drawn then some *principled* grounds for it must be articulated and (per hypothesis) these grounds cannot be exclusively *moral* grounds—on pain of leaving art on the wrong side of the boundary. From any point of view, therefore, whichever approach is taken, incompatibilists must give further attention to this set of problems. To the extent that incompatibilism is unable to come up with a satisfactory response, so to that extent their general position in relation to *morality* is suspect.

Although it remains open for incompatibilists to argue that free will is required for artistic achievement and merit, for reasons already given, this is not in my view the most promising strategy. Contrary to those who would extend their claims about free will beyond the bounds of morality, the best case for incompatibilism is to be made by arguing that morality is really different—whatever (superficial) parallels or analogies may be drawn between it and human agency and evaluation in the arts. The fundamental claim lying behind this approach is that the requirements of *fairness* are different in these two spheres. More specifically, morality—unlike art and athletics—requires fairness *all the way down*. Without this our moral evaluation would subject agents to the vagaries of *luck*, which would render morality *unfair as judged by its own standards*.

In order to understand what is (intuitively) at stake with regard to this claim, let us return to an example in the sphere of art. Consider a music competition or series of concerts involving piano players. In any situation of this kind the performers will clearly have different levels of (natural) talent, training, and so forth that have been made available to them. Moreover, as noted before, even their own levels of discipline and motivation may reflect these and other variables beyond their control or influence. Nevertheless, as we have argued, no person in ordinary life will claim that praise, recognition, or prizes awarded in these circumstances are inherently unfair because background variables involving luck of this kind are present. Having said this, it is also clear that any musical evaluation of this sort may indeed be deemed unfair if *certain* conditions are not met. The kind of standards we are actually concerned with are usually well-established and well-known. For example, a review or competition will be unfair if the judge or reviewer is incompetent and has no proper appreciation of the qualities and abilities that should be looked for. Similarly, if a pianist is asked to play on a faulty instrument or in circumstances where there is noise and distraction in the audience during the performance, we will consider the evaluation unfair. What we may say about this, therefore, is that the fairness of the evaluation is *relative* to these standards (which are themselves internal to and constitutive of an understanding of the art form). While these standards of *relative* fairness are themselves subject to adjustment and debate, they do not presuppose or aim at *absolute* fairness understood as the requirement of eliminating all background conditions of luck relating to talent, training, and the like. Clearly, it would be more or less impossible to create or secure conditions of absolute fairness, so interpreted, as a precondition for (fair) musical evaluation. In general, outside of morality most forms of evaluation of human activity and agency operate in a framework that permits and presupposes (inescapable) background distributive inequalities with regard to talent, ability, training, and opportunities. Our earlier examples of Mozart and Pele serve as evidence of this.

Why, then, should we not assume that morality is subject to the same structural features as the arts (and athletics), which depend only on *relative* fairness and allow for some measure of (background) luck? Clearly, we can give a compatibilist account of moral life, within the bounds of relative fairness, that still allows for luck in some degree. That is to say, we may begin with some scrutiny of the established moral standards of our community, in terms of which agents are evaluated. These may be adjusted and amended over time in light of reflection and criticism. Similarly, in particular cases we may ask if these standards have been properly interpreted and applied (e.g., is there proper impartiality, consistency, and clarity in the evaluations being made)? Are the circumstances in which agents are being evaluated and judged appropriate and suitable to the evaluations being made (e.g., do any of the usual and familiar excusing conditions apply, such as ignorance, accidents, and so on?) In cases of this kind, we assume that it lies broadly within the agent's *power of choice* to follow or reject the moral standards of the community. To this extent, in contrast with our experience in the arts and abilities, we assume that responsible agents can avoid blame and punishment *so long as they choose correctly.* Clearly, however, this set of conditions as described still falls short of *absolute* fairness. The reason for this, as familiar to incompatibilist concerns, is that *the way an agent chooses* may itself depend on background conditions that he has no (final) control or influence over. This is, indeed, exactly where worries about the implications of determinism enter the scene. On the assumption that the way an agent makes moral choices is a function of background factors over which he has no control (e.g., natural constitution, family, environment, etc.), then moral agency and evaluation fails the standard of *absolute* fairness.[20] In particular, the moral agent could not be said to have a genuine, open opportunity to avoid blame and secure praise in the absence of libertarian free will.

The fundamental incompatibilist concern here is that any effort to rest morality on foundations of *relative* fairness (as described above) places it on foundations that are flawed as judged *by its own standards.* That is to say, it is, according to the incompatibilist line of reasoning, essential that moral evaluations satisfy standards of *absolute* fairness whereby agents have a real, open possibility of satisfying or complying with moral standards, and thereby avoiding condemnation and blame and/or securing some measure of praise. As we have pointed out, this is not essential to art or athletics or the evaluations involved in those spheres of human activity. In the case of morality, however, according to this incompatibilist account, *there is no moral agency* where these conditions of *absolute* fairness are not met. Conditions of relative fairness may *masquerade* as allowing "deep" or "genuine" evaluations of agents but this serves only to *deceive* us. To present moral evaluation in these circumstances as indicative or responsive to "genuine desert" is to show a lack of understanding of the activity in question. To make this clear the incompatibilist may suggest another analogy. Imagine a piano recital where the performance involves a self-playing piano (e.g., a "Pianola"). In these circumstances any evaluation of the "pianist" and her "performance" would be based on an *illusion or misunderstanding.* There is no (real) pianist or performance to evaluate—to think

---

20. For an illuminating study relating to these concerns, see Gary Watson's discussion of the case of Robert Harris in Watson (2004, pp. 235f).

otherwise is fail to understand this art form and its associated standards. The same general observations hold, according to the incompatibilist in morality in circumstances of determinism, when standards of absolute fairness are not met. In these conditions there may be the *illusion* of (real) agency and action, but there is in fact nothing of this kind going on. The performance is little more than a tune played on a "Pianola."[21]

According to the incompatibilist strategy that has been described, the gap between morality, on one side, and the arts and similar (non-moral) activities on the other, reflects a gap between two general modes of agency evaluation that are committed to fundamentally distinct assumptions about what is required for fair evaluation and genuine desert. Whereas evaluation in the arts presupposes standards that do not require fairness *all the way down,* morality is more demanding than this. Morality, on this account, presupposes a notion of *absolute* fairness whereby a *moral* performance is by its very nature one whereby the agent has a real, open possibility of satisfying the standards in question. Where praise or blame are appropriate the agent's choices and conduct must not themselves result from background factors over which they have no control. In this way, morality, unlike art, is immune from the play of luck. Whereas we may admire Mozart as a great artist without concerning ourselves about free will or determinism, this perspective is not available to us in *moral* life properly understood. Moral life must be *absolutely* fair—otherwise it fails by its own standards and interpretation of what morality requires.[22]

Living with Luck: Morality, Compatibilism, and Relative Fairness

The question I want to consider in this section is how *compatibilists* should respond to the art/morality analogy in respect of the free will issue and what its significance is for their general position on this subject. On the face of it, compatibilists have every reason to *welcome* the analogy between art and morality. Our example of Mozart shows why this is so. We can and

---

21. When a tune is played on a "Pianola" we cannot say that the "pianist" has hit the "right" or "wrong" notes, as clearly the "pianist" is *not really playing the piano at all.*

22. There is, of course, a close connection between incompatibilism and what Bernard Williams has described as "the morality system." As Williams points out, "the morality system" lays stress on the "institution of blame" and the related notions of obligation, duty and voluntariness. For more on this, see Williams, (1985); see also Williams (1995, pp. 14–16).

do assess and evaluate artistic creations and merit without any worries about the presence or absence of libertarian free will. Worries of this kind (as argued in above) are simply *irrelevant* to our ordinary, everyday evaluation in these spheres. Evaluations of artistic performances and merit do not require absolute fairness or that the agent must have some real, open possibility of either success or failure. Luck plays a background role in all such evaluations. None of this discredits the evaluations we make or the way we assess genuine merit in this area. Granted that there exist clear and obvious parallels and structural analogies between artistic and moral activities and their associated evaluations, this gives considerable credence to the compatibilist view that moral evaluations, like artistic evaluations, do not depend upon or require *absolute* fairness. The presence of background luck, in the form of variables that may determine our character and choices, does not serve to discredit the *relative* fairness of the evaluations we make of agents *on the basis of their conduct and character.*

With this point in mind, we can construct a parallel case in moral life to that of our Mozart example in the sphere of the arts. Let us suppose that we can give a complete deterministic account of the life and work of Nelson Mandela.[23] Nothing about this hypothesis, the compatibilist will argue, discredits our (independent) assessment of his *moral* achievements (i.e., courageous acts, etc.) and the genuine merit he has acquired on this basis. Surely, the compatibilist may argue, it would be perverse, in this case, to refrain from making any judgment about his admirable deeds and moral merit until we can settle our metaphysical concerns about the presence or absence of libertarian free will—just as it would be in the case of our Mozart example. For the compatibilist, therefore, the analogy between art and morality is one that lends support to the general view that morality is no more *immune* from the background influences of luck than is art. In neither case does the presence of background luck discredit our evaluations and assessments or show they are somehow unjustified.

The compatibilist will also welcome the analogy between art and morality because, as our earlier discussion indicates, it generates significant difficulties for the incompatibilist. As we pointed out, the incompatibilist may hold, with Kane and others, that free will matters to us *beyond* the bounds of morality. Incompatibilists of this orientation *accept* there is some relevant analogy between art and morality, but deny that this tells

---

23. Once again this example is only hypothetical in character—the details of the actual case need not detain us.

against incompatibilism. They argue, on the contrary, incompatibilist worries do indeed extend to other spheres of human activity, such as the arts. On this approach, however, the incompatibilist then faces the difficulty of establishing some alternative (principled) boundary for the requirements of free will. The clear danger here is that this places them on a slippery slope that commits them to the view that even the most mundane human activities (e.g., a football game) involving the evaluation and assessment of agents presupposes the metaphysics of free will. Although it is possible to simply "bite the bullet" here, most incompatibilists will agree that this constitutes a *reductio* of their position.

Faced with this difficulty (as we pointed out further above) the incompatibilist may retreat to the citadel of morality and try and draw a principled boundary here—one that *excludes* art from the demands of free will. This is a strategy that commits the incompatibilist to *denying* that there is a relevant analogy to be had between art and morality as regards their incompatibilist conditions. More specifically, whereas art and other more mundane human activities do not require *absolute* fairness and the absence of luck, these conditions are *essential* to moral evaluation and moral merit. Having explained why incompatibilists find themselves pushed back into this position, the compatibilist may now use the art/morality analogy to further discredit it.

If the incompatibilist holds onto the view that requirements of free will apply specifically and exclusively to morality then they face another unattractive dilemma. On the one hand, if moral evaluation rests on some general requirement that "genuine desert" requires that the agent must have had real, open possibilities to avoid blame and/or secure praise, and that there can be no background role for luck (i.e., in contrast with the evaluation in the arts), then we must either construct some sort of metaphysical account of human agency in an effort to show how this demand can be satisfied, or we must accept the radical skeptical conclusion that (genuine) *moral* evaluation is never justified. The well-known problem with the first option is that, not only does it encourage obscure and problematic metaphysical system-building, it flies in the face of a considerable amount of (empirical) evidence that suggests that an agent's conduct and character is indeed subject to the background influence of factors beyond their control.[24] In moral life, the compatibilist will argue, no less than in other spheres of human agency, such as art, we see clear evidence that what the

---

24. See again Watson's observations on Robert Harris in Watson (2004, pp. 235f).

agent does, for good or for bad, depends on their natural constitution, upbringing, and the opportunities and obstacles they are presented with. The parallels seem clear and obvious here. To *conceal* this fact about moral life, by resting our evaluation on some illusory assumptions that *moral* agents must have real, open opportunities for moral success or failure, is a way of obscuring some of the more troubling and difficult truths about moral life.[25] Many incompatibilists are, of course, persuaded by these (compatibilist) criticisms in respect of the extravagant tendencies of libertarian metaphysics and associated tendency to deny the evident role that luck plays in moral life. However, the conclusion that these incompatibilists draw from this is one of *systematic skepticism* about all moral evaluation of agents. Since conditions of absolute fairness cannot be realized, they argue, it follows that there is no real "true" responsibility, understood in terms of "genuine desert" of some kind.[26]

Compatibilists generally regard this form of radical skepticism as clear evidence of philosophical pathology. While incompatibilism, on first appearance presents itself as an effort to *preserve* values that we care about (i.e., desert, merit, etc.), it nevertheless rapidly turns on itself and leads on to the *nihilistic* conclusion that these values are impossible to *realize*. As the requirements of libertarian metaphysics are impossible to satisfy— or perhaps even coherently state—we are invited to conclude that there are no well-founded evaluations of *moral* agents and their actions. All that survives on this (skeptical) view is some attenuated form of morality that employs moral *language* but lacks its true force and substance. From the compatibilist perspective, radical skepticism of this kind is disconnected from the realities of human life and experience. It is as perverse as any

---

25. In general, we usually acknowledge that there exist complex natural and social distributive inequalities that affect people's prospects in life, as shaped by the various abilities and opportunities that they receive in the "natural lottery." This observation, however, does not lead us into the (absurd) skeptical conclusion that there are no relevant distinctions to be drawn between people in respect of their achievements and merit in various areas of human activity (e.g., the arts). I note, beyond this, that there is, nevertheless, a certain ideological temper (e.g., as associated with hyper-capitalism) that encourages the view that "any one can be successful" so long as they have sufficient *willpower*—hence success and failure, even in non-moral activities are, ultimately, an indication of *moral* character. This is exactly what happens when the demands and presuppositions of incompatibilism—or "the morality system"—are (illegitimately) extended beyond the bounds of morality itself. As I have explained, among the distortions involved in this process, is the way it *conceals* conditions of *genuine inequality* in individuals' opportunities and initial circumstances—at least some of which are capable of social remedy.

26. For a view along these lines, see e.g., Galen Strawson (2003).

similar form of skepticism would be in relation to the arts, or athletics, or any other sphere involving human agents and their activities. In these other areas we see clear evidence that the evaluations we make, and the distinctions we draw, do not depend on foundations of free will. Nor are they compromised by the fact that our evaluations are made in the face of background conditions that allow scope for luck and its influence over the sorts of performances that agents produce. Morality, compatibilists maintain, is liable to similar sorts of constraints and limitations.[27] Indeed, the compatibilist response may take the stronger view that radical skepticism on these matters is actually *pernicious*—since it involves the nihilistic thesis that the clear evident distinctions we all draw in the moral sphere are somehow "unreal" or "illusory." The mistake that we need to resist here is the supposition that all fair (moral) evaluation must meet the standard of *absolute* fairness. We do not expect or need this in relation to art or athletics, and we have no reason to demand this in moral life either. Moral agents are similarly subject to background conditions that account for the specific way their agency is exercised and thus for their moral success and failures. To acknowledge this (familiar and evident) fact about the human predicament does nothing to show that there are no (real) moral agents or that all our moral evaluations lack any appropriate or relevant justification. The more we reflect on the art/morality analogy, the compatibilist may argue, the more obvious this conclusion becomes.

Presented in these terms it appears that the art/morality analogy is *wholly friendly* to the compatibilist position, whereas, at best, it is highly problematic for the incompatibilist. However, the situation is not so straightforward as this. More specifically, it may be argued that there are features of the art/morality analogy that are far from friendly to the compatibilist and actually serve to highlight its more significant vulnerabilities. If we abandon the requirements of absolute fairness—allowing a background role for luck whereby it is not the case that agents have a real open possibility for moral praise or blame—then moral evaluation occurs in a framework within which we must acknowledge that some agents are (ultimately) "fortunate" and others "unfortunate." Surely, incompatibilists will object, no plausible *moral* scheme can invite us to simply close

---

27. Indeed, this is something we should *expect* to be the case unless we operate on the implausible assumption that there is some simple and neat boundary to be drawn between the moral sphere and other areas of human activity. The "morality system" does nevertheless presuppose this (see notes 18 and 22, above).

our eyes or turn away from the evident *unfairness* of moral evaluation in these circumstances.[28] The relevant compatibilist reply to this objection is, I think, clear. Moral evaluation in these circumstance is *no more and no less fair* than the evaluation of artists and athletics in circumstances where we allow for background conditions of luck that influence what these agents do and how they are evaluated. There is no ideal, perfect plateau of *moral equality of opportunity*—any more than there is in art or athletics. We must reconcile ourselves to these features of the human condition rather than conceal them or collapse in nihilistic despair when we reflect upon them. Some may be born to be a Nelson Mandela, others to be Saddam Hussains. Most of us fall somewhere in between. Although the way we exercise our agency and take advantage of our abilities and opportunities will determine where exactly we fall in this continuum, *ultimately* this will depend on factors over which we have no (final) control. Nevertheless, the fact remains that *internal* to these practices (i.e., in morality, as in art) there are relevant standards that enable us to draw evident and significant distinctions relating to success or failure in these spheres. The important point is not to *distort* these standards in the direction of the requirements of *absolute fairness* so that these standards collapse under their own weight. This is the fundamental error of incompatibilism.

It is still arguable that this line of compatibilist thinking remains too *complacent*. The incompatibilist worries about *absolute* fairness suggest that without libertarian free will agents are inevitably vulnerable to background luck in respect of the formative conditions on their conduct and character.[29] There is, therefore, an important sense in which compatibilism must accept that *morality is unfair at this absolute level*. We all accept that the

---

28. Here we may be reminded of the *weight* and *importance* of moral evaluation, in contrast with other forms of evaluation. We may also be reminded that moral evaluation carries with it (more) weighty and significant sanctions—in the form of our retributive practices (i.e., punishment).

29. From the point of view of worries about luck, understood as background features beyond the control of the agent that determine what they do and how they will be evaluated, it may be questioned whether *libertarian* free will eliminates all relevant sources of worry here. For example, even agents who have powers of libertarian free will may still be subject to what Thomas Nagel describes as "circumstantial luck" (Nagel 1979). Although these agents are able to categorically act otherwise, the sorts of moral challenges they face may vary greatly—so free will is no guarantee of *equality of moral opportunity*. What this shows is that incompatibilist concerns about what is required for *absolute* fairness, depending on how strictly they are interpreted, may well be impossible to satisfy *whatever kind of free will powers we attribute to human agents*.

human predicament is such that we are all subject to the "natural lotteries" of life, whereby certain distributive inequalities are generated (e.g., in looks, abilities, character traits and so on). This is troubling enough when it concerns good or bad fortune outside the sphere of morality—but when it falls within the sphere of morality, as compatibilists allow, then we can hardly regard this as an "optimistic" solution to incompatibilist concerns. On the contrary, compatibilists do not so much solve the problem as simply ignore it or dismiss it as based on confusions of some kind.[30]

Compatibilists may reply to this objection by way of noting that optimism cannot be vindicated on this issue by falsifying or misrepresenting the human condition with respect to morality. Incompatibilists, as we have noted, do this by either generating illusory metaphysical systems or, when that fails, falling into skepticism and nihilism. Further, the compatibilist need not be complacent in the face of background inequalities that shape the way agents' lives unfold. Once again, the art/morality analogy can help us understand why this is so. In the face of background inequalities that shape the way artistic or intellectual abilities and talents may or may not be developed, social policies can help to foster and cultivate talent in this sphere (i.e., promote and encourage success rather than failure). There is no reason why the same attitude of concern cannot be manifest as regards morality. We can take many steps to encourage and promote healthy moral development and avoid moral failure of various kinds. However, in taking steps of this kind we should be understood not to be aiming at the (impossible) goal of *absolute* fairness, nor, on the other side of the same coin, should we abandon our confidence in the relative fairness or "depth" of the moral evaluations and assessments that we make. It may, in some *absolute* sense, be "unfair" that some individuals are born to be Mozarts and Mandelas and others are not.[31] Be this as it may, the distinctions that we draw in respect of these individuals, their achievements and their merit do not depend on any standard or presuppositions of absolute fairness. When this standard is set aside it becomes clear that morality does not

---

30. See, for example, Daniel Dennett's (complacent) attitude to luck in Dennett (1984), Chap. 4, Sect. 3. For more general discussion of compatibilist complacency (as manifest in Dennett and others), see Russell (2002, pp. 242–48).

31. I note that the nature of absolute unfairness is to be accounted for not simply in terms of the unequal distribution of talents, abilities, opportunities and so on, but in terms of our *evaluations* of agents where these background factors that agents do not control nevertheless influence and affect what they actually do and how their agency is evaluated.

rest on the foundations of free will metaphysics and that it can survive all (pessimistic) reflections and observations we may entertain concerning the role of luck in human life—morality included.

Conclusion

The discussion in this chapter began with some general observations concerning the structural parallels or analogies that exist in the spheres of human agency involving artistic and moral activity. With this in view, we considered the specific question of whether libertarian free will is required for the evaluation of artistic achievement and merit. Contrary to the claims of some distinguished contemporary incompatibilists, we concluded that this is not the case. Given this conclusion, it was suggested that an alternative incompatibilist strategy may argue that some relevant *boundary* must be drawn between art and morality, whereby free will is required only for moral evaluations but not for those in the sphere of the arts. The basis of this incompatibilist position is that in the case of morality, unlike the arts and other more mundane forms of human activity (e.g., athletics), we require *absolute* fairness. Absolute fairness is not satisfied in circumstances where the agent's performance, and the resultant evaluations of the agent's merit, depend on background factors that the agent has no control over (e.g., as per the Mozart example). More specifically, for absolute fairness whether an agent succeeds or fails to comply with relevant moral standards must (ultimately) depend on the *agent alone*. While standards of *relative* fairness may suffice in the arts and athletics—where free will concerns are plainly out of place—this is not how things stand with morality. The compatibilist rejoinder to this is that this approach commits us to either a *falsification* of moral life—along with the associated systems of extravagant metaphysics—or collapses into radical skepticism and nihilism. According to compatibilism, the way to avoid this unattractive dilemma is to look more closely at the significance of the art/morality analogy. What this analogy shows us is that the distinctions and evaluations that we draw in morality, like their counterparts in the arts, rest on a background that allows scope for luck to influence the way our moral agency is actually exercised. While this observation does not serve to discredit or in any way systematically undermine our confidence in the basic distinctions and evaluations that we make, neither does it lend itself to any easy or complacent optimism. What it reveals is that in respect of the human predicament, luck has a role to play in *all* dimensions of human life, and it is an illusion to suppose that human agency in general, and moral agency in particular, is immune or can be insulated from the influence of luck in the way that our lives unfold.

Philosophy should leave us strong enough to recognize and accept this truth about human existence without us having to cling to either metaphysical illusions to sustain some form of false optimism or falling into an exaggerated pessimism that offers us only nihilism and despair. The world we have is the world we must live in. There is no escape from this world into a realm whereby our actions and activities can be unshackled from the particularities and contingencies of each and every individual human existence. This is a reflection that should license neither deep pessimism nor complacent optimism. At least one source for resilience, in the face of all this, is the thought that both art and morality can survive even when this feature of the human condition is made entirely transparent to us.[32]

REFERENCES

Dennett, Daniel. 1984. *Elbow Room*. Oxford: Clarendon.

Kane, Robert. 1996. *The Significance of Free Will*. Oxford: Oxford University Press.

Nagel, Thomas. 1979. "Moral luck." Reprinted in *Mortal Questions*. Cambridge: Cambridge University Press.

Nietzsche, F. 1966. *Beyond Good and Evil* (trans.: W. Kaufmann). New York: Random House.

Popper, Karl. 1972. "Of clouds and clocks." In *Objective Knowledge*. Oxford: Clarendon. Press.

Reid, Thomas. 1969. *Essays on the Active Powers of the Human Mind*. Cambridge: MIT Press.

Russell, Paul. 2002. "Pessimists, pollyannas and the new compatibilism." In *The Oxford Handbook of Free Will*, ed. R. Kane. Oxford: Oxford University Press.

Strawson, Galen. 2003. "The impossibility of moral responsibility." Reprinted in *Free Will*, ed. by G. Watson, 2nd ed. Oxford: Oxford University Press: 212–28.

Strawson, P. F. 2003. "Freedom and resentment." In *Free Will*, ed. by G. Watson, 2nd ed. Oxford: Oxford University Press: 72–93.

---

32. Earlier versions of this chapter were read at the Bled Philosophical Conference on Freedom and Determinism, Slovenia (2006); the Moral Sciences Club, Cambridge University (2007); and Kwantlen College, British Columbia (2007). I am grateful to members of the audience at these talks for their comments and discussion.

Watson, Gary. 2004. "Responsibility and the limits of evil." Reprinted in *Agency and Answerability*. Oxford: Clarendon.

Williams, Bernard. 1985. *Ethics and the Limits of Philosophy*. London: Fontana.

Williams, Bernard. 1995. "How free does the will need to be?" Reprinted in *Making Sense of Humanity*. Cambridge: Cambridge University Press.

Woody, J. Melvin. (1998) *Freedom's Embrace*. University Park: Penn State University Press.

9

Selective Hard Compatibilism

MANIPULATION AND MORAL STANDING

RECENT WORK IN compatibilist theory has focused a considerable amount of attention on the question of the nature of the capacities required for freedom and moral responsibility. Compatibilists, obviously, reject the suggestion that these capacities involve an ability to act otherwise in the same circumstances. That is, these capacities do not provide for any sort of libertarian, categorical free will. The difficulty, therefore, is to describe some plausible alternative theory that is richer and more satisfying than the classical compatibilist view that freedom is simply a matter of being able to do as one pleases or act according to the determination of one's own will. Many of the most influential contemporary compatibilist theorists have placed emphasis on developing some account of "rational self-control" or "reasons-responsiveness."[1] The basic idea in theories of this kind is that free and responsible agents are capable of acting according to available reasons. Responsibility agency, therefore, is a function of a general ability to be guided by reasons or practical rationality. This is a view that has considerable attraction since it is able to account for intuitive and fundamental distinctions between humans and animals, adults and children, the sane and the insane, in respect of the issue of freedom and responsibility. This an area where the classical account plainly fails.

In general terms, rational self-control or reasons-responsive views have two key components. The first is that a rational agent must be able

---

1. See, e.g., Dennett 1984; Wolf 1990; Wallace 1994; and Fischer and Ravizza 1998. For a critical discussion of these theories (and others) see Russell 2002b.

to *recognize* the reasons that are available or present to her situation. The second is that an agent must be able to "translate" those (recognized) reasons into decisions and choices that guide her conduct. In other words, the agent must not only be aware of what reasons there are, she must also be capable of being *moved* by them. This leaves, of course, a number of significant problems to be solved. For example, any adequate theory of this kind needs to be able to explain just how strict and demanding this standard of practical rationality is supposed to be. On the one hand, it is clearly too demanding to insist that agents must *always* be able to be guided by available reasons—otherwise an agent could never be held responsible for failing to be guided by the available reasons. On the other hand, more is required than that the agent is occasionally or intermittently guided by her reasons. An agent of this kind is not reliably and regularly rational to qualify as a free and responsible agent. So some set of conditions needs to be found that avoids both these extremes. This is not, however, the problem that I am now concerned with.[2]

Let us assume, with the proponents of compatibilist theories of rational self-control, that there is some account of these capacities that satisfies these various demands. We may call these the agent's RA capacities, as they provide for *rational agency*. This account still faces another important set of problems as presented by incompatibilist critics. One famous problem with classical compatibilist accounts of moral freedom ("doing as we please") is that agents of this kind could be *manipulated* and *covertly controlled* by other agents and yet, given the classical compatibilist account, still be judged free and responsible. This is, as the critics argue, plainly counterintuitive. Agents of this kind would be mere "puppets," "robots," or "zombies" who are "compelled" to obey the will of their covert controllers. Agents of this kind have no will of their own. They are not *real* or *genuine* agents. They only have the facade of being autonomous agents. When we discover the origins of their desires and willings—located with some other controlling agent—then our view of these (apparent) agents must change. The deeper problem with these (pseudo) agents, incompatibilists argue, is that although they may be "doing as they please" they have no control over their own will (i.e., they cannot shape or determine their own will).

---

2. See Fischer and Ravizza 1998, which aims to provide an acceptable answer to this problem.

It is, therefore, an especially important question whether compatibilist accounts of rational self-control can deal effectively with objections of this kind.[3]

Rational self-control theories have two ways of approaching this problem. The first is to argue that what troubles us in situations of this kind, where manipulation and covert control is taking place, is that the agent's capacity for rational self-control is in some way being impaired or interfered with. The process of brainwashing, neurological engineering, or some other form of mind-control operates by way of damaging the agent's capacity to recognize and/or respond to the relevant reasons that are available.[4] The situation may, however, be more subtle and complicated than this. The manipulation or covert control, incompatibilists argue, can also work *without* impairing the agent's rational capacities but by controlling the way those capacities are actually *exercised* in particular circumstances. This sort of case is much more problematic for the compatibilist. Per hypothesis, the agent continues to operate with the relevant rational dispositions (recognition, reactivity, etc.). The way that this capacity is actually exercised in particular circumstances—that is, whether the agent's conduct succeeds or fails to track the available reasons—is not under the agent's control, as this would require libertarian free will to act otherwise in identical circumstances. In normal circumstances, the explanation for success or failure will rest with natural causes that involve no external controller or manipulation. The incompatibilist objection, however, is that there could be a situation whereby the agent is controlled in this way and the compatibilist has no *principled* reason for denying that the agent is free and responsible. It follows, therefore, that compatibilist accounts of rational self-control cannot provide an adequate account of conditions of free and responsible agency. Agents who are manipulated and covertly controlled are obviously not free and responsible despite the fact that they may possess a general capacity for rational self-control of the kind that compatibilists have described.

---

3. In relation to this problem, see Dennett's well-known discussion of the "nefarious neurosurgeon" (Dennett 1984, 8). See the related discussion in Fischer and Ravizza 1998: 196–201.

4. In these circumstances the agent is no longer sensitive or capable of being guided by any consideration other than the implanted desire. For example, a hypnotized agent may start to act in some arbitrary or random manner when some relevant psychological "trigger" is pulled. This way of dealing with problems of manipulation and behavior control is discussed in Wallace 1994, 176ff., 197ff.

1. Libertarianism and the Implantation Standard

According to incompatibilists, the problem with manipulation and covert control is one that indicates a more fundamental and general weakness in the compatibilist position. Following some prominent compatibilist accounts, let us assume that our power of rational self-control presupposes that the agent possesses some relevant "mechanism" M, whereby the agent who possesses M is able to recognize and react to reasons.[5] Incompatibilists argue that cases of implantation highlight aspects of compatibilism in relation to the way that M is acquired and operates that is problematic even when manipulation and covert control is *absent* (i.e., in the "normal case"). Let us assume that M may be "implanted" by natural, normal causal processes that involve no manipulation or covert control by other agents. Implantation of M in these circumstances is "blind" and without any artificial interference of any kind. What still troubles us about these cases is that although the agent may be a rational self-controller, she nevertheless lacks any control over the way these capacities are actually *exercised* in specific circumstances. Whether M is such that in conditions C the agent will succeed or fail to track the available reasons is not something that depends on the agent. Even in these "normal" cases the agent is still subject to *luck* regarding the way M is actually exercised in C. In order to avoid this problem the agent must be able to choose or decide differently in the very same circumstances. An ability of this kind—let us call it *exercise control*—would require the falsity of determinism and some kind of libertarian free will. What ought to bother us about manipulation and covert control, therefore, is not simply that *some other agent* decides how the agent's will is exercised in conditions C, but that the agent himself lacks any such ability or power. It is a matter of luck how his powers of rational self-control are actually exercised. Clearly, then, the lack of exercise control is not a problem that arises only in (abnormal or deviant) cases of manipulation and covert control.

---

5. This terminology comes from Fischer and Ravizza (1998, p. 38): "although we employ the term 'mechanism', we do *not* mean to point to anything over and above the process that leads to the relevant upshot. . . ." In a note to this passage, Fischer and Ravizza go on to say that they "are not committed to any sort of 'reification' of the mechanism; that is, we are not envisaging a mechanism as like a mechanical object of any sort. The mechanism leading to an action is, intuitively, the way the action comes about; and, clearly, actions can come about in importantly *different ways*" (emphasis in original).

It may be argued that one way that compatibilists will be able to avoid this difficulty, without collapsing into libertarian metaphysics, is to give more thought to the problem of how *M* is *acquired* by the agent. That is to say, since the agent is held responsible for the upshots that issue from *M* (in particular circumstances), it surely must follow that the agent has some control over how *M* is acquired. Failing this, the agent will lack control not only over the particular way *M* operates in C, but also over the fact that it is this particular mechanism *M* that he is operating with. Another mechanism, *M#,* may produce a different upshot in *C.* The agent, on the suggested compatibilist account, has control over none of this. What is need, therefore, in the absence of exercise control, is some control over mechanism acquisition. The incompatibilist will argue, however, that the compatibilist cannot provide any plausible account of how this could be possible.

Although we can make good sense of having control over our actions on the basis of possessing some reasons-responsive mechanism (*M*), it is not at all obvious what it *means* to say that an agent controls the process of acquiring such mechanisms. The mechanisms that we acquire generally develop through a process of (moral) education that begins at a very early stage of life. For this reason, responsibility for the kinds of mechanisms that children acquire and develop rests more plausibly on the shoulders of the adults who have raised the child. Moreover, even at a later stage (e.g., adolescence) when a person becomes able to think critically about the way his own deliberative capacities actually operate, there is little or no question of the agent being able to radically modify or reform the mechanisms that he is (already) operating with. Control of this kind is not available even to mature adults, much less younger children.

Let us concede, nevertheless, that we can make some sense of the suggestion that the mature agent has control over mechanism acquisition. This form of control must itself depend on the agent's ability to deliberate and decide about mechanism selection on the basis of some mechanism he already has. This situation presents compatibilist theory with a serious problem. The selection of some mechanism must be based on some mechanism that the agent currently operates with. This mechanism must be either chosen or given (i.e., through processes that the agent does not control). At some point, the mechanism involved in the process of mechanism acquisition must itself have been "unchosen" or presented to the agent through a process that he did not control (natural or artificial). Any choice concerning mechanism acquisition, therefore, must eventually depend on unchosen mechanisms—even on the optimistic assumption that mature agents are able to make choices of this kind.

It is evident that incompatibilist criticism of compatibilist theories of rational self-control reach well beyond narrow worries about manipulation and covert control. The deeper worries that situations of this kind bring to light is that rational self-control provides no (final) control over mechanism acquisition, nor over the way that these mechanisms are actually exercised in specific circumstances (i.e., success or failure to track reasons in particular conditions is not open for the agent to decide). Given these criticisms, it follows that agents who operate with rational capacities of these kinds are subject to luck about what specific mechanism (M) they acquire and operate with, as well as luck about the way the mechanism they operate with is actually exercised. Although these problems are certainly manifest in manipulation cases, they are by no means limited to them. On the contrary, these problems of limited control and luck are *systematic* to all circumstances in which agents operate on the compatibilist rational self-control model.[6]

Incompatibilist libertarians will be quick to contrast their own situation with respect to implantation and manipulation issues. Let us suppose that it is possible to artificially (intentionally) implant a mechanism of some kind that supports a libertarian capacity for free will. (Here again, the ontological basis of this mechanism is not our concern. There could be a biological basis for this or some soul-substance, and so on.) We may call a mechanism of this kind an *ML mechanism*. The fact that ML is implanted by another agent (God, a neurosurgeon, etc.) will not trouble the incompatibilist, because implantation as such will not compromise the agent's ability to operate with control over the way her rational capacities of deliberation and choice are actually exercised. Although the ML mechanism has been implanted by another agent, this does not make it possible to covertly control the implanted agent by means of this process. On the contrary, since the implanted agent possesses exercise control over the way this mechanism operates (i.e., controls the way reasons move her), the source or historical origins of ML is irrelevant to the way that the agent chooses to exercise her ML powers in specific circumstances. So long as the agent is capable of *exercise* control—then it is possible to set aside the

---

6. For a more detailed discussion of this point, see Russell 2002a, esp. sect. v.

issue of mechanism acquisition as irrelevant because there is no threat of manipulation or covert control.

It is true, of course, that libertarian agents who operate with ML mechanisms could not themselves control the process of ML acquisition unless they first possessed some ML mechanism. It follows from this that even libertarian agents of this kind do not control the process by which they become capable of libertarian free will (this must be a "gift of nature" or "God-given," etc.). Nevertheless, as I have explained, whether the implantation process in this case involves natural (blind) processes or artificial (other agent) involvement is irrelevant. The nature of the mechanism implanted precludes manipulation and covert control. More importantly, it ensures that the agent is not simply "lucky" or "unlucky" in relation to the way reasons actually move her. Because the agent possesses an ML mechanism her will is truly her own. Her will is truly her own because (per hypothesis) she has the power to determine when and how reasons guide her conduct. That is to say, her will is truly her own not because she chooses to be a ML agent but because being an ML agent allows her to determine her own will.

The immediate significance of this libertarian response is that it serves to provide an *alternative standard* by which compatibilist theories may be judged. That is to say, the libertarian may argue that in the case of libertarian ML capacities it is possible to implant them without compromising the agent's freedom and responsibility. This is a standard, the incompatibilist argues, that the compatibilist cannot meet. Compatibilists cannot meet this standard because the implantation of reasons-responsive or rational self-control capacities (M) is consistent with the possibility of manipulation and covert control. Even if compatibilists reject worries about "luck" in relation to the way that these capacities are actually exercised, surely no compatibilist can allow that an agent is free and responsible in circumstances where she is being manipulated and covertly controlled by some other agent by means of some (abnormal) implantation process.[7]

2. *Soft Compatibilism and History*

Critics of libertarianism argue, as we know, that all efforts to make sense of libertarian powers that could deliver on exercise control run into problems

---

7. Philosophers of quite different views and commitments accept that it is simply intuitively obvious that a manipulated agent cannot be responsible. See, e.g., Kane 1996, 65ff.; Pereboom 2001, 112ff.; Fischer and Ravizza 1998, 194–202, 230–39; and Haji and Cuypers 2004.

of intelligibility and/or nonexistence. Even if this is true, however, the compatibilist is still left with the problem of manipulation and covert control. More specifically, compatibilists who rely on accounts of rational self-control need to take a stand on whether or not the presence of covert control and manipulation will necessarily compromise an agent's freedom and responsibility when it is clear that the agent's general powers of rational self-control are not impaired or damaged by this process. There are two different approaches that compatibilists may take to this issue. The first is that of the "soft compatibilist" who holds that the presence of manipulation or covert control by means of mechanism implantation rules out freedom and responsibility.[8] The difficulty that soft compatibilists face is that, on the account provided, we could find ourselves with two agents (P and P^*) who have identical moral capacities and properties and deliberate, decide, and act in the very same way, and yet one is judged responsible and the other is not. The basis for this distinction rests entirely with the fact that one agent, P, has her deliberative mechanisms produced by natural (blind) causes, whereas the other agent, P^*, has her deliberative mechanisms produced by some other agent. Though we may concede that there is some residual intuitive worry about P^*'s circumstances, the question is on what *principled* basis can the soft compatibilist draw such an important distinction? It will not suffice for soft compatibilists to simply assume that the contrast in causal origins matters and then to construct an ad hoc set of principles to rule out manipulation and covert control cases. This leaves their position vulnerable to the criticism that they have failed to identify the real root difficulty in their position (i.e., that these agents lack exercise control).

The most convincing soft compatibilist reply to this problem that I know of is provided by John Fischer and Mark Ravizza.[9] They argue that reasons-responsiveness or powers of rational self-control will not suffice for moral responsibility. This is because it is also necessary that agents *own* the mechanism they are operating with. The problem of manipulation and covert control concerns the issue of ownership, not that of the agent's capacity for rational self-control. Briefly stated, an agent owns the

---

8. Kane 1996, 67–69. This terminology is Kane's.

9. Fischer and Ravizza 1998, ch. 8. Fischer and Ravizza defend their "historicist" views against a number of critics in Fischer and Ravizza 2004. For an earlier "historicist" (or "externalist") account of the conditions of responsible agency see, e.g., Christman 1991. See also Mele 1995, esp. ch. 9.

deliberative mechanisms that issues in her conduct only if the mechanism has the right history or causal origins.[10] When a mechanism is implanted by some other agent, using artificial techniques of some kind, "ownership" is compromised. On the other hand, when the mechanism is produced by means of normal causal processes, ownership is not compromised. In the case of artificial implantation involving deviant causal processes, the problem is not that the agent's rational self-control is compromised but that the agent does not *own* the mechanism that issues in her conduct.

The question we now face is: does this appeal to ownership and history provide a secure basis for soft compatibilism? The first thing to be noted here is that there is no suggestion that ownership depends on control over mechanism acquisition or requires that the agent has somehow *consented* to the mechanism that she possesses and operates with. In fact, for reasons we have already considered, any requirement of this kind is highly problematic and will inevitably run into regress difficulties. Clearly, then, the distinction between acceptable and unacceptable processes of mechanism acquisition cannot depend on considerations of this kind. Nor is it obvious why one agent is said to own her own mechanism when it is naturally produced whereas the other does not because it has been artificially produced. In both cases the agents clearly *possess* these mechanisms and *operate* with them, and in neither case have they consented to or chosen their own mechanisms.[11]

These considerations suggest that it remains unclear why anyone should *care* about the different histories of mechanism acquisition when the "current time-slice" properties of both agents P and P^* are exactly the

---

10. Fischer and Ravizza (1998) describe this required history in terms of a process of "taking responsibility." There are, they maintain, three required conditions for this process. The first begins with a child's moral education, as she comes to see herself "as an agent" (1998, 208, 210–11, 238). At this stage the child sees that certain upshots in the world are a result of her choices and actions. When this condition is satisfied, the child is then in a position to see herself as "a fair target for the reactive attitudes as a result of how [she] exercises this agency in certain contexts" (211). Finally, Fischer and Ravizza also require that "the cluster of beliefs specified by the first two conditions must be based, in an appropriate way, on the evidence" (238). As I explain, my general doubt about a historicist approach of this kind is that it fails to show that the agent has any (final) control over the process of mechanism acquisition— and to this extent it fails to answer incompatibilist objections. I discuss these issues in more detail in Russell 2002a.

11. The account of "ownership" that Fischer and Ravizza (1998) provide is one that leans on the analogy of Nozick's (Lockean) historical entitlement conception of justice (see Fischer and Ravizza 1998, ch. 7; cf. Nozick 1970, esp. ch. 7). The general idea, in both cases, is that ownership of something (e.g., a "mechanism") depends on the historical process involved

same. From the perspective of both the agent herself, as well as those she is engaged with in her moral community, there is *no difference* at all between P and P*. There is no ability one has that the other does not also have, and both agents exercise these abilities in the exact same way. In other words, from both the internal and external perspective these two individuals are "interchangeable" in respect of all powers and abilities that matter (per the compatibilist hypothesis) to moral responsibility. In the absence of some further explanation for why "history" matters, therefore, the soft compatibilist way of dealing with manipulation and covert control cases seems arbitrary and ad hoc. Given that the soft compatibilist position depends on placing weight on historical considerations, we may conclude (for our present purposes) that the soft compatibilist strategy fails.

3. Should Hard Compatibilists Just "Bite the Bullet"?

Where do these observations about contemporary compatibilist strategies that rely on accounts of rational self-control leave us? I think it is clear that compatibilist accounts of this kind face the following dilemma. Either they must provide a more convincing account of why the history or causal origins of reasons-responsive mechanisms matters, *or* they must accept that, since history is irrelevant, some version of hard compatibilism is the right course to take. I have explained that there is some reason to be skeptical about the prospects of the first alternative, so let us take a brief look at the hard compatibilist alternative. Robert Kane has noted that hard compatibilists are willing to "bite the bullet" and so deny that the presence or theoretical possibility of covert control or manipulation in any way compromises an agent's freedom and responsibility.[12] This position certainly

(as opposed to "current time-slice" considerations). That is to say, what matters to *ownership* is the *way* something was acquired. The difficulty with this analogy, as it relates to Fischer and Ravizza's "soft compatibilism," is that on a Nozickean/Lockean theory of property, individuals may (legitimately) come to own property through processes that do not necessarily involve their own activities or consent (e.g., gift, inheritance, etc.). In these circumstances ownership is possible even though the person concerned did not choose the property or select the mechanism—and so may view what is owned as *imposed* upon him. In general, from the point of view of the analogy with Nozickean/Lockean property theory, mechanism ownership is entirely consistent with a lack of control over acquisition.

12. Kane 1996, 67. Among the more recent and valuable defenses of "hard compatibilism are Watson 2004 and McKenna 2004. For two other interesting compatibilist counterarguments to the incompatibilist "global control" examples, see Vargas 2006 and also Berofsky 2006.

has some advantages when it comes to defending the compatibilist corner. One of these advantages is that it avoids a gap between libertarianism and compatibilism when it comes to the "implantation standard" that we considered above.

Recall that incompatibilist libertarians raised the following problem for compatibilist views. Compatibilist accounts of rational self-control exclude a power of exercise control, and because of this it is possible for the relevant mechanisms to be implanted in the agent by some artificial means that would permit manipulation and covert control. Granted that manipulation and covert control compromise an agent's freedom and responsibility, it follows that these compatibilist accounts fail to meet the implantation standard. In contrast with this, the implantation of libertarian deliberative mechanisms, which provide exercise control, will not leave any scope for manipulation or covert control by another agent. It is entirely irrelevant whether the libertarian mechanism is implanted by means of some natural, normal process or by some artificial intervention by another agent. Implantation in this case does not make possible manipulation or covert control. This opens up a significant gap between the two views—one that soft compatibilists have tried to close (unsuccessfully) by appealing to history.

The hard compatibilist response is to deny the (incompatibilist and soft compatibilist) assumption that manipulation or covert control necessarily compromises freedom and responsibility. Their claim is that, provided a suitably rich and robust account of moral capacity has been articulated and shown to be possible within compatibilist constraints (i.e., deterministic assumptions), then the mere fact that the agent may be covertly controlled or manipulated by this means is no more evidence that the agent is not free and responsible than it would be if natural, normal causal processes were at work and were the source of the agent's deliberative mechanisms. In other words, the hard compatibilist runs the argument in reverse. If we can provide a suitable account of rational self-control, where the relevant mechanism is *not* implanted by some other agent or a deviant causal process, it follows (since origins are irrelevant to the functioning of this mechanism) that, even if the mechanism has been implanted in a "deviant" manner that permits manipulation and covert control, there is no legitimate basis for denying that the agent is free and responsible. (E.g., if I discover later this evening that God, not nature, has implanted my deliberative mechanism and controls me through it, I still have no reason to change my fundamental conception of myself as a free and responsible agent. After all, I am unchanged and unaffected in all respects relating to my abilities, deliberations, and conduct. There is nothing I was able to do then that I cannot do after being informed about the causal history of my deliberative mechanism.) If we opt for compatibilism, therefore, we must accept the hard compatibilist implications that go with it. If we can't live with this, then we need to turn to incompatibilism and/or libertarian metaphysics to avoid these worries about manipulation and covert control.

My view is that this is the right general strategy *up to a point.* However, I want to suggest a significant amendment or qualification to this hard compatibilist alternative. Assuming that some suitably rich and robust account of moral capacity can be developed within compatibilist constraints, must we accept *unqualified* hard compatibilism? It is clear, I think, that there is something more to the basic intuition that covert control and manipulation compromise responsibility than the straight "bite the bullet" view allows for. It may be possible, however, to provide an alternative explanation for the *source* of our intuitive discomfort with this situation. We may begin by noting that the whole point of developing a theory of moral capacity is to describe the circumstances in which our moral sentiments of praise and blame, and the retributive practices associated with them, may be deemed appropriate or *fair.*[13] The basic idea here is that the agent who is held responsible is a legitimate target of the moral sentiments of other members of her moral community in virtue of possessing the relevant set of capacities and abilities (i.e., rational self-control). Consider now some different scenarios that may arise in circumstances where deviant implantation and covert control is present.

Consider, first, an agent A_m with relevant (reasons-responsive) moral capacity M. M is such that, bracketing off any worries about manipulation and covert control by others, it is reasonable and legitimate for another person B^1 to hold A_m responsible for the conduct that issues out of M. In other words, we assume some satisfactory compatibilist account of M, in circumstances where worries about manipulation by others do not arise. Now consider another scenario where agent A_m^* has the very same (time-slice) moral capacity M and the very same conduct issues from M. In this case, however, A_m^* is subject to manipulation and covert control by another agent B^2 who uses implantation processes of some deviant kind. What seems clear about this case is that A_m^* cannot be legitimately *held*

---

13. See, e.g., Wallace 1994, 5–6, 15–16, 93–95.

responsible by B^2, since B^2 is in fact covertly controlling A_m^*. If this situation was made transparent to A_m^* or any third party, it would be correct to say that the demands and expectations that B^2 is making on A_m^* are ones that B^2 decides will be met or violated. B^2 is, therefore, in *no position* to criticize, evaluate, or react to A_m^* in these circumstances.[14] We might say that since B^2 controls A_m^*'s agency there is *insufficient causal distance* between them to sustain the reactive stance. Moral communication and responsiveness presupposes that agents are not related to each other as controller and controllee. When a controller takes up an evaluative/reactive stance toward an agent that he controls there is plainly an element of fraud or self-deception going on. The controller B^2 can only praise or blame *himself* for the way in which the agent A_m^* succeeds or fails to be guided by available reasons.

These limitations do not apply to the relationship between A_m^* and (noncontrolling) B^1. B^1 may be aware that there is some (deterministic) causal story to be told about how A_m^* acquired the mechanism that she is operating with, but whatever it is (a natural or artificial process) all that matters is that A_m^* is rationally competent and B^1 does not control her. The contrast in the relations between these individuals may be illustrated as shown in Figure 9.1 (below).

It is clear, per hypothesis, that A_m is responsible to B^1, and there is no responsibility-compromising relationship between them. Moreover, since A_m^* possesses the same mechanism as A_m (i.e., M), and B_1 stands in the same (nonmanipulative) relation to A_m^* as he does to A_m, there is no principled basis for B_1 treating A_m but not A_m^* as responsible (i.e., since the causal origins of M do not alter or impair how A_m or A_m^* deliberate and act, nor result in any relevant change in the relationship between B^1 and A_m^*). When we turn to the situation of B^2, however, there is a relevant difference in his relationship with A_m and A_m^*. Although the situation of B^2 in relation to A_m is no different from B^1's situation, his relation to A_m^* is that of controller to controllee. Clearly, then, what is compromised in these circumstances is not the responsibility of A_m^* as such (since *both* A_m and A_m^* stand in the *same* relation to B^1); it is the stance that B^2 takes toward A_m^* that is compromised by the relationship of manipulation and covert control.

---

14. In the language of P. F. Strawson, we may say that B^2 must take an "objective," not a "reactive," stance to A_m^* (cf. Strawson 2003, esp. sect. iv). Since B^2 is manipulating A_m^* by deciding when and which reasons will or will not move A_m^*, it would be *fraudulent* or *self-deceptive* for B^2 to adopt a reactive stance. B^1 is not, however, constrained in these ways.

FIGURE 9.1 Agents, moral judges, and manipulators.

Putting this point in the familiar language of P. F. Strawson, we may say that when the relationship between two individuals is one involving covert control (e.g., through deviant implantation procedures of some kind) then the *participant stance* on the side of the *controller* is compromised. The controller is not *entitled* to take a participant stance in circumstances where he (B^2) decides when reasons, criticisms, and so on succeed or fail to move the agent (e.g., A_m^*). For the controller to retain some commitment to the participant stance in these circumstances would clearly be fraudulent or self-deceptive. However, in the absence of any relationship of this kind (e.g., as with B^1 to A_m^*) the participant stance is not compromised. Granted, therefore, that A_m and A_m^* are identical in respect of their capacity for rational self-control, there is no reason to treat one as responsible and the other as not responsible, *unless* the stance being taken is compromised by a relation of covert control (e.g., as in the case of B^2 but not B^1). If the hard compatibilist strategy is to succeed then it must, I suggest, draw some relevant distinction along these general lines. A distinction of this kind will enable us to explain why manipulation and covert control is intuitively unsettling, without driving us away from the basic hard compatibilist stance.

The position that I have suggested that compatibilists should take in relation to manipulation examples and circumstances of covert control may be described as *"selective* hard compatibilism." Selective hard compatibilism accepts that there is some basis to our intuitive worries arising from circumstances of manipulation and covert control. Unlike soft compatibilism, however, the selective hard compatibilist does not concede that agents in these circumstances are not responsible because of the (deviant or abnormal) "history" involved in the way they acquired their reasons-responsive mechanisms. What is compromised in these cases is not the agent's responsibility, as such, but the legitimacy of the stance of *holding* an agent responsible *on the part of those who covertly control him* through the (deviant) implantation process. Assuming, however, that the agent's capacity for rational self-control is otherwise unimpaired by the process involved, the stance of those individuals who do not stand in the relation of controller to controllee is not affected or compromised by the agent's history of deviant implantation (i.e., in relation to others). Since the agent has all the time-slice properties and abilities of an agent who is fully responsible given a normal history (i.e., in the absence of manipulation and covert control) there is no relevant basis for refusing to take the participant stance toward an agent of this kind (e.g., A_m^*).

4. *God, Walden Two, and Frankenstein: Modes of Implantation*

Having explained the general principles of selective hard compatibilism, it will be useful to consider a few further examples in order to test our intuitions about such cases. Perhaps the most obvious example—one that has an established place in the history of philosophy—is the theological case involving God as a cosmic covert controller, through the act of divine Creation. On one side, some compatibilists have taken the "hard" view that conditions of (divine) covert control or manipulation do not compromise (human) freedom and responsibility. They *deny*, therefore, that it is intuitively obvious that if God creates this world and ordains all human action, then we cannot be held accountable to him or anyone else.[15] On the other side, there are compatibilists who are clearly less than comfortable with this position. We find, for example, that Hume, in a well-known passage, considers the implications of his own necessitarian doctrine for Christian theology. In particular, he considers the objection that if the series of causes and effects can be traced back to God, then it follows that God and not humans are responsible for any crimes that occur.[16] Hume's reply to this objection oscillates between the suggestion that in these circumstances God *alone* is responsible for all that flows from his act of Creation (since he is their ultimate "author") and the distinct view that in these circumstances God must *share* responsibility with humans for any actions that we perform. Hume, in other words, oscillates between hard and soft compatibilist commitments on this issue.[17] The source of Hume's

---

15. For a classical statement of this ("hard compatibilist") view, see Hobbes 1839–1845, IV, 248ff.

16. Cf. Hume 1999, 8.33–8.36.

17. See my discussion of this point in Russell 1995, 160–63.

discomfort is that he cannot concede, consistent with his general compatibilist commitments, that (blind) *natural* causes of an agent's character and conduct would compromise freedom and responsibility. At the same time, there is something "absurd" about the suggestion that God holds humans accountable (in a future state) for events that he ordains. Clearly the unqualified hard ("bite the bullet") response is not one Hume is willing to accept in this case.[18]

Although I doubt that Hume was sincerely troubled by this issue, it should be clear that selective hard compatibilist principles provide a solution to this problem in a way that is consistent with Hume's *irreligious* intent on this topic. That is to say, the selective hard compatibilist view of this situation is that it is indeed illegitimate and inappropriate for *God* to hold humans accountable in these circumstances, insofar as God covertly controls us and all we do (as per the Creation hypothesis). On the other hand, this concession does nothing to compromise our basic (hard) compatibilist commitments. More specifically, it does not follow from the fact that God is in no position to hold us accountable that we are not (fully) accountable to our fellow *human beings* in these circumstances. Since we are not covertly controlled by other human beings, it is strictly irrelevant whether our conduct and character is ultimately determined by (blind) Nature or by (a personal) God. Nothing about our current abilities or our qualities of character and conduct is altered or affected either way. Therefore, to us (*qua* humans) this is not a consideration that fundamentally changes our relation with each other or compromises the participant stance that we take toward each other.

The incompatibilist and soft compatibilist critics may find this theological example less than convincing when we try to redescribe it in terms of purely human circumstances and conditions. For example, suppose that instead of God serving as a "global manipulator" we imagine a world like Walden Two, where individuals are "engineered" by the methods of implantation or some related technique adopted by the state for its "utopian" ends.[19] How will the principles of selective hard compatibilism fare in this situation?

---

18. Hume's strategy was to show that this dilemma reveals the *absurdity* of the "religious hypothesis." To this extent his apparent worry about this problem is insincere.

19. Skinner 1962. See also Kane's illuminating discussion of the significance of *Walden Two* from an incompatibilist perspective: Kane 1996, 65–69.

In cases like Walden Two, selective hard compatibilism draws the following distinction. Insofar as *within* human society there are covert controllers and those who are controlled by them, the former are not in any position to hold the latter responsible or take a participant stance toward them. Given their relationship, the participant stance I s not appropriate, since it is the state controllers who are determining how their subjects deliberate, decide, and act (e.g., through controlled implantation procedures). Any stance of evaluation and criticism is, for them (the controllers), not in order.[20] However, on the assumption that the subjects of Walden Two are not related to each other in this way (i.e., they play no role in the process of implantation and covert control), and still possess unimpaired powers of rational self-control, no restriction of this kind applies. These individuals have every reason to continue to view themselves as free and responsible agents (as they would if they were created through the processes of blind nature) and to take the participant stance toward each other. In this way, and to this extent, *within* Walden Two conditions of freedom and responsibility will survive.

As in the theological case of divine Creation, the subjects of Walden Two could wake up one morning and be told, by the relevant authorities, that they are all covertly controlled. Though they may well be surprised by this, they have no more reason to suddenly regard themselves as standing in fundamentally different relations *with each other* in respect of their status as responsible agents than their theologically conditioned counterparts (or, indeed, than they would if they were informed that they are all determined products of blind, natural processes). In neither case do these agents find that their abilities or qualities have been altered or changed. There is nothing that they were able to do yesterday that they cannot do today. What has changed is that these individuals will no longer view themselves as appropriate targets of moral sentiments in relation to the state authorities who control and condition them—since there is evidently something "absurd" about the authorities criticizing and condemning agents whom they are covertly controlling.

---

20. A similar situation may be imagined when an author enters into a dialogue with one of his own (fictional) characters. Should the author adopt a critical, reactive stance toward such characters, *we* might suggest to the author: "If you don't like this character, why criticize him—just *change* him." (It is true, of course, that the author may take up the reactive stance insofar as he *pretends,* to himself and others, that he is *not* the creator and controller of this character—then his reactive stance may seem more appropriate.)

The incompatibilist and soft compatibilist may remain unconvinced and argue that the chosen examples continue to obscure the real problems here. In both the divine Creation and Walden Two examples we are presented with circumstances of *global* manipulation, whereby all agents (i.e., "normal" or "ordinary" agents) are being covertly controlled. However, if we consider an isolated individual case of covert control, our intuitions may change. Viewed from this perspective, the case of an artificially designed agent who is covertly controlled by his creator is obviously problematic. Let us call cases of this sort "Frankenstein-type examples," in order to highlight this familiar and "troubling" theme in both literature and film.[21] Cases of this kind, it may be argued, make clear that something "abnormal" and "disturbing" is taking place. Surely, our critic continues, no one will claim that Frankenstein-type agents, as described, can be viewed as free and responsible. "Biting the bullet" in cases of this kind is an act of philosophical despair—or at least a sign of an inability or unwillingness to think imaginatively about cases of this kind.

The first thing we must do, in order to get clear about the significance of these Frankenstein-type examples, is to eliminate features of the example that are strictly irrelevant or misleading.[22] In the first place, it is important to note that the moral qualities of the *covert controller* may vary—they may be good, evil, or mixed. (The same is true in cases of global manipulation, as described above: e.g., either God or the Devil may rule the world.) The case, as described, leaves this issue open. Second, the literature concerned with examples of this kind often not only suggest the shadow of *evil* manipulators operating in the background, but also they typically conjure up the image of a "monster" or "freak" who serves as the agent involved (e.g., as in *Frankenstein*). However, cases of this kind are strictly irrelevant since, per hypothesis, we are concerned with individuals who have time-slice properties that are entirely "normal" and present them as otherwise fully functioning and complete agents (i.e., in the absence of any worries about manipulation and covert control). With these distortions removed, we are now in a better position to test

---

21. What I have described as "Franken*stein*-type examples" should not, of course, be confused with widely discussed "Frank*furt*-type examples," as associated with Harry Frankfurt's influential paper, "Alternate Possibilities and Moral Responsibility," reprinted as Frankfurt 2003. Frankenstein-type scenarios have more in common with cases like the "nefarious neurosurgeon" referred to in note 3.

22. Cf. Dennett 1984, 7–10, which is especially effective in identifying the (incompatibilist) misuse of "bogeymen" in cases of this general kind.

our intuitions about such cases and the intuitive force of the principles of selective hard compatibilism.

Clearly, selective hard compatibilism does not license any unqualified hard compatibilist approach to these cases. The individual who covertly controls the agent is in no position to take up the participant stance toward this individual—no matter how "complex" or "robust" the capacities and qualities of the (created) agent may be. Having said this, similar constraints and limitations do not apply to other individuals who stand in a relevantly different relation to the agent ("Frankenstein"). Given that the agent is not in any way impaired in his powers of rational self-control (i.e., he is not "abnormal" or "monstrous" in time-slice terms), and he is not covertly controlled by these other individuals, then the agent remains an appropriate target of *their* reactive attitudes. For these individuals, therefore, the participant stance is not ruled out or compromised simply on the ground that some other individual covertly controls him. From the perspective on other noncontrolling individuals, it is immaterial whether the agent's mechanism M is blindly implanted by Nature or implanted by a covert controller. How the agent functions, and how he relates to those of us who do not covertly control him, is entirely unaffected. Indeed, the case for selective hard compatibilism may be put in stronger terms. Any policy that *demands* that this agent be treated with a systematic "objective" attitude, simply on the basis of the *origins* of his (artificially implanted) mechanism, is itself intuitively *unfair.* Such a policy fails to recognize and acknowledge the agent *as an agent* and treats this individual as if he lacks capacities that he clearly possesses (and as such constitutes a form of *discrimination*).[23]

Our critic may persist that the relevant points have still not been covered. Consider, for example, discovering that *you* are a creation of Dr. Frankenstein and that he has implanted *you* with some mechanism M and thereby covertly controls you. Even if you do not assume that Dr. Frankenstein is evil, and you accept that this discovery in no way implies that you have suddenly been transformed into a "monster" of some kind (i.e., as judged by time-slice criteria), surely there remains something *deeply* disturbing about this discovery from the point of view of *the agent*? More specifically, what we find disturbing about this situation has nothing to do with the stance of the people who may

---

23. Keep in mind here that, per hypothesis, if the mechanism M were *blindly* implanted by natural processes the agent would be regarded as *fully* responsible and a fit target of reactive attitudes.

or may not hold the agent responsible; it has everything to do with how the agent must regard *himself.*

If there is something about the discovery that we find disturbing, from the agent's point of view, it must be judged in relation to cases where the mechanism *M* has been blindly implanted by natural processes and there is no possibility of covert control. So the relevant question we should be asking in this situation is: what does the agent have to worry or care about in these circumstances? The agent may well find the discovery of a history of *artificial* implantation and covert control disturbing on the ground that the *moral* qualities of the covert controller will indeed matter to the way that he functions and operates as an agent. In respect of this issue, the agent may be lucky or unlucky. Naturally, in these circumstances the agent would want to be created and controlled by a benevolent and good creator (just as in the parallel theological situation we would prefer that God and not the Devil is arranging the order of things). In general, if we are being covertly controlled the best we can hope for is a controller who directs our reasons-responsive capacities in some desirable way, as judged from our own point of view and that of those other individuals who must deal with us. Notice, however, that an agent who is *blindly* implanted through *natural* processes, without any possibility of covert control, will also have a parallel worry about whether he has been lucky or unlucky in the way these (blind) forces of nature shape his character and conduct. He will want to discover what these forces are and he will hope that they are benign and not malevolent in their outcomes (i.e., as judged from his own point of view and that of the people he is dealing with).[24]

It is clear, then, that the agent's discovery that he has been implanted and is covertly controlled will raise some distinct issues for him—concerns that do not arise in the "normal" case. However, it is by no means obvious that this discovery must lead the agent to cease viewing himself as a free and responsible agent. On the contrary, if he thinks carefully about his situation he will see that his (time-slice) capacities are not changed or impaired in any way. Moreover, any worries he may have about the (artificial) causal factor that conditions and directs the process of mechanism acquisition have clear counterparts in the case of agents who are subject to a process of blind, natural implantation—such as he took himself to

---

24. Related to this, consider how we may be lucky or unlucky in the parents we have, insofar as they may greatly influence the process of mechanism *M* acquisition. Evidently we *care* about this—and we all hope to have had good parents (and, more generally, we want to be "lucky" in respect of the way we have been brought up).

be until the moment of discovery. Finally, the agent in question may also recognize that his situation does not *necessarily* leave him worse off than his "normal" counterpart who is not covertly controlled. It may well be that the "normal" agent is (deeply) unlucky in the natural causes that shape the process of mechanism acquisition, whereas it remains an open question whether the agent who is implanted and covertly controlled is lucky or unlucky. Nothing about the agent's circumstances, as described, determine *this* issue, and it is this issue that the agent has most reason to care about.

These observations suggest that when Frankenstein-type scenarios are accurately described, they are not disturbing in any way that implies that the agent involved must lose all sense of himself as a free and responsible individual (i.e., not unless he has similar reason for this worry based on *blind* implantation processes). Faced with these observations, the critic may try one last maneuver. If we turn to our perspective as *observers* in these circumstances—where we are neither controller nor controllee—we may find the principles of selective hard compatibilism are unconvincing. According to this position, the critic continues, conditions of covert control are relevant only to the individual who actually covertly controls the agent. More specifically, this situation is otherwise irrelevant to all third-party observers, since they can continue to take up the participant stance unconcerned about the circumstances of convert control. Surely the knowledge that an agent has been artificially implanted by another individual, who covertly controls him on this basis, cannot be dismissed as *irrelevant* to our attitude and (third-party) perspective on this agent. Once this relationship becomes transparent it will matter to us—in our capacity as *observers*.

Once again, this line of objection is mistaken. For reasons made clear in my earlier replies, it may be important for us to know that an agent is *artificially* implanted and covertly controlled, given that the *moral nature* of the *controller* (e.g., the aims and purposes involved) will indeed matter to us—just as this will also matter to the agent. The covert control may be benign and benevolent, or it may not. We certainly have reason to care about *that*. At the same time, however, even if no artificial implantation or covert control is present, we have good reason to care about and investigate the blind, natural causes that may condition and shape the agent's powers of rational self-control. The nature of these causal origins, and the character of the upshots that they bring about, will matter to us *either way*. It is, therefore, a mistake to think that because we have reason to care (and worry) about whether an agent is being covertly controlled, and what the character and purposes of his covert controller may be, it follows that we cannot view this individual as a responsible agent. No such conclusion is implied, any more than it follows that because we care about the nature of the blind causal forces that may shape and condition an agent's mechanism we must cease to view him as a free and responsible individual. The observer or third-party interest in both cases is similar. Whether the process involved is artificial or natural—whether it leaves open the possibility of covert control or not—the agent continues to enjoy the same capacities and abilities either way. Nor is our own relationship with the agent changed or altered in any relevant way by this discovery. We have, therefore, no relevant grounds for abandoning the participant stance toward this individual simply on the ground of the history of artificial implantation and covert control (i.e., unless we also entertain some *further* skeptical doubts about the implications of *any* process of implantation, be it blind or covertly controlled). In these circumstances all that has changed is our specific understanding of the *particular history* involved in the agent's mechanism acquisition—something that is of interest and importance to us (and the agent) whether covert control is involved or not.

The examples that we have considered in this section make clear that selective hard compatibilism involves a distinct set of commitments from those of either soft or hard compatibilism. Unlike hard compatibilism, selective principles acknowledge that circumstances of implantation and covert control have implications that *are* relevant to issues of responsibility. The way that it *interprets* these issues is, however, very different from the soft compatibilist approach. Whereas the soft compatibilist follows the incompatibilist in holding that responsibility in these circumstances is *systematically* undermined, the selective hard compatibilist maintains that what is compromised is not the agent's responsibility as such, but the legitimacy of the *stance* of holding the agent responsible *on the part of those who covertly control him.* Beyond this, however, there is no general failure of responsible agency. It follows from this that compatibilist accounts of rational self-control cannot be said to fail simply on the ground that they permit covert control (i.e., just as orthodox hard compatibilists have maintained). In this way, selective hard compatibilism blocks the fundamental conclusion that incompatibilists are anxious to establish—a conclusion that motivates soft compatibilist attempts to add historical requirements to conditions of responsible agency.

5. *Nothing Too Hard to Swallow—Some Final Thoughts*

Let us now review the argument of this chapter. We began with a discussion of the problems that contemporary compatibilist theories of rational self-control face when presented with cases of implantation and covert control by another agent. One way of trying to deal with this problem is to embrace soft compatibilism and accept that situations of this kind do indeed compromise the agent's freedom and responsibility. The soft compatibilist claims that what this shows is that we must also care about the "history" involved in the way that we have *acquired* our reasons-responsive dispositions. Considerations of this kind, they suggest, will allow us to draw the relevant distinctions we need to make in this area. I have expressed skepticism about this approach on the ground that it remains unclear why, on this account, we should *care* about the agent's history when it makes no difference to the way that the agent actually deliberates, decides, and acts. Having the "right" history does not provide any form of "enhanced freedom," nor will it satisfy incompatibilist worries about having effective control over the process of mechanism acquisition (i.e., given regress problems, etc.).[25]

Granted that the strategy of soft compatibilism based on history fails, we must choose between incompatibilism and some form of hard compatibilism. The hard compatibilist accepts the "implantation standard": any adequate account of the capacities associated with freedom and moral responsibility must be such that they could be implanted by either natural or artificial processes without compromising the agent's standing as free and responsible (this being a standard that libertarians claim they are able to satisfy). The obvious difficulty for the hard compatibilist, however, is that this seems to open up the door to covert control and manipulation. I have argued that it will not do for hard compatibilists to *simply* "bite the bullet" on this issue. Something more plausible must be said about the

---

25. I take this observation to apply not just to the particular historicist approach that Fischer and Ravizza (1998) defend, but also to a number of other historicist approaches that I have not directly discussed. This includes, for example, the approaches of Christman (1991); Mele (1995), esp. chs. 9 and 10; and Haji and Cuypers (2004). These "historicist" (or "externalist") approaches vary in significant and interesting ways, and each deserves consideration in its own right. Nevertheless, my primary concern in this chapter is not to provide a series of refutations of these various historicist/externalist strategies but rather to sketch an *alternative* compatibilist approach that avoids the need for any historicist/externalist commitments (and also avoids simply "biting the bullet").

basis of our intuitive discomfort with this situation and why we resist this suggestion.

The strategy I have defended involves drawing a distinction between those who can and cannot legitimately hold an agent responsible in circumstances when the agent is being covertly controlled (e.g., through implantation processes). What is intuitively unacceptable, I maintain, is that an agent should be held responsible or subject to reactive attitudes that come from another agent who is covertly controlling or manipulating him. This places some limits on who is *entitled to take up the participant stance* in relation to agents who are rational self-controllers but are nevertheless subject to covert control.[26] In this way, what is compromised by conditions of covert control is not the responsibility of the agent as such. It is, rather, the participant stance of those other agents who covertly control him. Clearly it is possible to establish *these specific limits* on who can *hold* these agents responsible without denying that the agents themselves remain free and responsible. When we take this approach we will find that we are no longer faced with an unattractive choice between simply "biting the bullet" or having to "spit it out." All we need to do is chew carefully, until there is nothing left that we find too hard to swallow.

Acknowledgments

I am grateful to audiences at the Fifth European Congress for Analytic Philosophy (Lisbon, 2005); the Inland Northwest Philosophy Conference (Moscow, Idaho, and Pullman, Washington, 2006); University of British Columbia, McGill University, and Queen's University at Kingston, for their helpful comments and discussion relating to this chapter. For further discussion and correspondence I would also like to thank Joe Campbell, John Fischer, Arash Farzam-kia, Ish Haji, Josh Knobe, Rahul Kumar, Alistair

---

26. Josh Knobe has suggested to me (in correspondence) that this general conclusion of "selective hard compatibilism" receives some significant support from experimental data. More specifically, the data concerned show that people who stand in different relationships to the agent have different views about whether or not the agent is morally responsible. One way of reading this is that they just disagree with each other about whether or not the agent really is responsible. However, another way of interpreting the data is that although everyone agrees about the agent's moral status, they also believe that the agent may be held morally responsible by some but not by others (i.e., depending on their relationship). For more on this see Knobe and Doris (2010).

Macleod, Storrs McCall, Michael McKenna, Alfred Mele, Jeff Pelletier, Saul
Smilansky, and Kip Werking.

REFERENCES

Berofsky, B. 2006. Global Control and Freedom. *Philosophical Studies* 87:419–45.

Christman, J. 1991. Autonomy and Personal History. *Canadian Journal of Philosophy* 21:1–24.

Dennett, D. 1984. *Elbow Room: The Varieties of Free Will Worth Wanting.* Cambridge, MA: MIT Press.

Fischer, J. M. 1986. Responsibility and Control. In *Moral Responsibility.* Ithaca: Cornell University Press.

Fischer, J. M., and M. Ravizza. 1998. *Responsibility and Control: A Theory of Moral Responsibility.* Cambridge: Cambridge University Press.

Fischer, J. M., and M. Ravizza. 2004. Responsibility and Manipulation. *Journal of Ethics* 8:145–77.

Frankfurt, H. 2003. Alternate Possibilities and Moral Responsibility. In *Free Will,* 2nd ed. Ed. G. Watson. Oxford: Oxford University Press.

Haji, I., and S. Cuypers. 2004. Moral Responsibility and the Problem of Manipulation Reconsidered. *International Journal of Philosophical Studies* 12:439–64.

Hobbes, T. 1839–1845. Of Liberty and Necessity. In *The English Works of Thomas Hobbes,* 11 vols. Ed. W. Molesworth. London: John Bohn.

Hume, D. 1999. *An Enquiry Concerning Human Understanding.* Ed. T. Beauchamp. Oxford: Oxford University Press.

Kane, R. 1996. *The Significance of Free Will.* Oxford: Oxford University Press.

Knobe, J., and J. Doris. 2010. Strawsonian Variations: Folk Morality and the Search for a Unified Theory. In *The Oxford Handbook of Moral Psychology.* Ed. J. Doris, G. Harman, S. Nichols, J. Prinz, W. Sinnott-Armstrong, and S. Stich. Oxford: Oxford University Press.

McKenna, M. 2004. Responsibility and Globally Manipulated Agents. *Philosophical Topics* 32:169–92.

Mele, A. R. 1995. *Autonomous Agents: From Self-Control to Autonomy.* Oxford: Oxford University Press.

Nozick, R. 1970. *Anarchy, State, and Utopia.* New York: Basic Books.

Pereboom, D. 2001. *Living without Free Will.* Cambridge: Cambridge University Press.

Russell, P. 1995. *Freedom and Moral Sentiment.* Oxford: Oxford University Press.

Russell, P. 2002a. Critical Notice of John M. Fischer and Mark Ravizza. *Responsibility and Control. Canadian Journal of Philosophy* 32:587–606.

Russell, P. 2002b. Pessimists, Pollyannas, and the New Compatibilism. In *The Oxford Handbook of Free Will.* Ed. R. Kane. Oxford: Oxford University Press: 229–56.

Skinner, B. F. 1962. *Walden Two.* New York: Macmillan.

Strawson, P. F. 2003. Freedom and Resentment. In *Free Will,* 2nd ed. Ed. G. Watson. Oxford: Oxford University Press: 72–93.

Vargas, M. 2006. On the Importance of History for Responsible Agency. *Philosophical Studies* 87:351–82.

Wallace, R. J. 1994. *Responsibility and the Moral Sentiments.* Cambridge, MA: Harvard University Press.

Watson, G. 2004. Soft Libertarianism and Hard Compatibilism. In *Agency and Answerability: Selected Essays.* Oxford: Clarendon Press: 197–215.

Wolf, S. 1990. *Freedom Within Reason.* Oxford: Oxford University Press.

PART IV

Pessimism and the Limits of Free Will

10

Compatibilist-Fatalism

FINITUDE, PESSIMISM, AND THE LIMITS OF FREE WILL[*]

To escape pessimism is, as we all know, no easy task.
WILLIAM JAMES, "The Dilemma of Determinism"

COMPATIBILISTS ARGUE, FAMOUSLY, that it is a simple incompatibilist confusion to suppose that determinism implies fatalism. Incompatibilists argue, on the contrary, that determinism implies fatalism, and thus cannot be consistent with the necessary conditions of moral responsibility. Despite their differences, however, both parties are agreed on one important matter: the refutation of fatalism is essential to the success of the compatibilist strategy. In this chapter I argue that compatibilism requires a richer conception of fatalistic concern; one that recognizes the *legitimacy* of (pessimistic) concerns about the origination of character and conduct. On this basis I argue that any plausible compatibilist position must concede that determinism has fatalistic implications of some significant and relevant kind, and thus must allow that agents may be legitimately held responsible in circumstances where they are subject to fate. The position generated by these compatibilist concessions to incompatibilism will be called "compatibilist-fatalism."

* I am grateful to Ton van den Beld, Richard Double, Richard Gale, Walter Glannon, David Gauthier, Saul Smilansky, Jay Wallace, and Allen Wood for helpful comments and suggestions on earlier drafts of this chapter. For further helpful comments and discussion I would like to thank audiences at Simon Fraser, Washington (Seattle), British Columbia, Edinboro (Pennsylvania), Virginia and, especially, the Utrecht conference on "Moral Responsibility and Ontology" (1998).

I

Compatibilist-fatalism has two key components:

(1) It claims that the truth of determinism is compatible with conditions of responsibility. I will call this the "responsibility-compatibilist
claim." (Its contrary will be called the "responsibility-incompatibilist
claim.")
(2) It claims that determinism implies conditions of universal fatalism.
I will call this the "fatalism claim."

There is near unanimous agreement in both compatibilist and incompatibilist camps that it is incoherent to combine these two claims, since an
agent cannot be both responsible and subject to fate. Compatibilists and
incompatibilists have, nevertheless, very different reasons for taking this
view. Indeed, their superficial agreement conceals fundamental differences about the nature and significance of *fatalism* itself.

With remarkable consistency compatibilists have been very clear about
why they believe that the fatalistic claim should be rejected. It is, they
maintain, a product of simple confusion—a confusion that gives illegitimate support to incompatibilism. The compatibilist argument against the
fatalism claim—let us call it the "refutation argument"—is very familiar.
In an influential statement of classical compatibilism R. E. Hobart gives
the following brief account of the refutation argument:

> Fatalism says that my morrow is determined no matter how I strug-
> gle. This is of course a superstition. Determinism says that my mor-
> row is determined through my struggle.... The stream of causation
> runs through my deliberations and decisions, and if it did not run
> as it does run, the event would be different.[1]

According to this view, then, determinism is the thesis that everything that
occurs, including our deliberations and decisions, are causally *necessitated*
by antecedent conditions. Fatalism, by contrast, is the doctrine that our
deliberations and decisions are causally *ineffective* and make no difference

---

1. R. E. Hobart, "Free Will as Involving Determination and Inconceivable Without It,"
reprinted in Bernard Berofsky, ed., *Free Will and Determinism* (New York: Harper & Row,
1966), 82.

to the course of events. In circumstances of fatalism what happens does not depend on how the agent deliberates. The relevant outcome will occur no matter what the agent decides. Clearly, however, determinism does not imply fatalism. While there are some circumstances in which deliberation is futile (i.e., "local fatalism"), deliberation is nevertheless generally effective in a deterministic world.[2]

Let us call those who accept the responsibility-compatibilist claim but reject the fatalist claim "orthodox-compatibilists." Orthodox-compatibilist understanding of the relationship between responsibility and fate seems clear enough—indeed, one of its attractions is its simplicity. In circumstances where a person is subject to fate, her deliberations and decisions cannot change the course of events. Whatever occurs in these circumstances does not depend on the agent's deliberations. Accordingly, if it were true that determinism implied universal fatalism then it would follow that no one would be responsible—since no one would be able to influence or alter what occurs.[3] However, as the refutation argument makes plain, none of these consequences follow from the truth of determinism. Responsibility-incompatibilism, therefore, has no legitimate foundation in the fatalism claim that incompatibilists mistakenly try to draw from the thesis of determinism.

Incompatibilists defend the fatalism claim and reject the (orthodox) compatibilist's refutation-argument.[4] The incompatibilist reply to the refutation argument turns, crucially, on an alternative interpretation of *fate*. The incompatibilist maintains that compatibilist accounts of "fate,"

---

2. Daniel Dennett is the most prominent contemporary defender of the (classical) refutation argument. As an example of "local fatalism" he describes circumstances where a person has thrown himself off the Golden Gate Bridge and then asks if this is really such a good idea. For this person, Dennett observes, "deliberation has indeed become impotent." Dennett, *Elbow Room: The Varieties of Free Will Worth Wanting* (Oxford: Clarendon Press, 1984), 104. The point is, however, that these circumstances are "abnormal" in a deterministic world and deliberation is generally effective, not futile (106).

3. The sort of fatalistic circumstances that the refutation argument is concerned with (i.e., situations that concern the "causal impotence" or "futility" of deliberation—*Elbow Room*, 15, 104, 106) may nevertheless vary in significant ways. Compare, for instance, Dennett's "bogeymen" examples such as being controlled by "the Peremptory Puppeteer" and "the Hideous Hypnotist" (*Elbow Room*, 8–9). As Dennett points out, the phenomenology of agency/fatalism is very different in these cases.

4. There are exceptions to this generalization. See, e.g., Isaiah Berlin, *Four Essays on Liberty* (Oxford: Oxford University Press, 1969), xiii. Although Berlin accepts the refutation argument and its associated understanding of fatalism, he nevertheless argues for the responsibility-incompatibilist claim on independent grounds.

interpreted in terms of the causal ineffectiveness of an agent's deliberations and actions, is wholly inadequate, and that in consequence it evades
not only real difficulties of a fatalistic character, but also related difficulties about the conditions of moral responsibility. Incompatibilist concern
about fate is not—as on the refutation argument—directed to the issue
of the causal influence *of the agent,* but rather at the issue concerning the
causal influence on the agent. An agent is said to be subject to "fate," on
this account, if her character and conduct does not (ultimately) originate
with the person concerned. The incompatibilist maintains that determinism implies universal fatalism in the sense that—however complex the
mechanisms at work may be—the causal chains eventually reach outside
the agent, and hence no person is *the real originator or ultimate source* of
her conduct and character. When an agent is not the (ultimate) source of
her actions then, the incompatibilist argues, the person is subject to fate.

Compatibilists and incompatibilists, evidently, conceive of "fate" in
quite different terms. For the compatibilist a person is subject to fate only
if their circumstances are such that they are unable to causally *contribute*
to the course of events in some relevant respect. Let us call this account of
fate, as developed in the refutation argument, the concept of "contributory-
fate." Incompatibilists do not (or need not) deny that contributory-fate is
one mode of fatalistic concern, nor need they suppose that determinism
implies that contributory-fatalism holds universally.[5] What the incompatibilist maintains is that there is another mode of fatalistic concern that
arises from a backward-looking perspective (and is, as I will explain, intimately linked with problems of responsibility). The question that concerns
us from this perspective is whether or not the agent is the ultimate source
or true originator of her character and conduct. An agent is subject to "fate,"
in this sense, if her circumstances are such that her character and conduct
have origins and sources that (ultimately) extend beyond her.[6] Let us call
this alternative, incompatibilist conception of fate "origination-fate." The

---

5. Some incompatibilists, of course, object to deterministic metaphysics on the ground that it
implies "mechanism," and this is incompatible with the sort of purposive explanations that
are essential to responsible agency. This distinct and more radical line of incompatibilist
reasoning (which Dennett labels as worries about "sphexishness"; *Elbow Room,* 10–14) is not
essential to their position.

6. For a discussion and interpretation of the relevance of the origination/contribution distinction for the free will debate see Robert Nozick, *Philosophical Explanations* (Oxford: Oxford
University Press, 1981), 313. Nozick interprets fatalism as denying that our actions have any
"contributory value," and the problem of causal determinism as the suggestion that our
actions would be left without "originatory value."

essence of the incompatibilist position is that determinism implies that origination-fate is the universal condition, and thus renders responsibility impossible.[7]

Issues of responsibility and fatalism are intimately and inextricably woven-together on the standard incompatibilist account. Incompatibilists object to the compatibilist's refutation argument on the ground that it constitutes a superficial response on this issue (i.e., fate), and argue that it reflects a one-sided, forward-looking pragmatic perspective that fails to capture—or even acknowledge—difficulties arising from the backward-looking perspective (i.e., matters of origination as opposed to contribu-tion). According to the incompatibilist, the very same shortcomings can be found in compatibilist views on responsibility, and for reasons that are rooted in and run parallel to the failings of the refutation argument.[8] Incompatibilists grant that it is possible to advance a "superficial" concep-tion of responsibility that is essentially pragmatic and forward-looking in nature, and this can be reconciled with determinism. What cannot be rec-onciled with determinism, however, is deep responsibility.[9] Deep responsi-bility is concerned not with the causal efficacy of the attitudes and practices of blaming and punishing, but rather with whether these attitudes and practices are deserved or merited. To understand (deep) responsibility in these terms involves a change of perspective from forward-looking to backward-looking considerations. Only from this perspective can we understand the retributive aspects of responsibility which the compatibil-ist's (superficial) forward-looking account cannot capture.

It is at this point that incompatibilists draw on their defense of the fatalism claim, and use it to support their responsibility-incompatibilist

---

7. For an influential and illuminating discussion that articulates these incompatibil-ist intuitions see Thomas Nagel, "Moral Luck," reprinted in Gary Watson, ed., *Free Will* (Oxford: Oxford University Press, 1982); esp. 183 on "genuine agency" and "shrink-ing" responsibility. Another similarly important and interesting discussion of these mat-ters is presented in Gary Watson, "Responsibility and the Limits of Evil: Variations on a Strawsonian Theme," reprinted in J. M. Fischer & M. Ravizza, eds., *Perspectives on Moral Responsibility* (Ithaca & London: Cornell University Press, 1993); esp. 143–44 on "origination" and the "historical dimension" of responsibility. Both Nagel and Watson (consistent with usual incompatibilist concerns) emphasize the relevance of worries about "origination" for issues of responsibility.

8. It is no coincidence, for example, that Dennett's account of responsibility is wholly prag-matic and forward-looking in character (*Elbow Room*, 156–65). On this see Gary Watson's review of *Elbow Room* in the *Journal of Philosophy*, 83 (1986), 517–22.

9. Susan Wolf, *Freedom Within Reason* (New York & Oxford: Oxford University Press, 1990), 40–45.

conclusion. Attributions of desert, claims the incompatibilist, rest with an agent's capacity for *self-determination,* and this requires the metaphysics of indeterminism. The incompatibilist maintains, in other words, that it will not suffice to establish a person's responsibility to show, simply, that her deliberations and conduct are causally effective in the world. On the contrary, what is required is to show that the choices and actions originate with the agent—and that is why we hold the agent accountable. Clearly, then, since determinism implies universal origination-fatalism, it makes responsibility impossible. It is in this manner that the responsibility-incompatibilist claim and fatalism claim are inextricably bound together on the standard incompatibilist account.[10]

II

The success of any compatibilist strategy depends on showing that "origination," understood in terms of indeterministic metaphysics, is not a necessary condition of moral responsibility, and that a suitably "deep" account of responsibility can be provided within the restrictions imposed by compatibilist commitments. It is not possible in this context to provide any full-scale defense of the case for responsibility-compatibilism. For our purposes, however, this is not necessary. All that is necessary is to describe the general structural features of the case for responsibility-compatibilism in order to assess its significance for the *distinct* prospects of compatibilist-fatalism (as contrasted with orthodox-compatibilism). Suffice it to say, that if there is nothing of a convincing nature to be said in support of the responsibility-compatibilist claim then both orthodox-compatibilism *and* compatibilist-fatalism collapse—since this claim is common to both.

There are two independent but merging strands in contemporary compatibilist thinking that promise a "deeper" and more "robust"

---

10. See, in particular, Nagel's remarks on "the contributions of fate" and their tendency "to erode most of the moral assessments we find it natural to make" ("Moral Luck," esp. 176, 180, 182). I note in passing that not all incompatibilists would accept that their position should be interpreted in terms of concerns about "origination." Some, for example, may articulate their incompatibilism in terms of the issue of "alternate possibilities" or "freedom to do otherwise." Incompatibilist concerns of this nature, however, depend on a particular ("categorical") interpretation of these requirements which on analysis, it may be argued, reflect (deeper) concerns about origination. It suffices, in any case, that concerns about origination constitute a standard incompatibilist perspective on the free will issue. For the purpose of concise presentation, therefore, I will not elaborate on these complexities.

compatibilist account of moral responsibility. Both these strands can be described under the general heading of "naturalized responsibility." The first strand is closely associated, in the contemporary context, with P. F. Strawson's highly influential paper "Freedom and Resentment."[11] The view advanced is that circumstances of responsibility must be understood in terms of the natural workings of moral sentiment. Human beings, it is argued, are inescapably subject to moral emotions under certain conditions, and no general "theoretical" considerations concerning the truth of determinism can discredit—much less dislodge—our human commitment to these emotional responses. To suppose otherwise is to "over-intellectualize" these matters. The most notable strength of this strand of naturalized responsibility is that it distances itself from the cruder utilitarian, forward-looking features of classical compatibilism, without making any concessions to the metaphysics of libertarianism. The Strawsonian strategy, therefore, plugs a significant "gap" in the compatibilist position, and provides a substantial basis for accounting for backward-looking, desert-based considerations consistent with compatibilist commitments. To this extent, compatibilists are better placed to provide their account of responsibility with the kind of "depth" which it plainly requires.

Although the Strawsonian strand of naturalized responsibility (plausibly) addresses a number of traditional incompatibilist objectives, it has its own significant vulnerabilities. The most important of these is, perhaps, that taken by itself it fails to explain on what basis individuals are or are not appropriate objects of moral sentiment.[12] More specifically, without some account of the relevant *capacities* required of moral agents, the theory remains entirely open to the incompatibilist counter-argument that what is required is some mode of contra-causal freedom. The second strand of contemporary naturalized responsibility, however, appears to plug this gap in the position very neatly. What is required is an account of moral capacity that can account for freedom of the *will*, as well as freedom of action.

---

11. P. F. Strawson, "Freedom and Resentment," reprinted in Watson, ed., *Free Will*, 59–80. Strawson's paper is also reprinted in Fischer & Ravizza, eds., *Perspectives on Moral Responsibility*; see also the editors' introduction for a helpful discussion of various responses and criticisms of Strawson (4–25).

12. I develop this line of criticism of Strawson in "Strawson's Way of Naturalizing Responsibility," *Ethics*, 102 (1992), 287–302 (see esp. 296–97, 300–01). See also Watson's related discussion of Strawson's difficulties in accounting for "exempting conditions"; "Responsibility and the Limits of Evil," esp. 125–26.

Various models of "hierarchical" or real self theories provide this.[13] Moral freedom, it is argued, is not simply a matter of being able to act according to your own will, unimpeded by external constraints. It also involves a capacity to reflect on the structure of your own will and form preferences about which desires move you to action. On the basis of a higher-order capacity of this kind agents are able to "identify" with or "repudiate" their own will—something that is essential to being capable of moral conduct and an appropriate object of moral sentiment. It is a general capacity of this nature that distinguishes fully responsible human adults from animals and children who (in some degree) do not enjoy such a capacity and thus are not (fully) responsible. The crucial point remains, however, that this sort of higher-capacity involves no contra-causal or libertarian metaphysical commitments.

Although it would be entirely premature to declare this two-pronged defense of the responsibility-compatibilist claim a success (as clearly the matters raised continue to be strenuously debated), it is nevertheless fair to say that this general approach provides substantial support for the position taken.[14] Let us say, therefore, that the responsibility-compatibilist claim has substantial (although not conclusive) support. The issue that concerns us is what the implications of this are for the compatibilist position in respect of the matter of fatalism. The view that is most widely accepted on this issue is plain. If responsibility-compatibilism is accepted, then the fatalism claim must be rejected, as both cannot be accepted.

Let us call the assumption that responsibility and fate *exclude* each other the "exclusion thesis." Both orthodox-compatibilists and incompatibilists accept the exclusion thesis although, as I have explained, they accept it for very different reasons. The exclusion thesis, however, provides a very

---

13. Dennett's *Elbow Room* is an important contribution to this aspect of contemporary compatibilist thinking. Other influential accounts of this kind include Harry Frankfurt, "Freedom of the Will and the Concept of a Person," and Gary Watson, "Free Agency," both reprinted in Watson, ed., *Free Agency*. Closely related to the second strand of naturalized responsibility is the issue of "reflexivity" and "reason-responsiveness." Dennett, among others, devotes considerable attention to this matter. See esp. *Elbow Room*, ch. 2.

14. There is considerable variation in the specific ways that these two strands of naturalized responsibility are developed and articulated. Compare, for example, the Humean way of developing and blending these themes as presented in Paul Russell, *Freedom and Moral Sentiment: Hume's Way of Naturalizing Responsibility* (New York & Oxford: Oxford University Press, 1995), with the essentially Kantian account presented in R. Jay Wallace, *Responsibility and the Moral Sentiments* (Cambridge, MA: Harvard University Press, 1994). It is also important to note that not all contemporary compatibilists accept both of the two strands described above (see, e.g., note 8 above on Dennett).

quick way of dealing with the issue of fatalism once the responsibility-compatibilist claim is established. The exclusion thesis eliminates the possibility that conditions of universal fatalism could persist in conditions when agents are still morally responsible. Hence, if agents are responsible, conditions of universal fatalism cannot hold. In short, if we accept the responsibility-compatibilist claim, and the exclusion thesis, then we *must* reject the fatalism claim. If this is correct, then compatibilist-fatalism is an untenable position.

If a case can be made for compatibilist-fatalism it must be able to show that there is some basis for accepting the fatalism claim without compromising the responsibility-compatibilist claim (thereby showing the exclusion thesis to be false). Another way of expressing this is to say that there must be issues of fatalism that survive the (assumed) success of responsibility-compatibilism. On the face of it, however, this is odd, as incompatibilist concern about the fatalistic implications of determinism (i.e., in respect of origination-fate) are generally motivated by worries about responsibility-incompatibilism. The puzzle is that if determinism has no responsibility-incompatibilist implications then the issue of origination-fatalism seems to be empty.[15]

III

In order to explain the distinctive commitments of compatibilist-fatalism it will be useful to employ the terminology of "optimism" and "pessimism."[16] These labels are illuminating for understanding the free will debate because they indicate that the various parties involved have certain concerns or interests that motivate the positions that they take. In other words, these labels make plain that the issues at stake are not merely theoretical (conceptual) puzzles that require clarification but, rather, they are matters that are in some sense emotionally charged. The language of "pessimism," in particular, is indicative of the fact that incompatibilists

---

15. Some incompatibilists may argue that their pessimism about the fatalistic implications of determinism are not entirely based on worries about responsibility, although this is their primary concern. In so far as incompatibilists have fatalistic concerns independent of the issue of responsibility they share common cause with compatibilist-fatalists—as I will explain.

16. This terminology is a prominent feature of Strawson's discussion in "Freedom and Resentment," where it is used to describe the positions of the major parties in the free will dispute: incompatibilists being "pessimists," compatibilists being "optimists."

find some implications of determinism troubling or disturbing.[17] For the incompatibilist determinism suggests a picture of human beings that is (somehow) disillusioning, and thus the incompatibilist wants this thesis to be false. Compatibilists, by contrast, do not share these concerns, and believe, indeed, that they are misguided and a product of (philosophical) confusion. Since compatibilists find nothing "troubling" or "disturbing" about the thesis of determinism—and nothing about it motivates a desire that it be false—they may be characterized as "optimists."

Any position that accepts the fatalism claim seems to be committed to pessimistic motivations of some kind. In the case of incompatibilism these pessimistic motivations, as we have noted, are closely tied to concerns about the conditions of responsibility. These concerns are not endorsed by compatibilist-fatalists since they accept the (contrary) responsibility-compatibilist claim. The obvious question arises, therefore, given their commitment to the fatalism claim, what are the pessimistic motivations of the compatibilist-fatalist? Clearly compatibilist-fatalists hold that determinism implies universal origination-fatalism and there is something "troubling" or "disturbing" about this which lies beyond the scope of issues of responsibility. However, the source of this pessimism remains obscure.

What is essential to compatibilist-fatalism is the view that while origination-fatalism does not undermine or discredit our (natural) commitment to moral responsibility, it nevertheless does not leave our conception of ourselves as real agents in the world undiminished. A well-known passage of Spinoza's *Ethics* identifies this source of pessimistic concern and describes it in the following terms:

> Most of those who have written about the emotions and human conduct seem to be dealing not with natural phenomena that follow the common laws of Nature but with phenomena outside Nature. They appear to go so far as to conceive man in Nature as a kingdom within a kingdom. They believe that he disturbs rather than

17. In *Elbow Room* Dennett interprets his own defense of compatibilism as a vindication of "optimism" over "pessimism" (18–19, 169). His discussion makes clear that, from an orthodox-compatibilist perspective, incompatibilist claims are not innocuous, as they generate negative emotions such as "fear," "anxiety," "dread" and so on. Dennett's general conclusion is that all such incompatibilist "pessimism" can be effectively discredited and shown to be motivated by various kinds of (philosophical) confusion and/or illusion. This includes, notably, pessimism about fate.

follows Nature's order, and has absolute power over his actions, and is determined by no other source than himself.[18]

Spinoza's observations appear in a context in which he is seeking to explain the source of deep *resistance* to any naturalized, deterministic conception of human life. Although much of this resistance is motivated by incompatibilist concerns about the threat to the fabric of moral responsibility, Spinoza's remarks bypass them. Instead, his remarks are addressed directly at the issue of agency. The specific dimension of pessimistic concern is captured through the metaphor of "sovereignty." In conceiving of human beings as "a kingdom within a kingdom" we conceive of ourselves as subject, not to the alien laws that govern all nature, but rather to laws that pertain uniquely to human (rational) life. Our sense of "sovereignty," therefore, is tied to our belief that we are distinct from nature, not (a reducible) part of it. Through our capacity for sovereignty, so conceived, we are not only independent of nature, but also *above* it. We are above it—qua sovereign—because we govern nature without being governed by it (i.e., we are not subject to its laws).[19] From this perspective we take ourselves to be something more than (sophisticated and complex) causal intermediaries. We conceive of ourselves as starting points that intervene in the order of things. Finally, the metaphor of sovereignty brings with it a conception of beings who are worthy of a particular kind of dignity—the dignity due to beings who are sovereign over both themselves and nature.

Clearly, from this perspective, we want much more than simply to be morally accountable to each other. What is at stake here is our conception of ourselves as (actively) *ordering nature*, rather than being (passively)

---

18. Spinoza, *Ethics* (Indianapolis & Cambridge: Hackett, 1992), 102 (Part III, Preface); translation by Samuel Shirley.

19. The metaphor of being "governed by nature" may be taken to suggest that Nature (somehow) "controls" us for its own ends and purposes. This would involve confusion and should be avoided. For this reason it is important to distinguish worries about origination-fatalism from worries about supernatural fate. In the case of supernatural fate it is argued, not only that the ultimate source of character and conduct does not lie with the agent (and thus has an external source) but, moreover, that the external source is some supernatural agent or cosmic being who "manipulates" or "directs" our (human) lives according to some (alien) design or plan. Worries about loss of "sovereignty," however, need not presuppose any such "bogeyman" to be at work. In general, there is no reason to suppose that a mistake of this kind is required to motivate pessimistic concerns about origination-fatalism. (One of the unsatisfactory aspects of Dennett's efforts to defuse worries about fatalism is that he tends to assimilate worries about origination with worries about supernatural fate: see *Elbow Room*, 7–17, and ch. 3.)

ordered by nature. This distinction depends on a capacity for spontaneous self-determination and thus cannot be sustained in conditions of universal origination-fatalism. Any optimism secured on the basis of responsibility-compatibilism, therefore, must be significantly tempered by a pessimism rooted in these reflections. Although we may concede that universal origination-fatalism poses no threat to the fabric of responsibility, it nevertheless has troubling implications for aspects of our self-conception that lie outside this sphere (something that is obscured by incompatibilist arguments that focus exclusively on issues of responsibility). Only those who are unmoved by the issue of "sovereignty," and place no value on it, can draw any other conclusion.

What reply can orthodox-compatibilists offer to this line of reasoning? The first point to note is that it will not do to fall back on the refutation argument. The pessimistic concerns of the compatibilist-fatalist are not motivated by any simple confusion between determinism and contributory-fatalism. On the contrary, compatibilist-fatalists (along with incompatibilists) object to the refutation argument on the ground that it fails to draw the relevant distinction between origination and contributory fate and is, consequently, blind to the very different concerns that arise from the former. Furthermore, the entire line of reasoning that develops from the refutation argument proceeds from the same one-sided, forward-looking perspective that generated serious shortcomings in the efforts of classical compatibilists to address incompatibilist concerns about responsibility. Since compatibilism has overcome its blindness to backward-looking claims in respect of responsibility, so too it must face the issues raised by origination-fatalism in a more direct manner.

The orthodox-compatibilist may argue that it is possible to address these concerns about origination without accepting the fatalism claim. It may be argued, for example, that the resources of naturalized responsibility provide an effective basis from which to discredit the specific concerns that the compatibilist-fatalist has raised. What is supposed to be troubling about determinism is that it makes genuine origination or (true) self-determination impossible. If there is any foundation to the pessimistic concerns that support the fatalism claim, this seems to be it. Against this, however, it can be argued that hierarchical or real self theories of freedom provide a substantial account of self-determination and self-control without any appeal to indeterministic metaphysics. All that is required is a suitably complex description of the higher-order capacities of human beings to reflect on their own character and motivation and restructure their own wills on this basis. It is simply incorrect, on this account, to suppose that any agent in a deterministic framework is incapable of altering or amending his character and the structure of his own will. Agents with the relevant capacities of the sort described (i.e., two-level freedom) are not passive in these respects. Indeed, with capacities of these (natural) kinds we can, to a large extent, conceive of ourselves as "self-made-selves."[20] Whatever residue of pessimistic concern survives responsibility-compatibilism, therefore, is effectively discredited by these considerations.

Does this orthodox-compatibilist counter-argument—let us call it the *"revised* refutation argument"—serve to discredit the distinct pessimistic concerns that motivate the compatibilist-fatalist? The revised refutation argument is obviously an improvement on the original argument. It does not, for example, suggest that the defender of the fatalism claim makes the crude mistake of supposing that determinism implies universal *contributory*-fatalism. More importantly, this revised effort to refute the fatalism claim does not deny the general legitimacy of concerns that arise from a backward-looking perspective about the issue of origination of character and conduct. What is argued is that determinism provides no basis for pessimistic concerns of this kind and to this extent the concerns are unreasonable. The resources of higher-order capacities are more than adequate to account for talk of self-determination and self-control (i.e., some form of "sovereignty") and they do so without relying on the obscure metaphysics of libertarianism to fill this particular gap.

The strength of the revised argument is that it shows that compatibilists can provide a more sophisticated account of self-determination and freedom of will, which is a clear improvement on the more limited (classical) compatibilist accounts of freedom understood in terms of unimpeded action. Nevertheless, it is not evident that the case against the fatalism claim can be secured by means of the revised refutation argument. The (higher-order) moral capacities described may well serve as the relevant basis on which to distinguish individuals who are appropriate objects of moral sentiment from those who are not. (Indeed, for reasons that have been explained, the case for responsibility-compatibilism depends on this.) However, capacities of these kinds are not capable of addressing the

---

20. The expression is Dennett's (*Elbow Room*, ch.4, esp. 100) and it is indicative of the extent of his "optimism" on such matters. See also the papers by Frankfurt and Watson cited in note 13 above.

specific difficulties that are suggested by reflection on the implications of (universal) origination-fatalism.

First, the compatibilist-fatalist may grant that human beings have capacities of self-determinism of the sort described without in any way conceding that these capacities are of such a nature as to allow agents to reinvent themselves as they please. Any account of these capacities, so construed, is self-evidently an exaggeration. Clearly there are many other forces of an external nature that condition character and the conduct that flows from it. Accordingly, the scope and extent of the human capacity for self-determination of this sort is much more limited and restricted than orthodox-compatibilist talk of "self-made-selves" suggests.[21] Second, and more importantly, even if these powers of self-control were as extensive as defenders of the revised refutation argument imply, they entirely fail to address the more basic concern that sustains the fatalism claim. The specific concern is that ultimately nothing that the agent is or does originates with the agent—the causal source can always be traced to factors lying outside the agent. Granted a deterministic framework, when and how an agent actually *exercises* such capacities of rational self-criticism and redirection will depend, ultimately, on factors that lie beyond the agent.[22] This brings us back full-circle to the specific implication of determinism that compatibilist-fatalists find disturbing: determinism implies that no agent is the ultimate source of her own character and conduct.[23]

---

21. Dennett notes himself (*Elbow Room,* 85, 156) that "a completely self-made self, one hundred per cent responsible for its own character, [is] an impossibility." The question arises, however, what percentage is required for a self to be "self-made"—will any percentage do? It should also be noted that Dennett does not claim that we avoid worries about fatalism to the extent that we are "self-made-selves." On the contrary, since he accepts the (classical) refutation argument, and its narrow conception of fate as contributory fate, all that is required to avoid worries about "fate," he claims, is for deliberation and action to be causally effective.

22. There are variations on this general problem in compatibilist literature. Wallace, for example, suggests that "powers of reflective self-control" constitute the relevant moral capacities required for responsible agency. (See the discussion concerning moral capacities above.) These powers, he says, involve the possession of the ability to grasp and apply moral reasons and to regulate behavior on this basis.(*Responsibility and the Moral Sentiments,* 157). However, as Wallace concedes, agents may possess these powers and yet have no ability to determine the way that they are exercised in particular circumstances (180–94, 201–14). This is, however, precisely what is required for "sovereignty." Hence, even if Wallace's defense of responsibility-compatibilism is accepted, the concerns about origination-fatalism remain unanswered.

23. For a brief account of this matter see Russell, *Freedom & Moral Sentiment,* 128–30.

This basic concern is, of course, very familiar in literature critical of compatibilist efforts to account for self-determination. It is, however, particularly important to note that while libertarian efforts to explain what ultimate agency consists in may be judged hopelessly obscure, the aspiration itself is motivated by a general worry that is clear enough: namely, that compatibilist accounts of self-determination are essentially superficial, since such agents are, inescapably, conditioned by factors that they have no control over. Clearly, then, the revised refutation argument fails to discredit this fundamental concern. It may be argued, furthermore, that this conclusion is especially disturbing if the compatibilist is right, and our natural commitment to responsibility persists in the face of these (fatalistic) conditions.[24]

IV

In face of this reply to the revised refutation argument, orthodox-compatibilists may suggest another way of discrediting the pessimistic concerns that seem to sustain the fatalism claim. What is not clear, they may argue, is what sort of "origination" or "self-determination" is required to avoid these fatalistic anxieties. More specifically, the desire to be a (pure) self-determinator, so conceived, is simply incoherent, and thus no real sense can be made of the pessimistic concerns that lie behind the fatalism claim.[25] Moreover, in so far as any sense can be made of this desire for

24. In respect of this, consider Watson's illuminating and suggestive reflections on the significance of the case of Robert Harris. ("Responsibility and the Limits of Evil," 137–46). Harris was a notably brutal Californian killer (i.e., when viewed as a "victimizer") and also the product of an exceptionally brutal childhood (i.e., when viewed as a "victim"). Watson interprets the significance of the "historical" considerations relating to Harris's childhood and moral development in terms of their tendency to influence our reactive attitudes (i.e., to produce "ambivalence," 137–38). There is, however, another way of looking at this case, more in keeping with compatibilist-fatalism. Reflection on such circumstances presses the thought upon us that who we are, and what we are responsible for to other human beings, depends ultimately on factors that we have no control over. These reflections are even more troubling when, as Watson puts it, we "turn our gaze inward" and recognize "that one's moral self is such a fragile thing" (139). In contrast with this view, orthodox-compatibilism suggests that historical considerations of this kind are untroubling so long as they do not discredit or dislodge our (natural) commitment to reactive attitudes.

25. It is, in particular, a notorious stumbling-block of libertarian metaphysics that it is unable to make clear what is required for "genuine agency" beyond simple indeterminism. The difficulties facing the libertarian are well described in the closing passages of Nagel's "Moral Luck"; Nagel's *The View from Nowhere* (New York & Oxford: Oxford University Press, 1986, ch. 7); and also Galen Strawson, *Freedom and Belief* (Oxford: Clarendon Press, 1986, ch. 2).

(pure) self-determination it appears, on examination, less than desirable. So the orthodox-compatibilist reply is this: the objective of "overcoming" origination-fate in the terms suggested is neither coherent, nor obviously attractive in itself. To this the orthodox-compatibilist may also add that it is important to note that the problem of fate, conceived in terms of worries about origination (rather than contribution), is not limited to the metaphysics of determinism. On the contrary, the metaphysics of indeterminism generates its own "fatalistic" worries in this regard. That is, even if there are real "breaks in the causal chain," and "spontaneous willings" occur, it is not evident that this serves to secure "genuine agency." This is because (pure) "spontaneity" seems to undermine genuine agency no less than the chains of causal necessity. The underlying point is, of course, that the ideal of "genuine agency" is simply a confused illusion that cannot stand up to critical scrutiny. Given this, the pessimistic concerns that are supposed to sustain the fatalism claim can be dismissed as wholly unreasonable.

This rejoinder seeks to discredit the pessimistic motivations of the compatibilist-fatalist by arguing that there is no plausible *alternative* metaphysics that could overcome these difficulties (i.e., regarding ultimate self-determination or origination). In my view, however, this is not a convincing way to discredit these concerns about origination-fatalism. The obvious point is that it may be granted that there is no alternative metaphysics that serves to insulate us from these pessimistic concerns about the ultimate origination of character and conduct, but this does not show that these concerns are somehow bogus or without foundation. Consider, for example, the analogous debate concerning the doctrine of the immortality of the soul. Many philosophers—especially religiously minded philosophers—have argued that we have reason to want to be immortal, to exist for all eternity. Accordingly, faced with arguments for human mortality (i.e., naturalistic conceptions of human beings) these philosophers maintain that mortalism has pessimistic implications. Against pessimism of this nature, defenders of mortalism may argue (in parallel reasoning with orthodox-compatibilists) that the desire for immortality is neither coherent in itself, nor an obviously attractive ideal—to the extent that we can conceive of it being realized.

Clearly, however, those who find mortalism a source of pessimism (i.e., troubling, difficult, disillusioning, and so on) may readily grant the truth of the mortalist's claims concerning the doctrine of immortality. Nevertheless, it simply does not follow that if one grants that the desire for immortality involves an ideal or aspiration that is doubtfully coherent and (on reflection) doubtfully attractive, then there is no basis for being troubled by reflections on human mortality.[26] On the contrary, reflection on this specific aspect of the human condition provides a reasonable basis for being troubled *whatever view we take.* There is no guarantee that some trouble-free optimistic alternative must be "available" to us. Indeed, in the case of human mortality/immortality the truth seems otherwise. What is troubling about human mortality is that it confronts us with the limits of human existence—our inevitable and inescapable *finitude* as beings in the world. Clearly, then, while we may not want to be immortal, and we may agree there is no coherent account of what we would want if we sought immortality, we may still have some reasonable basis for finding the limits of human existence and individual finitude to be matters that unsettle and disturb us in important respects (so long as we are tolerably reflective on the matter). This feature of the human condition is something that we cannot contemplate with optimistic calm and serenity.[27]

Parallel reasoning is available to the compatibilist-fatalist. Against this position it is argued that concerns about the fatalistic implications of determinism rely upon an ideal of (pure) self-determination that is neither coherent nor, on reflection, attractive. From this the orthodox-compatibilist concludes that there is no basis for the pessimistic anxieties that are supposed to sustain the fatalism claim. To this, however, the compatibilist-fatalist may reply that, however incoherent and unattractive the ideal of pure (unconditioned) agency may be, what is troubling about origination-fatalism is that it confronts us with the limits of human agency—the inescapable fact that the ultimate source of our character and conduct lies beyond us.[28] Our finitude and place in the order of nature has implications for our conception of ourselves as genuine agents. We may not want to be (God-like) self-creators, and we may agree that there is no

---

26. The many difficulties associated with making sense of the thesis of immortality are well-known. An interesting discussion of the desirability of immortality is presented in Bernard Williams, "The Makropulos Case," in *Problems of the Self* (Cambridge: Cambridge University Press, 1973).

27. "We cannot look squarely at either death or the sun." LaRochfoucauld, *Maxims*, no. 26.

28. The only way to evade these pessimistic reflections about origination-fatalism is to provide some (coherent) account of "genuine agency" that is premised on indeterministic metaphysics. For recent libertarian efforts along these lines see the various papers in Timothy O'Connor, ed., *Agents, Causes & Events: Essays on Indeterminism and Free Will* (Oxford: Oxford University Press, 1995).

available coherent interpretation of this ideal, and yet consistently maintain that reflections on these limits concerning the origination of human
agency are disturbing and troubling in ways that are analogous to reflections about human mortality. To insist on (easy) optimism in face of such
thoughts about the human condition is a form of "superficiality" to which
(orthodox) compatibilists are much too prone.

V

There is one final reply to the compatibilist-fatalist that may now be presented. The fatalism claim receives whatever support it has on the basis of
the pessimistic concerns that it generates from reflections about origination. The orthodox-compatibilist may simply insist that none of these concerns move him, or *trouble* him, in the least. It may be argued, moreover,
that it is the compatibilist-fatalist who is guilty of "over-intellectualizing"
this whole issue by appealing to "theoretical" considerations regarding
origination in order to *compel* a particular affective response (i.e., pessimism)—but this cannot be done.

   This reply, however, is one that the orthodox-compatibilist should be
reluctant to employ. The orthodox-compatibilist has tried to *discredit* the
fatalism claim by showing that, in some way or other, it depends on confusion and/or illusion. In reply it has been shown that these attempts to
refute the fatalism claim are themselves confused, or manifest a shallow
appreciation of fatalistic concern. The compatibilist-fatalist may grant, at
this stage, that their concerns may not be shared by everyone, and that it
is impossible to argue someone into the relevant attitude (i.e., pessimism)
once all relevant considerations have been made clear. Nevertheless, if it
is impossible to compel pessimistic attitudes in the face of such considerations, it is no less impossible to compel optimism. As there seems to be
no identifiable confusion lying behind either the optimistic or pessimistic
attitude in these circumstances, a stalemate results. This situation, however, leaves orthodox-compatibilists unable to discredit the pessimism that
sustains the fatalism claim. All that can be said in reply is that the orthodox-
compatibilist does not share it, which is clearly a different matter. It suffices, therefore, that the pessimism that motivates the commitment to the
fatalism claim has not been discredited, and the orthodox-compatibilist is
mistaken to suppose that it can be.

   The compatibilist-fatalist may also argue that the best explanation for
the fact that orthodox-compatibilists are unable to share this pessimism

is that they have not sufficiently exercised their reflective imagination. To remedy this, they may suggest that appropriate reflection on especially striking cases will help to make clear why pessimistic concerns about origination are called for.[29] As I have explained, however, it would be a mistake to represent the pessimistic concerns that sustain commitment to the fatalism claim as simply the end-result of a process of pure reasoning, as clearly such concerns also require some relevant *sensibility*. (Consider, again, the analogy with pessimistic reflections on death.) This is why the cultivation of artistic imagination is of such obvious significance in this context; since many great works of literature and drama are devoted to the central message of compatibilist-fatalism (i.e., that responsibility and fate come fused together in human life).[30]

Another possibility is to show that the orthodox-compatibilist's inability to share this mode of pessimism is rooted in confusion about the *quality* of the pessimism involved. Pessimism varies in its quality as well as its source. The quality of pessimism generated by contributory-fatalism may be characterized as one of *despair*, produced by a sense of impotence. To conceive of ourselves as "puppets" or "dolls," for example, would certainly be awful and justify despair.[31] The pessimism associated with origination-fatalism, however, is not of this character.

Origination-fatalism, I have argued, focuses on our awareness of human finitude and its relevance to agency. This basic concern is well captured by John Macquarrie in the context of a discussion of existentialist philosophy.

> Man is thrown into existence, each one is thrown into his own particular existential situation. From the human point of view, it is rather like the throw of a dice. . . . As we see it from the purely human point of view, we all start out as different people with different endowments in different situations, and there is as little

---

29. Consider, for example, Watson's discussion of Robert Harris, as cited in note 24 above.

30. The compatibilist-fatalist, as explained, interprets the specific way that responsibility and fate "come fused together in human life" in terms of (rejecting) the exclusion thesis, and distinguishing between origination and contributory fatalism.

31. Dennett associates the pessimism generated by the "bugbear" of fatalism with the condition of "puppets" or "dolls"—something that really is a "terrible condition" (*Elbow Room*, ch. 1).

assignable reason for the differences as there is for the dice turning up one number rather than another.[32]

As these remarks suggest, the pessimism of compatibilist-fatalism is not so much a sense of despair rooted in impotence, but rather one of being *disconcerted,* rooted in awareness of finitude and contingency.[33] Closely associated with the sense of finitude and contingency is, I suggest, a sense of the absurdity of human life.[34] In this context it takes the form of an (uncomfortable) awareness of the gap between our aspiration to "sovereignty" and being "self-made-selves," and the recognition, as conveyed by the fatalism claim, that this is an illusion. It is evident, therefore, that the pessimism involved in endorsing the fatalism claim, so interpreted, is of a very different kind than the pessimism associated with contributory-fatalism (i.e., as featured in the refutation argument). Much of the orthodox-compatibilist resistance to the pessimism of compatibilist-fatalism is based, I suggest, in a confusion between these two very different modes of fatalistic concern, and the distinct sensibilities associated with them.

It should now be clear what the optimistic and pessimistic commitments of compatibilist-fatalism come to. In respect of the issue of responsibility, the compatibilist-fatalist maintains that the resources of naturalized responsibility are rich enough to provide firm support for the responsibility-compatibilist claim. (This is an issue that I have left open, except for the proviso that a strong enough case can be made for this claim to give it considerable credibility.) In respect of the fatalism claim compatibilist-fatalists hold that the refutation argument is blind to pessimistic concerns about origination. Moreover, even the more substantial revised version of the refutation argument (employing the resources of naturalized responsibility) cannot discredit or dislodge the source of pessimism that sustains commitment to the fatalism claim. So interpreted, compatibilist-fatalism involves *mixed* optimistic and pessimistic elements,

---

32. John Macquarrie, *Existentialism* (Harmondsworth, Middx., Penguin, 1973), 191.

33. This sense of the contingency of human existence, and its relevance to our view of ourselves as (responsible) agents who are nevertheless "thrown" into our own particular circumstances, is something that many moral theories (most notably Kantianism) strongly resist. On this see Bernard Williams, "Moral Luck: A Postscript," reprinted in *Making Sense of Humanity* (Cambridge: Cambridge University Press, 1995), 246.

34. My comments here draw on Thomas Nagel's influential discussion of the our sense of the absurd as it relates to human life: "The Absurd," reprinted in *Mortal Questions* (Cambridge: Cambridge University Press, 1979).

and to this extent it addresses both compatibilist and incompatibilist concerns.

VI

My objective in this chapter has not been to defend compatibilist-fatalism, but to consider its merits in relation to orthodox (non-fatalistic) compatibilism. Both forms of compatibilism accept the responsibility-compatibilist claim: that is, the claim that determinism does not discredit the attitudes and practices associated with moral responsibility. Where they diverge is on the matter of fatalism. Compatibilist-fatalists accept a claim that is generally associated with incompatibilism: namely, that determinism has fatalistic implications. The discussion in this chapter, therefore, has been primarily concerned to provide an interpretation and defense of the fatalism claim from the perspective of those who are already (i.e., independently) committed to the responsibility-compatibilist claim. For reasons that have been explained, this is an unusual and controversial position for any compatibilist to adopt.[35]

I have described a number of different approaches that the orthodox-compatibilist may take in order to discredit the specific pessimistic motivations associated with the fatalism claim. All of them, I argue, are unsuccessful. It follows from this that any plausible compatibilism must take the form of—or accept the legitimacy of—compatibilist-fatalism.[36] An obvious corollary of this is that a plausible compatibilism must reject the

---

35. Despite this, some may be tempted to question the freshness of compatibilist-fatalism on the ground that each of its two component claims are (very) familiar. It should be clear, however, that the particular interest of this position does not rest with its two component claims considered in isolation from each other, but rather with the effort to combine two claims that have traditionally been treated by both the major parties in the free will dispute as incompatible—a thesis which compatibilist-fatalism rejects. I am unaware of any compatibilist thinker who has defended the "mixed" optimist/pessimist position of compatibilist-fatalism as described. See, however, Saul Smilansky, "Does the Free Will Problem Rest on a Mistake," *Philosophical Papers*, 22 (1993), 173–88. Smilansky pursues themes that are very relevant to the position taken in this chapter.

36. The qualifying clause in this sentence (i.e., "or accept the legitimacy of") provides scope for the weaker position that allows that some compatibilists, after due reflection, may remain untroubled by any considerations regarding origination. (See section V above.) On the assumption that there is no confusion about the source and quality of the pessimism at issue, nor any failure of due reflection in such cases, but only a divergence of sensibility, then orthodox-compatibilism may be judged no less—and no more—legitimate than compatibilist-fatalism. As I have indicated, however, it may be argued that a failure to be

exclusion thesis.[37] A particular merit of compatibilist-fatalism is that it recognizes the (deep) source of incompatibilist as rooted in backward-looking concerns about the origination of character and conduct and, related to this, it avoids the one-sided superficiality of the (classical) refutation argument. When these points are properly established, I maintain, the compatibilist is better placed to provide a more nuanced and appropriate response to the (pessimistic) concerns of the incompatibilist.

A plausible compatibilism, I conclude, must embrace a richer conception of fatalistic concern and allow for the possibility that agents may be legitimately held responsible in circumstances where they are subject to fate. The significance of this should be clear. Hitherto all forms of compatibilism have been orthodox in character: they reject the fatalism claim and are homogeneously "optimistic." The central thesis of this chapter is that compatibilism can (or must) take the form of compatibilist-fatalism, and thereby accept that determinism has fatalistic implications without compromising its commitment to naturalized responsibility.

troubled by considerations regarding origination is best explained in terms of a lack of appropriate reflection, and that a suitable sensibility can be cultivated on the basis of such reflection.

37. Incompatibilists, of course, remain committed to the exclusion thesis in so far as it is essential to their defense of the responsibility-incompatibilist claim.

11

Pessimists, Pollyannas, and the New Compatibilism[*]

> *If a man is a pessimist, he is born a pessimist, and emotionally you cannot make him an optimist. And if he is an optimist, you can tell him nothing to make him a pessimist.*
>
> CLARENCE DARROW

THE AIM OF this chapter is to examine a number of influential recent contributions to compatibilist literature on freedom and responsibility. Although the views of several authors will be considered, discussion will be organized primarily around Daniel Dennett's *Elbow Room*, an important work in the evolution of the "new compatibilism."

1. Cheerful Compatibilism and the Bogeymen of Pessimism

Dennett's discussion of the free will problem begins with the observation that this is a subject that people care about—it is not simply an intellectual puzzle looking for a solution. One group believes that if determinism is true, and "every deed and decision is the inexorable outcome . . . of the sum of physical forces acting at the moment," then the human condition would be a "terrible" and "frightening" existence (Dennett 1984: 1–5). Freedom would be an illusion, and we would be reduced to "awful" circumstances similar to those of individuals who find themselves imprisoned or paralyzed, or subject to (hidden) control and manipulation by others.

Incompatibilist views of this kind generate, and reflect, strong emotional responses that can be labeled as "pessimistic." Dennett's fundamental objective in *Elbow Room* is to discredit incompatibilist pessimism and to

[*] I am grateful to Robert Bunn, Ish Haji, Saul Smilansky, and Robert Kane for their helpful comments and suggestions.

vindicate a more "optimistic" position (19, 169). According to Dennett, the thesis of determinism has none of these bleak implications for the human condition, and we do not require the metaphysical system building of libertarianism to "ward off non-existent evils" (4; and compare Strawson 1962).[1]

The opening chapter of *Elbow Room* provides a vivid and lively account of how incompatibilist pessimism acquires its psychological grip over us. Our worries and anxieties about determinism, says Dennett, are the product of "fearmongery" by philosophers. It is philosophers who have "conjured up a host of truly frightening bugbears and then subliminally suggested, quite illicitly, that the question of free will is whether any of these bugbears actually exist" (Dennett 1984: 4). The arguments of these pessimistic "gloomleaders," says Dennett, rely on thought experiments that serve as "intuition pumps" designed to produce the same relevant negative emotional response (Dennett 1984: 12, 18). According to Dennett, however, these thought experiments do not so much illuminate the problem as artificially create it by means of misleading analogies and metaphors.

In Dennett's view, the analogies and metaphors concerned "do not in the slightest deserve the respect and influence they typically enjoy" (7). His method in *Elbow Room* is to examine carefully these incompatibilist intuition pumps and to show how they are systematically misleading. In this way, Dennett plays the part of a philosophical therapist, trying to release us from the set of worries and anxieties produced by these misleading analogies.[2] If the therapy succeeds, then the free will problem, as traditionally conceived, "dissolves."[3]

---

1. Dennett's way of associating incompatibilism with "pessimism" is also a prominent feature of Strawson's influential essay "Freedom and Resentment" (Strawson 1962). Although this perspective on the free will debate reflects dominant tendencies in incompatibilist literature, there are some important complications to be noted. For example, the incompatibilist pessimist may well be an "optimist" about the existence of (libertarian) free will. Moreover, some incompatibilists would argue that our everyday beliefs and attitudes concerning freedom and responsibility are not worth salvaging, and so they find nothing "frightening" or "awful" about doing without them. As we will see, at times this attitude surfaces in Dennett. For the purposes of this chapter, however, I will work within the pessimist/optimist framework that Dennett (and Strawson) have constructed.

2. Dennett's methodology is self-consciously modeled after the ordinary language techniques of predecessors such as Ryle and Wittgenstein (Dennett 1984: 6, 18). (*Elbow Room* is dedicated to the memory of Ryle.)

3. Dennett argues that worries about free will are "an almost exclusively Western preoccupation" and that for most people "metaphysical freedom has just not been worth worrying about" (Dennett 1984: 4). Clearly, then, Dennett sees his audience as composed primarily of philosophers, who are victims of their own " induced illusions."

A particularly important subset of the bugbears that Dennett wants to discredit are various "bogeymen," viewed as agents who are really in control of us. The class of bogeymen can itself be subdivided into distinct groups. The first are those analogies that imply that our will somehow fails to govern our conduct, effectively disconnecting us from any (causal) influence on the world. These cases include, for example, imagining ourselves as living in a prison run by an invisible jailer, or being in the clutches of a puppeteer who controls our every movement no matter how we may struggle against him. These versions of the bogeymen control us not by controlling our will but by moving our bodies directly and rendering our efforts and preferences inert.

Closely related to these bogeymen are more general worries about fate, the view that all our efforts and deliberations are futile. The concern here is that if determinism is true, and everything that we think and do is governed by causal laws, then we are subject to conditions of universal fate. This bugbear, says Dennett, "looms large" in the free will debate, and the intuition pumps described above do much to support and promote it.

Another subset of bogeymen operate on us in a different way. In these cases the worry is not that our wills fail to guide our conduct, but rather that the way we deliberate and will is controlled by another agent. In these cases, although actions are produced by our will, our will is not truly our own. Examples of this anxiety include cases of hypnosis, or manipulation by an evil neurosurgeon using electronic implants to control us. In such cases we may not even be aware that we are being controlled by another agent. We have the illusion of freedom.

A further worry—in some ways the opposite of the bogeymen anxieties—is that if determinism is true then there is no agent in control at all, since we are really nothing more than mere machines or automata responding in predictable ways to stimuli in our environment. On this view of things, human beings are not much different from simple insects, which can be easily manipulated by more sophisticated beings who control their environment. A wasp, for example, may look as if it makes choices and decisions, but it is really just biological machinery operating according to established causal laws—no real agent is at work. If determinism is true, says the incompatibilist pessimist, then human beings are not much better off than an insect operating in this fashion.

Dennett's objective is to show that all these intuition pumps are, in various ways, misleading. For the purpose of understanding his project, I will focus on his examples of bogeymen and the two different ways that they threaten human freedom. In order to distinguish among the various categories of pessimistic concern, I will introduce a spatial metaphor of distance. Close-range pessimism concerns those cases where the worry is that our will fails to guide our conduct. Middle-distance pessimism is the set of worries we have in circumstances where we believe that we are unable to properly regulate our own will, either because we cannot respond to available reasons or we are subject to manipulation of some kind. I also consider worries that our will is ultimately determined by causal antecedents that we cannot control. I refer to this concern as "pessimism at the horizon." (See the diagram at the end of this chapter.)

2. Classical Compatibilism and Close-Range Pessimism

A number of Dennett's basic arguments to discredit the bugbears of incompatibilism are taken straight from the shelf of classical compatibilism as developed by empiricist thinkers from Hobbes and Hume to Schlick and Ayer. (Classical compatibilism still has distinguished defenders. See, for example, Davidson 1973.)[4] The classical arguments deal primarily with close-range pessimism. The position taken is that the traditional free will debate is a "pseudo-problem," the product of a series of conceptual or terminological confusions. The distinction that is fundamental to this position is that between caused and compelled action. According to this view, free actions are caused by our desires or willings. In contrast to this, unfree actions are brought about by "external" causes, independent of the agent's desires or will. Under these circumstances, the agent is forced or compelled and therefore not responsible for the action. In this way, the classical compatibilist position maintains that free action is to be distinguished from unfree action not by the absence of causes, but rather by the type of causes at work.

Another aspect of the classical position is a diagnosis of the source of incompatibilist confusion on this subject. The "metaphysical" interpretation of the causal relation is supposed to imply that a cause somehow forces or compels its effect to occur. Since freedom is, properly understood, opposed to compulsion, this would imply that an action that is

---

4. "Hobbes, Locke, Hume, Moore, Schlick, Ayer, Stevenson, and a host of others have done what can be done, or ought ever to have been needed, to remove the confusions that can make determinism seem to frustrate freedom" (Davidson 1973.

caused must also be compelled, and so unfree. However, when the causal relation is properly understood in terms of a regular succession or constant conjunction of like objects, then all suggestion of causes forcing or compelling effects is removed. To say an action is caused by some antecedent willing by the agent is to say only that events of the first kind regularly follow events of the second kind—nothing more is involved.[5]

The classical compatibilist position also employs the distinctions introduced above to dismiss incompatibilist worries about fatalism. Incompatibilists argue that if determinism is true then all human beings are subject to fate, and any effort to alter or change the future is futile. According to classical compatibilism, this simply confuses two distinct issues.[6] Determinism is the thesis that everything that occurs, including our deliberations and decisions, are causally necessitated by antecedent conditions. Fatalism, by contrast, is the thesis that our deliberations and decisions are causally ineffective and make no difference to the course of events. Although there may be particular circumstances when we find that our efforts are futile ("local fatalism"), nothing about the thesis of determinism implies that this is the universal condition. On the contrary, as Dennett puts it, "deliberation is (in general) effective in a deterministic but nonfatalistic world" (Dennett 1984: 106).

Moral freedom, as the classical compatibilist understands it, involves being able to act according to the determination of our own will—that is, doing as we want to do or as we please (Hobbes 1962: 1, 66–68; Hume 1955: 95). On this account, therefore, freedom is a matter of freedom of action, the absence of any external impediments or obstacles. Accompanying this positive doctrine is the negative thesis that incompatibilist attempts to provide some account of free will, as distinct from free action, are radically mistaken and confused. More specifically, the notion of free will, it is claimed, is simply meaningless and absurd (Hobbes 1962: 1, 61–62). The only freedom that we need or want, according to this view, is to be able to guide our conduct by means of our own desires and willings. Any effort to go beyond this and explain moral freedom in terms

---

5. There are, in my view, significant problems with the efforts of (empiricist) compatibilists to defend their position on the foundations of a regularity theory of causation. For more on this, see Russell (1988).

6. "Fatalism says that my morrow is determined no matter how I struggle. This is of course a superstition. Determinism says that my morrow is determined through my struggle...." (Hobart 1934: 82). For criticism of this doctrine, see Russell (2000).

of control over our own will inevitably leads to either metaphysical obscurity or the absurdity of an infinite regress.

3. Reason, Self-Control, and Middle-Distance Pessimism

On the face of it, the classical compatibilist arguments deal effectively with close-range pessimist worries about being unable to regulate conduct through our own will. A determined world should not be assimilated to conditions of an invisible jail or being a puppet, since we can still distinguish circumstances where we act according to our will from those in which we do not.

These observations and reflections, however, fall far short of dealing with middle-distance pessimism. The most obvious difficulty facing any conception of moral freedom identified with the ability to act according to the determination of an agent's desires or willings is that such freedom is something that an animal, a child, or a mentally ill person might enjoy—all paradigmatic cases of individuals who lack moral freedom. Related to this point, some individuals, such as the kleptomaniac, appear to act according to compulsive desires. In cases of this kind, the agent's desires constitute *internal* obstacles to doing what the agent (reflectively) truly wants to do. Clearly, then, classical accounts of freedom understood simply as free action cannot draw the sorts of distinctions that we need to make in this sphere.[7]

These familiar incompatibilist objections to classical compatibilist accounts of freedom seem closely related to some of the worries raised by Dennett's "bogeymen." In the case of middle-distance pessimism, the concern is not that our will does not guide our behavior, but rather that we are unable to regulate our will according to reason or our own true values. Two of Dennett's examples speak directly to this problem—hypnotism and manipulation through neurological implants. The specific way that

---

7. The usual point of criticism of classical compatibilism is that freedom o faction does not imply freedom of will. Rogers Albritton, drawing on the same distinction, argues that an agent who is unable to act according to his own will (that is, faces "obstacles" of some kind) may nevertheless enjoy "perfect and unconditional" freedom of will (Albritton 1985). Indeed, Albritton is skeptical about the very possibility of unfree will. Even the addict or compulsive, he claims, lacks only strength of will, which is a different matter. However, Albritton does not discuss "bogeymen" cases of the kind that Dennett describes, and these, in my view, show that his unqualified skepticism concerning the possibility of unfree will is misplaced.

we interpret these cases, and the worries associated with them, will shape the way we judge the prospects of the "new compatibilism."

Dennett's interpretation of these cases, and the fears that they generate, center on two closely related issues. The first concerns the worry that we are not able to regulate our will in light of reasons that are available to us. The second is that our will is in some way being manipulated by another agent, and so our conduct is being indirectly controlled through control of our will. Under these circumstances our conduct reflects, not our own reasons and interests, but rather those of our manipulator. If Dennett can show that determinism has none of these unpleasant and disturbing implications then, he believes, he has discredited middle-distance pessimism.

The first step in his approach is to explain the nature of the relationship between our capacity for reason and the kind of freedom that is worth wanting. What we want, says Dennett, is to be the sort of creatures that are able to be "moved by reasons" (Dennett 1984: 25). Our reasons for acting are interpreted in terms of our fundamental interest in "self-preservation" and "self-replication." As finite beings, of course, our ability to represent all such reasons to ourselves is limited, but this does not mean that our sensitivity to relevant changes and variations in our environment is not significantly greater than that of other creatures. What is especially important to us, Dennett argues, is our ability not only to consider the direct objects of our desires, but also to reflect on our beliefs and desires themselves. This kind of reflective capacity enables us to question the evidential credentials of our beliefs, as well as the soundness and coherence of our desires. This constitutes, Dennett suggests, "a major advance in the cognitive arms race" (37). (This account of our reflective capacity is, of course, closely related to other "hierarchical" or "real self" theories of freedom, as advanced by, for instance, Frankfurt 1971 and Watson 1975.)

According to Dennett, the particular importance of this "power of reflexive monitoring" is that it helps us to deal with worries about manipulation by others. An agent who is able to examine and monitor his own beliefs and desires will detect "abnormalities" in their causation (Dennett 1984: 30). With this ability, an agent can unmask "sneaky manipulators" or "evil tricksters," which makes it difficult to trap him in disturbing situations of the kind suggested by middle-distance bogeymen. These abilities to self-monitor and escape the clutches of (evil) manipulators evolve and develop naturally and gradually—both in the individual and in the species. Nothing about the thesis of determinism suggests that we do not possess and exercise such abilities. What is crucial, however, is that we do not allow ourselves to be deceived by "intuition pumps" that conceal the complexity of our rational and reflexive powers. For the purposes of understanding human freedom, Dennett argues, *complexity matters* (12, 34, 37–38).

Central to clarifying the nature of freedom—and escaping our worries about bugbears—is recognizing that what we want or value is control. "We want to be *in control*," says Dennett, "and to control both ourselves and our destinies" (Dennett 1984: 51, Dennett's emphasis). Any individual who is a "controller" must have states that include desires about the states of the "controllee," which must in turn have a variety of states that it can be in (52). Dennett uses the example of controlling an airplane to illustrate this point. By means of anticipating or predicting future states of the airplane, we can keep control of it. There are limits to the range of things that we can do with the plane (that is, degrees of freedom with respect to it). Nevertheless, if we judge things correctly, we can retain control over it. When it comes to self-control, this is what distinguishes us from "mere puppets." We are not helpless in using our foreknowledge and powers of deliberation to "take steps to prevent, avoid, preempt, avert, harness or exploit" wanted or unwanted circumstances. This power of control and self-control is what we want and value. Like the pilot of a airplane, we want to leave ourselves a "margin for error"—lots of "elbow room"—so we can keep control of the situation and do the things that we want to do (62-63).[8] Self-knowledge is essential to maintain and expand this freedom. While not "absolute" or unconditional, human beings enjoy a considerable amount of this kind of control. One implication of this understanding of control is that there are "degrees of freedom" (53; and compare Williams 1986: 5).

This account of freedom, as explained by Dennett, clearly goes well beyond the simple definitions suggested by classical compatibilism. On this account, it is not meaningless or absurd to say how free agents are able to control and regulate their own desires and wills. Our powers of reflection enable us to monitor our beliefs and desires, and, when necessary, to detect and "disconnect" unwelcome manipulators. Accompanying this positive doctrine, there are important negative theses about the nature of human freedom. First, a freedom that implies an ability to make arbitrary or causeless decisions or choices is not worth wanting, and not what we actually care about (Dennett 1984: 2). Second, and relatedly, the kind

---

8. According to Dennett, our deliberations about our "options" require only "epistemic openness" (Dennett 1984: 122–23).

of freedom that Dennett has described does not presuppose that agents "could have done otherwise." This claim is particularly controversial, although it is consistent with Harry Frankfurt's well-known critique of the doctrine of "alternative possibilities" (Frankfurt 1969).

Dennett endorses Frankfurt's strategy but also argues that it is "insufficiently ambitious" (Dennett 1984: 132). In the first place, Dennett argues, a person may truly state that he could not do otherwise, but not in order to disown responsibility (Dennett 1984: 133-35). Beyond this, if such a condition had to be satisfied to establish responsibility—that is, the agent could have done otherwise under the exact same circumstances—we could never know whether the agent was really responsible, given the epistemological difficulties involved. Finally, not only is the "traditional metaphysical question unanswerable"; even if we knew the answer, it would be useless. We want to know whether the agent is likely to repeat similar kinds of (undesirable) conduct again—and to know this we do not need to know if she actually had "alternative possibilities" available to her under the specific circumstances of her action. The question that matters to us is whether or not a flawed character trait needs to be corrected (Dennett 1984: 137–38).

There is, according to Dennett, another insidious (middle-distance) bugbear that needs to be exorcised from the overactive incompatibilist imagination—one with, he believes, an especially powerful hold over us: the worry that if determinism is true then we are (somehow) "controlled by nature" or "controlled by the past" (Dennett 1984: 50, 61, 72). This way of presenting the pessimist's anxieties does not rely on any fictional or hypothetical case of (evil) hypnotists or neurosurgeons at work. On the contrary, the source of the anxiety seems much closer to traditional theological worries about God's omnipotence and omniscience undermining the possibility of human freedom. Clearly God is not conceived of as evil, but vis-à-vis our aspiration to be true self-controllers, God may be viewed as a kind of cosmic bogeyman. In the secularized/naturalized version, however, the role of God is played by "Nature" or the "Past," but the same general worry persists: while we appear to be self-controllers, control nevertheless slips away through the causal chains to an external and alien source. Self-control, therefore, is really an illusion.

Dennett's reply is that such worries rest on simple confusion about the nature of control. To be a *controller*, as we have noted, involves being an agent with desires that can drive the controllee into some preferred state or another. The controller must also receive "feedback signals" from the object if it is effectively to control it (Dennett 1984: 72). All talk of being controlled by

Nature or by the Past plainly involves *personification* (57, 72). Without this, these bugbears disappear—neither Nature nor the Past can properly be said to be "controllers" of any kind, whether determinism is true or not. On Dennett's account this (basic) confusion about the nature of control motivates much of the incompatibilist's pessimism and accompanying resistance to the thesis of determinism.[9]

This analysis of incompatibilist worries covers three issues that we should carefully separate: (1) Do human purposes and choices have determining causes that ultimately originate externally? (2) Is the ultimate source of our purposes and choices another intentional agent, who is in control of us? and (3) If there is such an agent in control of us, is the quality of its moral character good or evil? Pessimist anxieties, according to Dennett, depend largely on the last two issues. It is especially horrible to imagine ourselves under the control of another demonic or evil agent (for example, a "hideous hypnotist" and the like). Nevertheless, even a benevolent controller, looking out for our interests, leaves us with a sense of chill, since there remains the fear that some other agent is "really in control of US."[10] When we consider the first issue by itself, Dennett maintains, we have no reasonable basis for being troubled or disturbed by the thought that the ultimate origins of our deliberations and choices lie outside of us.

Dennett associates worries about the ultimate origin of our deliberations and choices with the aspiration to "absolute agenthood"—to be a perfect, Godlike self-creator (Dennett 1984: 83–85). It is his position that this aspiration is both impossible and unnecessary, since it is not needed for the kind of freedom that we care about (that is, "self-control" as he interprets it). The incompatibilist view is that, contrary to Dennett, worries about ultimacy or "absolutism" are essential to our conception of ourselves as true self-controllers, and libertarians maintain that this kind of freedom (which rules out determinism) is something that human beings are actually capable of. The distinct set of worries associated with ultimacy are

9. Kane comments on this aspect of Dennett's strategy as follows: "[Dennett] plays the old compatibilist tune in a new key. Just as classical compatibilists distinguish constraint from mere causation, he says we must distinguish control from mere determination" (Kane 1996a: 70).

10. Kane points out, for example, that children, as they reach maturity, "want an autonomy and dignity that they associate with the power to run their own lives," even though they "know that their parents are well-intentioned toward them" (Kane 1996a: 69).

the basis of "pessimism at the horizon." The critical question that faces us is whether Dennett is justified in dismissing these concerns at the horizon as both incoherent and unnecessary.

4. *Middle-Distance Refinements and Difficulties*

It is clear that Dennett's version of the new compatibilism involves a number of controversial claims. At this stage, however, I want to consider some interesting amendments and modifications that have been suggested in two essays by Paul Benson. In "Freedom and Value" Benson argues that free agency requires another "equally significant ability" apart from control, the ability "to appreciate values." More specifically, to attribute free agency correctly in a given context depends, according to Benson, "partly on the content of the agent's normative understanding, not just on the agent's having some valuational point of view or other" (Benson 1987: 472). Benson maintains "that obstacles to competent appreciation of the norms that apply to our actions are as much impediments to full freedom as are certain obstacles to the expression of our evaluative judgments in our will or certain obstacles to the realization of our will in our conduct" (472).

Benson points out that the omission that he is concerned with in compatibilist accounts of moral capacity (that is, normative competence) is addressed in Susan Wolf's essay "Asymmetrical Freedom" (Wolf 1980; and see also 1990), but he argues that what is missing from her account "is any discussion of why specifically *freedom* involves the competent appreciation of value" (Benson 1987: 474). To answer this question, we need to reflect on why the power of control is so important to us. We care about control, Benson suggests, because we care about the values by which our actions are assessed. This, in turn, reflects our "deep seated desire to be able to justify our conduct" (Benson 1987: 475; and compare Scanlon 1988: 170–72). Since the norms governing our actions are important to us, so too must be the ability to regulate our conduct by means of our evaluative judgments. Benson continues:

> [If] we care deeply about the value of our actions, then we want more than the power to translate our own value judgments into effectual willing. We also want to be able to appreciate the relevant values and arrive at competent appraisals of the alternative courses of action we face. Our concern for those values would be practically

impotent if we could not bring them competently to bear in our deliberations about what to do.

Benson 1987: 475

Benson uses these observations about the importance of normative competence to shed light on another feature of fully free action that is intimately connected with it: the "enduring belief that a completely free act is fully our own" (Benson 1987: 475).

Free acts are fully our own, Benson argues, "only insofar as they potentially afford appropriate bases for normative assessments of us in face of which we have no excuse" (Benson 1987: 482). When we lack any control over what we do (for example, cases of compulsion), the action provides no basis for "moral disclosure" and thus cannot be fully our own. Similarly, when agents lack normative competence, Benson argues, their conduct cannot reveal their moral values and so cannot disclose what they are like as persons in the relevant respect. The incapacity involved may be severe enough to render the individual wholly ignorant of normative standards and when and how they apply (as in the case of infants or severe mental illness). In other cases, the agent may adequately *appreciate* the pertinent values but cannot use their normative insights to *regulate* or guide their conduct (for example, older children, the severely deprived, and so on). (For a different compatibilist perspective on the issue of deprivation and blameworthiness, see Klein 1990: esp. ch. 4, sec. 3. For another view closer to Benson's, see Wallace 1994: 231–35.) The general point, in all such cases, is that actions coming from agents who lack normative competence cannot reveal their moral values and, as such, cannot be said to be "fully their own."[11]

In a more recent essay, "Free Agency and Self-Worth," Benson modifies his position. He argues, in this context, that the "normative-competence condition" is too strong, insofar as it is "content specific." That is, Benson now accepts the view that "any desires, plans, values, beliefs, etc., can be involved in the motivation of free action"—free agents must be able to "commit themselves to whatever motives they please" (Benson 1994: 653, 663). On the new account, Benson refuses "to restrict substantively persons' desires, values, life plans or normative capacities in the name of

---

11. It may be objected that no action that we condemn can be judged as fully the agent's own—since it manifests a failure of normative competence. Benson denies this implication on the ground that "we can sometimes freely do what we believe we should not" (Benson 1987: 480).

freedom" (665; compare Christman 1991: 356–59).[12] However, this more "permissive" position is not wholly "neutral" about content. The weaker condition that Benson now advances is a "self-worth condition." Free agents must "have a certain sense of their worthiness to act, or of their status as [competent] agents, which is not guaranteed by their abilities to act freely" (Benson 1994:650).

The condition of self-worth, Benson argues, helps us to understand a variety of cases where agents do not face any of the "standard impediments" to free agency but are nevertheless not fully free. Among the cases that he cites are the effects of severe shaming and slavery, conditions that under-mine a person's confidence in their own competence as an agent and, as such, constitute an assault on their sense of "moral dignity as persons." One particularly important aspect of this condition is that it draws our atten-tion to the "social dimension of free agency" (Benson 1994: 661). Related to this point, this condition of free agency also clarifies that the value of free agency lies in part with "our sense of being in a position to answer for [our] conduct," which is itself "partly constitutive of [our] sociality" (Benson 1994: 668). "A blow to our freedom," Benson argues, "can obstruct our ability to express through our conduct who we are, but it can also be a blow to our sense of who we are as social creatures" (Benson 1994: 668).[13]

Another important set of issues that arise from Dennett's discussion concern the question of how freedom relates, in more precise terms, to our capacity to be guided by reason. Recent work by John M. Fischer and Mark Ravizza (1998) provides an influential and illuminating discussion of this problem. Fischer and Ravizza make clear that the relationship between "rea-son-responsiveness," on one side, and freedom and responsibility on the other, is open to very different interpretations. On the account that they pro-vide, our capacity to respond to reasons depends on our (natural) "human deliberative mechanisms" (Fischer & Ravizza 1998: esp. 34-41). A free agent, on a "strong" interpretation, operates with a mechanism that is always recep-tive and responsive to available reasons. Under these circumstances, the agent's reasons, choices, and actions reliably "track value" or "the reasons

---

12. Christman argues that to hold "that freedom is a value only in relation to correct moral norms is to ignore the obvious non instrumental value of self-mastery itself" (Christman 1991: 358).

13. Benson's interesting observations on the social dimension of responsibility, and how it relates to issues of normative competence, lead to further questions about the rele-vance of emotional competence to moral agency. I discuss these matters in more detail in Russell 2004.

there are" in every case (Fischer and Ravizza 1998: 42; compare Nozick 1981: 317–62). Clearly, however, this condition is too demanding, since we would then be unable to hold an agent responsible when "tracking" reason fails. So what is required is a weaker theory that can accommodate cases where the (actual) mechanism fails, as well as cases where it succeeds.

Fischer and Ravizza employ considerable ingenuity trying to develop a "weaker" or "moderate" account that can deal with worries of this kind. A plausible account, which can serve the purposes of compatibilism, must describe "mechanisms" that can fail under some conditions, without being *systematically* unreliable (that is, too "weak"). We need, therefore, some principled way of distinguishing and identifying mechanisms that are sufficiently reliable in responding appropriately to reasons. When it comes to recognizing what reasons there are (that is, receptivity), there must be, Fischer and Ravizza argue, some appropriate *pattern* of reason-receptivity. That is to say, "the actual mechanism that issues in [the agent's] action must be at least '*regularly*' receptive to reasons" (Fischer and Ravizza 1998: 70–71). This avoids the worry that the mechanism in question could be reason-receptive in an isolated case but otherwise fail systematically. When it comes to choosing in accordance with the available reasons (that is, reactivity), however, Fischer and Ravizza argue that the (stronger) demand for regular reactivity or a pattern is not required. All that needs to be satisfied, they maintain, is the weak condition that in a given case the mechanism has been shown to be reactive to available reasons (Fischer and Ravizza 1998: 73–76).[14]

This account of "moderate reason-responsiveness" introduces an "asymmetry" between the receptivity and reactivity requirements. Fischer and Ravizza describe this as follows:

> In the case of receptivity to reasons, the agent ... must exhibit an understandable pattern of reason-recognition, in order to render it plausible that his mechanism has the "cognitive power" to recognize the actual incentive to do otherwise. In the case of reactivity to reasons, the agent ... must simply display *some* reactivity, in order to render it plausible that his mechanism has the "executive power"

---

14. There are, as Fischer and Ravizza point out, difficulties associated with "judgments about mechanism individuation" (Fischer and Ravizza 1998: 40n, 51–2n, 113, 216n; 251n). They offer, however, no "general way of specifying when two kinds of mechanism are the same" and rely, instead, on our "intuitive judgments" about such matters.

to react to the actual incentive to do otherwise. In both cases the pertinent power is a general capacity of the agent's mechanism, rather
than a particular ability of the agent (i.e., the agent's possession of
alternative possibilities—the freedom to choose and do otherwise).

Fischer and Ravizza 1998: 75, emphasis in original

Two (related) difficulties arise from these claims. The first problem is that
it is unclear what justifies the "asymmetry." If a "pattern" or "regularity"
is needed for receptivity, why is this not the case with reactivity? Clearly,
Fischer and Ravizza hold that strengthening the reactivity requirement, in
line with the receptivity requirement, would be too demanding, since we
do not want to excuse agents whose mechanism is regularly receptive and
has shown that it can react to reason. The controversial assumption that
this position rests upon is that "reactivity is all of a piece in the sense that
the mechanism can react to all incentives, if it can react to one" (Fischer
and Ravizza 1998: 73–74). It may be argued, however, that this same reasoning can be applied to the receptivity requirement, which would result
in a return to a "weak reason-responsive" view. On the face of it, therefore,
the asymmetry that Fischer and Ravizza introduce, in order to arrive at a
"moderate" position, seems to depend on ad hoc adjustments rather than
principle-driven considerations.

There is, I believe, an even more fundamental difficulty for a reason-
responsive view of the kind that Fischer and Ravizza seek to defend. The
objection may be raised that it is unclear how the mere possession of such
reason-responsive mechanisms or capacities can render agents sufficiently
in control, unless they also have control over how the capacity is actually
exercised within the particular conditions of action. On this view of things,
the responsible agent needs more than simply the general capacity for
reason-responsiveness (under some interpretation). What is also needed
is a capacity of exercise control, which means that the agent is able to
direct the specific way that her capacity for rational self-control moves her.

Any attempt to satisfy this demand is, of course, liable to lead us back
into the conundrums associated with "ultimacy" and "absolute agency"
(as discussed later in this chapter). While it may well be that exercise
control is a demand that can never be satisfied, it will not suffice for the
compatibilist to argue this point since the "moral skeptic" or "hard determinist" may agree about this. The point that the compatibilist needs to
establish is that exercise control is *unnecessary* for responsibility, and that
the mere possession of powers of rational self-control will suffice. (For an

interesting, although I think unsuccessful, attempt to make this case, see Wallace 1994: 180–93; and 161–62, 201–14.)

The difficulties that we have been considering relate primarily to the possibility that reason-responsive mechanisms may sometimes fail to respond appropriately to available reasons, without excusing the agent. There are, nevertheless, also difficulties associated with "strong" mechanisms that cannot fail (that is, always "track value"). In cases of this kind, since the agent is guided flawlessly by reason and enjoys perfect practical reason, she may be viewed as perfectly free. This view, however, does not entirely square with all our intuitions on this subject. More specifically, it may be argued that an agent who is *naturally* governed by (moral) reason, and so does what is required of her *effortlessly*, does not deserve moral praise. Moral praise should be reserved for those who must "struggle" to be good and do the right thing. Certainly, this claim captures the spirit of important strands of neo-Kantian incompatibilism (Campbell 1951: 130–33). However, some compatibilists, such as Martha Klein, embrace this view and have made it an essential element of a compatibilist approach to moral responsibility (Klein 1990: 167–71; compare Wolf 1990: 138–42).[15]

The general point that these observations bring to light is that reflection on both the success and failure of reason-responsive mechanisms present compatibilism with difficulties, and the relationship between rationality and freedom is by no means straightforward. Dennett's tendency to present incompatibilist concerns as based on confusion and exaggerated worries of various kinds leads him to underestimate the (genuine) difficulties and obscurities involved in articulating a plausible compatibilism as it relates to middle-distance issues.[16]

Nevertheless, while significant "gaps" in Dennett's compatibilist position are apparent, it is evident that he succeeds in outlining how compatibilists can deal with middle-distance worries about self-control, as they relate to questions of rationality and manipulation. Moreover, as Dennett's

---

15. It may be argued that our interest in "moral effort" is closely connected with the question of how an agent actually exercises her rational capacities (that is, how she uses "exercise control"). The exact nature of this relationship is, however, open to a number of different interpretations.

16. Dennett claims that in the process of moral development "everyone comes out more or less in the same league" —unless they are "singled out as defective" (Dennett 1984: 96). According to this view, normal adults are all "gifted with powers of deliberation" and "self-control" and at this threshold can be treated as (fully) free and responsible agents (98). However, as indicated, this view leaves large problems unaddressed.

analysis of the "problem cases" suggests, these two categories are intimately connected, since cases of manipulation can be understood as "problematic" precisely because they involve a break-down in the agent's sensitivity to reasons. (See also Wallace 1994: 175–77, for a related account of how such "problem cases" can be interpreted in terms of a breakdown of rational self-control.) Dennett's strategy is to argue that our (natural) complexity, not indeterminism, provides us with the ability to be sensitive to available reasons and to guide our conduct on this basis. The same general ability gives us powers of "self-monitoring" that enable us to detect and escape from (threatening) manipulators. These incompatibilist bogeymen, therefore, need not frighten us anymore.

5. Ultimacy and Pessimism at the Horizon

Middle-distance pessimism, as we have seen, is generated by worries associated with intuition pumps and bogeymen that imply that we are somehow unable to regulate our will according to reason and what we reflectively care about. This is why we find (hypothetical) cases of manipulation disturbing: we want our will to respond to reason and we do not want another agent to control our will (in service of alien interests or reasons). Dennett maintains that in order to avoid these worries we do not need to be "absolute agents" capable of self-creation *ex nihilo*. More specifically, it is a false dilemma to suggest that either we are "a completely self-made self, one hundred per cent responsible for its own character" or we are "mere dominoes" in the causal chain (Dennett 1984: 10a, 156–57). All that we want, says Dennett, is "to be as immune as possible from manipulation and dirty tricks and as sensitive as possible to harbingers of future vicissitudes that might cause us to alter course in the right ways—so that we can face the world with as much elbow room (as large a margin for error and as little relevant uncertainty) as we can get" (Dennett 1984: 72–73).

Dennett refers to a number of philosophers who have presented objections that are supposed to show that our worries about determinism extend to issues on the horizon (Dennett 1984: 33, 75, 83–84). He cites, for example, A. J. Ayer's description of "implanted" desires and beliefs (Ayer 1954: 9); Paul Edwards's observation that if determinism is true then even our efforts at self-creation must be "the result of factors that are not of [our] making" (Edwards 1958: 121); and Thomas Nagel's worries about "luck" as it concerns even "the stripped-down acts of the will itself" (Nagel 1979: 183). Each of these critics raises variations on the problem of ultimacy. For the purpose of this essay, however, I turn to Martha Klein's particular account of this problem.

Although Klein defends a ("partial") compatibilist position, she maintains, nevertheless, that our ordinary moral intuitions support certain incompatibilist claims (Klein 1990: 3 and ch. 4).[17] More specifically, according to Klein, we generally accept "that one of the things which disqualifies an agent from blameworthiness is his not having been responsible for the causes of his decisions or choices" (51). This conviction commits us, she says, to a "U-condition" for agent accountability: the condition that "agents should be ultimately responsible for their morally relevant decisions or choices—"ultimately" in the sense that nothing for which they are not responsible should be the source of their decisions or choices" (51).[18] Klein's interpretation of the basic rationale behind the U-condition is that if agents' acts are caused by factors for which they are not responsible, it is not obvious how they can be responsible for acting as a result of those factors (50). (This way of interpreting the U-condition and its significance is open to revision. See, in particular, Kane 1996a: esp. chs. 3 and 5; and also the essays by Kane and Galen Strawson in Kane 2002, chs. 18 and 19.)

In support of the U-condition, Klein cites a number of "problem cases" that closely resemble Dennett's "bogeymen" examples (Klein 1990: 70–75, 89–90). These include victims of brain tumors, implantations, brainwashing, and hypnosis. The feature these cases share, Klein maintains, is that in each the agent's decisions can be traced to causes for which he is not responsible, and so he ought not to be blamed (70). The example of the brain tumor is especially important to Klein's case for the U-condition, because it highlights the point that the real source of concern is not the "implantation" of desires and beliefs by others, but rather that the agent is not the true source or origin of his own motivations, since "he did not choose (to have) these states of mind" (73).[19]

---

17. See esp. Klein (1990: ch. 7), for the details of her effort to (partially) reconcile compatibilist and incompatibilist principles.

18. One of Klein's particular concerns is to argue that the U-condition is distinct from incompatibilist worries about "could have done otherwise" (Klein 1990: ch. 2). I will not discuss this aspect of her position.

19. Classical compatibilists, of course, insist that worries about the source of our moral qualities are misplaced, as this does not change the value of the qualities themselves. See, for example, Hobart (1934: 84): "It is the stuff certain people are made of that commands our admiration and affection. Where it came from is another question. . . . Its origin cannot take away its value, and it is its value we are recognizing when we praise."

Klein extends this reasoning and applies it "to the relatively pedestrian and non-threatening-sounding causes of genetic endowment and environment." The U-condition theorist reasons, says Klein, that since the agent "is no more responsible for his genetic endowment and upbringing than he is for the designs of a malevolent demon or brainwasher," it follows that he "is no more responsible for a personality which (perhaps) depends on his brain in a normal state, than he is for the personality change attributable to the brain tumour" (Klein 1990: 75). From the perspective of the U-condition advocate, unless this condition is met, it will simply be a "matter of luck" whether or not an agent's will is governed by "good" or "bad" desires (Klein 1990: 165-66). Under these circumstances it would be *unfair* to impose unpleasant treatment such as blame and punishment on an agent who is the (undeserving) "victim" of bad desires.

Dennett's initial line of reply to these worries is that his observations on middle-distance pessimism, and the bogeymen that it conjures up, discredit Klein's concerns about "ultimacy" or "absolute agency." Take, for example, worries that we may have about "implantation" of desires and beliefs. According to Dennett, so long as the agent possesses the relevant degree of "complexity" to be capable of self-monitoring, then she will be able (eventually) to unmask "the process of conditioning" (Dennett 1984: 33–34). Of course, if this capacity is destroyed or damaged by the conditioning process, then the agent is not a self-controller in the full sense of the term—but determinism itself does not imply this. What is worrying about brain tumors is not fears of manipulation by others, nor that our thoughts and actions are caused, but rather that we may become insensitive to reasons and consequently act in irrational and unpredictable ways (compare Dennett 1984: 64–65). While this is frightening, there is no basis for supposing that determinism implies it. In sum, we do not need "absolute agency," says Dennett, to avoid the sorts of worries that Klein's "problem cases" present to us.

According to the U-condition theorist, this general line of reply entirely misses the point. It is not denied that agents may possess some relevant capacity to be "reason-responsive" and to revise and alter their character on the basis of reflection. We might well be able to distinguish agents of this kind from individuals who lack these capacities (as new compatibilism suggests). Nevertheless, all this only postpones the fundamental difficulty. While our beliefs and desires may be subject to self-monitoring activities of various kinds, it remains true that these activities are themselves conditioned by factors that are not of the agent's own making.[20] Reflection on this process, therefore, strips away our confidence that we are truly "self-creators" *even in the normal case*. For this belief to be sustained, we must presuppose some power to undertake "self-forming actions" that enable us to be the (ultimate) origin of our character and conduct.[21] The sorts of capacities that Dennett and other new compatibilists in his mould describe fall short of this, and so their strategy fails to relieve pessimistic worries at the horizon. Other lines of reply, however, are still available to Dennett. The first is to argue that many of these worries are motivated by confusion about "luck." It is simply a mistake, he claims, to suggest that individuals who are self-controllers of the kind that he has described are subject to "luck" because they fail the test of "absolute agenthood." These individuals are not "just lucky," he argues; they are "skilled" and "gifted" members of "the community of reason-givers and considerers" (Dennett 1984: 92-100). When we identify individuals with these abilities we do not—and should not—treat them as simply "lucky" or "unlucky." On the contrary, we provide them with reasons and treat them accordingly.

This response, I believe, fails to confront the real worries that the U-condition presents. Without ultimacy, two crucial modes of control are absent: (1) The actual "reason-responsive mechanisms" that we possess are *acquired* in ways over which we have no final control (in both the normal and abnormal case). The character of these mechanisms, however, plainly determines the kind of choices and decisions that we will actually make.[22] (2) Apart from worries about how we acquire our (given) reason-responsive capacities, we may also worry about our ability to control the way that these capacities are *exercised* in specific circumstances (as discussed earlier). If determinism prevails, then the way capacities for self-creation and self-monitoring are exercised in a given situation will ultimately be determined by factors the agent cannot control.[23] Dennett

---

20. This is, of course, a familiar objection to "hierarchical" models of free will, such as Frankfurt (1971). For further discussion of this and related points, see Fischer and Ravizza (1998) 25–33).

21. The terminology of "self-forming actions" is from Kane (1996a: esp. ch. 6). Klein is a skeptic about the (empirical) possibility of ultimate agency. Kane (1996a) is a sustained and sophisticated attempt to work out the details of a libertarian metaphysics of this kind.

22. For an interesting and important effort to deal with this general problem, see Fischer and Ravizza (1998: 230–36).

23. It is arguable that our basic concerns about the way we acquire our reason-responsive mechanisms can be reduced to worries about whether we control the actual exercise of

is clearly right to assert that this does not reduce us to the condition of a "domino" or "zombie" and so on, but it is still true that without ultimate or absolute agency of some kind we lack these vital modes of (self-) control. It may be argued, therefore, that Dennett is too complacent in face of these problems, and consequently his "considerable optimism" (Dennett 1984: 48) has the same pollyannaish appearance that plagues classical compatibilism.

Dennett has, nevertheless, more cards to play. Up to this point his methodology has been faithful to the aims of "descriptive metaphysics."[24] That is to say, his position has been that our everyday attitudes and practices associated with moral freedom and responsibility are not threatened by any (confused) pessimist worries at the horizon. This is consistent with Dennett's "ordinary language" effort to expose the "bugbears" and "bogeymen" for what they really are—artificial creations of professional philosophers in the Western tradition. However, when it comes to dealing directly with worries at the horizon as they relate to issues of responsibility, Dennett takes a sharp turn in the direction of "revisionary metaphysics."[25] The argument here is that worries about ultimacy may be motivated by a conception of *responsibility* that, although deeply rooted in the Western philosophical and theological tradition, is nevertheless hopelessly incoherent and implausible—and so ought to be jettisoned. What really sustains "absolutism," on this view, is an understanding of responsibility that is committed to a conception of "total, before-the-eyes-of-God Guilt" (Dennett 1984: 165–66; on related themes see also Bernard Williams 1986). An absolutist conception of *desert* of this kind takes issues of responsibility out of the relevant (human) practical contexts that should concern us and tries to place them on metaphysical foundations that are disconnected with these legitimate and intelligible concerns.

In opposition to the absolutist view, Dennett prefers a conception of responsibility that is thoroughly utilitarian and forward-looking, and he

---

these capacities in particular circumstances. Note, for example, that if we had (ultimate) control over how our reason-responsive mechanism is actually exercised in the context of specific conditions, there seems to be no reason to worry about how the general capacity was acquired (for example, even if it was implanted in some deviant manner).

24. The distinction between "descriptive" and "revisionary" metaphysics is introduced and explained in Strawson (1959).

25. "My conclusions are neither revolutionary nor pessimistic. They are only moderately revisionary: the common wisdom about our place in the universe is roughly right" (Dennett 1984: 19).

leans heavily on "engineering" metaphors when describing how this system operates (Dennett 1984: chs. 6, 7). Responsibility, he argues, should be understood in terms of "the rationale of punishment, "and its rationale is to support the criminal laws of society. That is to say, we punish individuals when we think they are "mentally competent" enough to be deterred or reformed by the threat or imposition of sanctions. All this is not only a highly "revisionary" approach; it also takes a (large) step back in the direction of classical compatibilism.

Although the utilitarian features of Dennett's position are very familiar, a more unusual and interesting aspect of his discussion draws attention to the question of how responsibility and character are related—a subject that is generally treated lightly in free will literature. The view that Dennett defends is that in the realm of responsibility, what really interests us is what an action reveals about the character of the agent. More specifically, what we want to know is what we can expect from the agent in the *future* (Dennett 1984: 137–38; compare Smart 1961: 300–305). Isolated actions may be "regrettable," but they are only of moral interest to us insofar as they suggest ways that we can "redesign" agents so they will avoid future "errors" (Dennett 1984: 139-44). The importance of action, on this view, is that it allows us to identify character flaws that can be corrected by means of some relevant sanctions. Actions that do not serve this purpose can be dismissed as "don't cares"—that is, as cases that it is "rational to ignore" (Dennett 1984: 141).

This view is plainly at odds with our ordinary moral assumption that agents are no less responsible for out-of-character action than for action that is in character. This certainly suggests that Dennett's "revisionism" is more radical than he acknowledges. Beyond this, the critic may also argue that, given that out-of-character action is still produced by the agent's own will, it is entirely reasonable to attribute such conduct to this agent, even if he is unlikely to repeat it in the future (compare Foot 1957: 105–6). Action that is produced through the agent's own will should not be treated the same way as action produced by another agent, or no (moral) agent at all.

The compatibilist can, of course, agree with Dennett that we ought to take the issue of responsibility for character more seriously, without endorsing his forward-looking, utilitarian perspective. Robert Audi has argued, for example, that agents can be held responsible for their character traits, but that this depends on the fact that their character is in some way generated or retained by more basic acts. According to Audi, "all (normative) responsibility traces to acts and ultimately to basic acts," (Audi 1991: 307) because a person cannot be responsible "for something over which one has no control" (312). We can be responsible for our traits of character, therefore, only because we have control over our actions, which in turn affects our acquisition or retention of traits (312–13). A view of this kind, Audi maintains, can account for responsibility for character, consistent with compatibilist commitments, but without utilitarian commitments of the kind that Dennett embraces (Audi 1991: 319).[26]

Although Dennett gives considerable attention to the question of control and "self-creation," he is not committed to Audi's view, that responsibility for character requires the agent to have control (either generative or retentive) over it. On the contrary, an agent's character could be "implanted" or "conditioned" in ways she could not control, and yet it may still be true that sanctions or moral engineering will be effective in altering or changing her future conduct in desirable ways. Clearly, then, Dennett's pragmatic, utilitarian approach severs any (assumed) link between control and responsibility for character.[27]

My analysis reveals a deep tension in Dennett's entire project in *Elbow Room*. On his account, the relevant authorities or powers in society can (and should) use the conditioning influence of rewards and sanctions to control the character of others. In this way, even though the individuals concerned may possess rational and reflective capacities, in a (deeper) sense they may be truly described as "selves-made-by-others." The irony in all this is that Dennett's pragmatic, engineering approach to responsibility allows real worries about manipulation and "conditioning" to resurface. (There is, indeed, something of the spirit of B. F. Skinner's *Walden Two* to be found in his views on this subject.) To this extent, the first part of Dennett's project, which aims to relieve us of pessimistic anxieties about manipulative "bogeymen," is undermined by the second, which defends a conception of responsibility that places heavy emphasis on the benefits of "social engineering." (A good discussion of why we should be troubled by circumstances of this kind is presented in Kane 1996a: 65–70, 201–4).

---

26. It is evident that worries about ultimacy return on the account of responsibility for character suggested by Audi. Given that we must be able to "trace" character traits to actions that the agent could control, it may be argued that these ("self-forming") actions must satisfy the U-condition. For a libertarian argument along these lines, see Kane (1996a: 38–40).

27. Dennett's views on this subject may be compared and contrasted with Hume's. Hume also holds that a person may be (morally) evaluated for character traits over which he has little or no control. Indeed, he takes the more radical view that this includes "natural abilities" (intelligence, imagination, and so on), understood as pleasurable or painful qualities of mind. For a discussion of Hume's views, see Russell (1995: ch. 9).

In a review of *Elbow Room*, Gary Watson suggests that Dennett's "treatment of responsibility is the least instructive part of the book," and that the weaknesses of his general position are well illustrated by P. F. Strawson in his important essay "Freedom and Resentment" (Watson 1986: 522; and compare Dworkin 1986: 424). A central theme of Strawson's essay is that compatibilists or "optimists" who emphasize only forward-looking, utilitarian considerations in their account of moral responsibility leave an important "gap" in their position. More specifically, according to Strawson, conditions of responsibility must be understood in terms of our natural disposition toward "reactive attitudes and feelings" or "moral sentiments." Such responses to the good or ill will that we detect in the conduct of our fellow human beings are an "essential part of moral life as we know it" (P. F. Strawson 1962: 23). To a limited extent, we can suppress these reactions in particular cases or circumstances: there is no possibility however, that we can *systematically* abandon or suspend our commitment to the whole "complicated web of attitudes and feelings."

These observations, Strawson argues, are highly significant for the free will debate because they reveal what is wrong with both (classical) compatibilist optimism, as well as incompatibilist pessimism. Pessimists are right in saying that a purely utilitarian approach to responsibility leaves out "something vital in our conception of these practices" (Strawson 1962: 23). It is a mistake, however, to conclude on this basis that what is required to fill this "lacuna" in the optimist account is some form of libertarian metaphysics that involves denying determinism (Strawson 1962: 23–25). Contrary to the pessimist, Strawson argues, no theoretical belief in the truth of determinism could lead us to abandon our commitment to the moral sentiments (Strawson 1962: 18: compare 10, 12). To suppose otherwise is "to over-intellectualize the facts" (Strawson 1962: 2, 3). When the role of moral sentiment is allowed its proper place in moral life, we can avoid both a crude utilitarian account of responsibility that is divorced from psychological reality, while at the same time avoiding the "panicky metaphysics" of libertarianism. Our sense of *desert* is founded, not on (incoherent) beliefs about undetermined conduct, but rather on the natural, emotional responses that are essential to human life as we know it.

A number of Strawson's followers have picked up on his "naturalistic" arguments and developed his twofold critique of utilitarian optimism, on one side, and of pessimistic worries at the horizon on the other side. (See Haji 2002 for further discussion of Strawsonian strategies.) Among these contributions to Strawsonian themes is the work of Kevin Magill, who advances arguments that are relevant to Dennett's "revisionary" views about responsibility. Magill maintains, in line with Strawson, that we must resist the temptation to provide a general "justification for punishment, desert and moral responsibility." The "impulse" to do this, he claims, is based on the (misguided) assumption that a utilitarian principle can be applied to a sphere where a distinct and independent retributive principle operates (that is, that the guilty should suffer). According to Magill, both the utilitarian and retributive principles are "foundational to our moral thought and practices," and so any attempt to justify one in terms of the other involves us in "a kind of category mistake" (Magill 2000: 193–94; compare Magill 1997: ch. 2 and Mackie 1985).[28]

Dennett, as we have already noted, dismisses worries about ultimacy on the ground that they depend on a traditional absolutist conception of responsibility (that is, "guilty-before-the-eyes-of-God") that is simply unintelligible and should be (moderately?) "revised" in favor of a pragmatic conception based on "moral engineering" by means of sanctions. Against this, Strawson and his followers (for instance, Magill) argue that if compatibilists paid more attention to the role of moral sentiments in this sphere they could provide a richer, nonutilitarian understanding of responsibility. To the extent that this approach remains closer to the original spirit of Dennett's descriptive project, it is more satisfying than the revisionary, pragmatic account of responsibility that Dennett defends. What is not so evident, however, is that the Strawsonian view succeeds in providing us with a sure and easy way of setting aside pessimist worries at the horizon.[29]

It may be argued by the incompatibilist, for example, that our moral sentiments must be targeted only on individuals who possess some relevant set of moral capacities, and that this includes a capacity for ultimate control. Agents who have no control over the specific reason-responsive

---

28. Magill does not claim, on this basis, that "there are no grounds for being troubled by the suffering caused by punishment and blame" (Magill 1997: 47). On the contrary, his point is that the "true problem" that we face is "a practical one about opposing strains within our moral framework and conflicting (nonmetaphysical) moral sentiments within ourselves" (49). Regarding this problem, he claims, "there can be no general resolution of the tension between the principle of well-being and the principle of desert" (52). Nevertheless, "if we keep in mind that it is what we care about, informed by our personal, moral and political feelings and sentiments, that generally informs whether we take the objective or the reactive attitudes, we will not be faced with a helpless dilemma every time we confront decisions about whether to blame or to understand" (52). On the subject of moral sentiment and retributivism see also Russell (1995: ch. 10).

29. For the details of this, see Russell (1992).

mechanisms that they have acquired, nor over how these mechanisms are actually exercised in particular circumstances, lack the kind of (ultimate) self-control that is required to sustain and support our moral sentiments. Human beings may possess reason-responsive mechanisms, and be (complex) self-controllers of the kind that Dennett and others have described, and yet still exercise these capacities in ways that stem ultimately from factors that they cannot control. In some sense, therefore, they have no final say about the moral quality of their own character and conduct.[30] It is not obvious, says the pessimist, that moral sentiments can be sustained when such considerations are pressed upon us.[31]

6. Pessimism and the Unbearable Limits of Finitude

In my view, the important and significant issues facing the new compatibilism of the kind advanced by Dennett lie primarily with problems of ultimacy at the horizon. The spatial metaphor of distance is helpful in this connection because it indicates that these horizon problems do not immediately present themselves to us in everyday moral life. Close-range and middle-distance issues differ in this respect. In our everyday moral dealings, we ask ourselves whether the conduct we are presented with is a product of the agent's own will and, if so, if the agent is a rationally competent (normal) adult, free from manipulation or coercive pressure. Concerns of this kind are part and parcel of ordinary moral life. Nothing about them is "artificial" or a peculiar product of the Western philosophical tradition.

The situation is not so straightforward at the horizon. Regarding worries about ultimacy, Dennett's general diagnosis of the free will problem seems more plausible. When action is produced by the agent's will, and the agent is clearly capable of rational self-control (that is, reason-responsive), further worries about the ultimate origin or source

---

30. There are a number of important complexities here that I cannot pursue. Suffice to note in passing, however, that this way of interpreting what is needed to satisfy ultimacy (that is, the forms of control missing from new compatibilist accounts) may set a standard that some suggested libertarian accounts of ultimacy still fail to meet.

31. An illuminating discussion of this problem is presented in Watson (1987); but compare McKenna (1998).

of the agent's will—in the absence of any worries about manipulation—seem remote from our usual concerns and interests. Worries of this kind seem likely to leave a typical moral audience unmoved. One reason why horizon concerns about ultimacy appear disconnected from ordinary moral life is that, unlike close and middle-distance issues, there is no obvious or decisive way to settle them. That is to say, when we raise questions about ultimacy, as distinct from issues of rationality and manipulation, there seems no way to *prove* that an agent was their ultimate source. The skeptic can always challenge such claims by arguing that any appearance of ultimate agency simply reflects our ignorance of the relevant causes at work. We become trapped, consequently, in issues and claims that can never be resolved. Beyond this, the skeptic is also likely to argue that it is not even clear what ultimacy *demands*—so how can we ever *verify* that it is satisfied in a given case? Clearly, general considerations of this kind lend credence to Dennett's claim that horizon problems are the artificial product of (overintellectualized) Western philosophy and theology.

There are, nevertheless, a number of reasons for rejecting this complacent attitude to horizon problems. First, worries of this kind—reaching beyond middle-distance problems of rationality and manipulation—emerge in legal contexts, where the problems are by no means the product of artificial philosophical reflection. On the contrary, lawyers and judges are plainly interested in evidence showing that a person accused of a crime had no control over factors that led to it.[32] Second, and relatedly, our understanding of the influence of genetic endowment and the environment on human conduct and character is constantly advancing, and this presses horizon issues on us with increasing force—to refuse to consider them seems mere evasion (compare Klein 1990: 75 and Greenspan 1993).

Most important, it will not do to argue, as Dennett and others have done, that because we are unable to provide a coherent account of how ultimate agency is possible, that we can therefore dismiss worries that agents

---

32. See, for example, Clarence Darrow's classic "hard determinist" defense of Leopold and Loeb (Darrow 1924). It is significant that Darrow did not argue that his clients did not understand what they were doing or lacked general powers of rational self-control. On the contrary, his defense is based largely on the (assumed) existence of causes of their character and conduct that were ultimately beyond their control. It is also significant, however, that he refers to several different "bogeymen," which tends to obscure the exact nature of his case.

have no final control over their character and conduct. On the contrary, it should be obvious that a convinced skeptic on the subject of "libertarian metaphysics" may draw thoroughly pessimistic conclusions from this (as in the views of the "moral skeptic" or the "hard determinist"). Arguing from the impossibility of ultimate agency to the conclusion that there is no basis for pessimism in the realms of freedom and responsibility is an egregious example of pollyannaism.

There are interesting structural similarities between pessimism as it relates to the free will problem and the question of human mortality. Consider, for example, Pascal's profoundly pessimistic description of the human condition in the following passage:

> Imagine a number of men in chains, all under sentence of death, some of whom are each day butchered in the sight of the others; those remaining see their own condition in that of their fellows, and looking at each other with grief and despair await their turn. This is the image of the human condition.

Pascal 1966: 165 n434

The conclusion that Pascal draws from this analogy is that "the only good thing in this life is the hope of another life" (157/#427). For our purposes, the interesting thing about this passage is that Pascal uses an "intuition pump" to justify extreme pessimism about the human condition. If there is no immortal soul and future state, he suggests, then human life is nothing better than a painful period during which we wait to be executed, along with everyone else.

The obvious reply to all this is that it grossly exaggerates and distorts the limits and miseries of human life. Pascal is guilty of the same sort of abuse of intuition pumps that Dennett objects to in the free will problem. However, while we may grant that Pascal's pessimism is *exaggerated*, it does not follow that all worries about human morality and finitude are without foundation. We may, for example, discredit Pascal's pessimism by pointing out (close and middle-distance) pleasures and sources of happiness that can be found within the span of human life. These show that, typically, our experience of human life does not resemble being chained up and waiting to be executed. At some point, however, those of us who are skeptical about the possibility of immortality must confront the reality of the limits of human existence—the duration of a human life is finite. Such reflections do not impose themselves on us in our everyday concerns, so we are not usually depressed or troubled by them. Nevertheless, to the extent that we have the occasion, opportunity, and temperament to think about such matters, most people will find them sobering or rather melancholy to contemplate.[33] The important point is that we may not share Pascal's extreme pessimism on this subject and yet still appreciate why these reflections on human mortality occasion pessimism of some kind. The reasonable position on this subject, therefore, seems to lie somewhere between Pascalian pessimism and pollyannaish optimism.

These observations on Pascal's pessimism shed light on both what is right and wrong in Dennett's attempt to discredit incompatibilist pessimism. The incompatibilist pessimism that Dennett has challenged is essentially Pascalian. It involves analogies and metaphors that are more misleading than illuminating. However, it does not follow from this that reflection on the limits of human agency is not disconcerting or unsettling. On the contrary, when we look beyond the close and middle-distance issues that are the focus of Dennett's attention, we must still confront horizon worries about ultimacy. Even if the worries here are not Pascalian, they provide no basis for pollyannaish optimism.[34]

What these observations show is that, regarding the free will problem, we must carefully identify the source and *quality* of our pessimism and note the way they are related. More specifically, it is obvious that the quality of our pessimism will vary with the (perceived) *source* of worry. For example, Dennett is surely right to say that if close-range worries were justified (for example, we are in chains), then this would be a "terrible" condition. Much the same is true of middle-distance worries, which would also be "awful." It is not evident, however, that worries at the horizon have this quality or license an extreme negative

---

33. "Neither the sun nor death can be looked at steadily" (LaRochfoucauld 1678: #26). Although we generally assume that people have some shared sensibility about such matters, variations of response can always be found. This need not imply, however, any kind of intellectual confusion about the relevant considerations or issues involved.

34. It may be argued, of course, that the only way to escape from pessimistic worries of this kind, is to embrace libertarian metaphysics, much as some maintain that the only way to escape pessimism about the finitude of human life is to embrace the doctrine of the immortality of the soul.

emotional response. In the first place, concerns of this kind will vary depending on how lucky/unlucky individuals are with respect to their character and conduct.[35] A person of admirable character may occasion no feeling that her condition is "terrible" or "frightening"—unless, of course, we confuse horizon issues with close and middle-distance pessimism. Even a person whose character and conduct is deplorable cannot be assimilated to the condition of a person who is manipulated or incapable of rational self-control. The sort of pessimism occasioned by a lack of ultimacy must be qualitatively different (that is, reflecting a difference in the source of our concern). An awareness of finitude and contingency, as it relates to the (assumed) impossibility of ultimate agency, licenses a more modest sense of being *disconcerted*, rather than any form of Pascalian despair.[36] In general, it is a mistake to assume that incompatibilist pessimism must take the form of an all-or-nothing, homogeneous, and extreme sense of despair at the thought of the implications of determinism. The alternatives available to both the pessimist and the optimist are surely more subtle and nuanced than this.[37]

---

35. Compare, for example, our sense of luck regarding the distribution of other qualities such as beauty or intelligence. It is not obvious that the beautiful or intelligent person will feel any sense of "despair" or "fear" when she contemplates her situation although the (unfortunate) ugly or stupid person may view things differently.

36. Although I believe that reflection on horizon issues of ultimacy generate a sense of disconcertment, my reason is not that it threatens, systematically, to discredit our moral sentiments. On the contrary, when we reflect on considerations about the finitude of human agency, the thought that presses upon us is that who we are, and what we are responsible for to other human beings, depends ultimately on factors that we cannot control. This sobering thought makes us aware of the (uncomfortable) gap between our aspiration to be self-made selves and the evidence that this is an illusion. Such problems concern the relationship between fate (understood in terms of the issue of origination) and responsibility. A plausible compatibilism, I maintain, must acknowledge the legitimacy of concerns about origination and accommodate them by allowing for the possibility that agents who are subject to fate may nevertheless be justifiably held responsible. On this see Russell (2000).

37. There is, of course, a considerable amount of room to be found between Pascalian pessimism and pollyannaish optimism in respect of the issues of determinism and origination. Other (divergent) positions of this general kind in the contemporary literature can be found in, for example Honderich (1993), Pereboom (1995), and Smilansky (2000), as well as Russell (2000). Smilansky's position, which involves the claim that illusion about libertarian free will is desirable and "morally necessary," is described in Smilansky 2000).

Free Will and Pessimism at the Horizon

Range	Scope of Concern
Close	*Freedom of Action*
	Is the agent's conduct regulated by his will?
	Are the agent's deliberations and choices futile?

↓

Range	Scope of Concern
Middle	*Rational Self-Control*
	Is the agent's will responsive to the available reasons and his true values?
	Is the agent subject to control or manipulation by others?

[*** The unstable boundary of ordinary moral life ... ***]

↓

Range	Scope of Concern
Horizon	*Ultimate Agency*
	Is the agent's character and will ultimately determined by factors that he does not control?
	Does the agent have a final say about the nature of his character and conduct?

↓

Range	Scope of Concern
Cosmic	*Self-Creation*
	Is the agent an absolute, unconditioned (Godlike) self-creator?

∞

BIBLIOGRAPHY

Albritton, Rogers. 1985. "Freedom of the Will and the Freedom of Action." Presidential Address. *Proceedings of the American Philosophical Association* 59: 239–51.

Audi, Robert. 1991. "Responsible Action and Virtuous Character." *Ethics* 101: 304–21.

Ayer, A. J. 1954. "Freedom and Necessity." In *Philosophical Essays*. New York: St. Martin's Press, 3–20.

Benson, Paul. 1987. "Freedom and Value." *Journal of Philosophy* 84: 465–87.

———. 1994. "Free Agency and Self-Worth." *Journal of Philosophy* 91: 650–68.

Berofsky, Bernard, ed. 1966. *Free Will and Determinism*. New York: Harper & Row.

Campbell, C. A. 1951. "Is Free Will a Pseudo-Problem?" *Mind* 60: 446–65. Reprinted in Berofsky, 1966, 112–35.

Christman, John. 1991. "Liberalism and Individual Positive Freedom." *Ethics* 101: 343–45.

Darrow, Clarence. 1924. "Freedom and Responsibility: Leopold and Loeb." In *Virtue and Vice in Everyday Life*, edited by C. H. Sommers. San Diego: Harcourt Brace Jovanovich, 319–26.

Davidson, Donald. 1973. "Freedom to Act." In Honderich, 1973, 67–86. Reprinted in Davidson, 1980.

———. 1980 *Essays on Actions and Events*. Oxford: Clarendon Press.

Dennett, Daniel. 1984. *Elbow Room*. Cambridge, MA: MIT Press.

Dworkin, Gerald. 1986. Review of *Elbow Room* by Daniel Dennett. *Ethics* 96: 423–25.

Edwards, Paul. 1958. "Hard and Soft Determinism." In Hook, 1958, 117–25.

Fischer, John Martin, and Mark Ravizza. 1998. *Responsibility and Control: A Theory of Moral Responsibility*. Cambridge: Cambridge University Press.

Foot, Philippa. 1957. "Free Will as Involving Determinism." *The Philosophical Review* 66: 439–50. Reprinted in Berofsky, 1966, 95–108.

Frankfurt, Harry. 1969. "Alternate Possibilities and Moral Responsibility." *Journal of Philosophy* 66: 829-39.

———. 1971. "Freedom of the Will and the Concept of a Person." *Journal of Philosophy* 68: 5–20.

Greenspan, Patricia. 1993. "Free Will and the Genome Project." *Philosophy and Public Affairs* 22: 31–43.

Haji, Ishtiyaque. 2002. "Compatibilist Views of Freedom and Responsibility." In Kane, 2002.

Hobart, R. E. 1934. "Free Will as Involving Determinism and Inconceivable without it." *Mind* 43: 1–27. Reprinted in Berokfsky, 1966, 63–95.

Hobbes, Thomas. 1962. *The English Works of Thomas Hobbes*. Vol. 5. Edited by W. Molesworth. London: Scientia Aalen. (First published in 1654.)

Honderich, Ted, ed. 1973. *Essays on Freedom of Action*. London: Routledge & Kegan Paul.

———. 1993. *How Free Are You?* Oxford: Oxford University Press.

Hook, Sidney, ed., 1958. *Determinism and Freedom in the Age of Modern Science.* New York: Collier-Macmillan.

Hume, David. 1955. *An Enquiry Concerning Human Understanding.* Edited by L. A. Selby-Bigge. Oxford: Clarendon Press. (First published in 1748.)

Kane, Robert. 1996a. *The Significance of Free Will.* Oxford: Oxford University Press.

———. 1996b. "Free Will, Responsibility and Will-Setting." *Philosophical Topics* 24:2: 67–90.

———, ed. 2002. *The Oxford Handbook of Free Will.* Oxford: Oxford University Press.

Klein, Martha. 1990. *Determinism, Blameworthiness and Deprivation.* Oxford: Oxford University Press.

LaRochfoucauld, Francois. 1959. *Maxims.* Translated by L. Tancock. Harmondsworth: Penguin. (First published in 1678.)

Mackie. J. L. 1985. "Morality and the Retributive Emotions." In *Persons and Values,* Vol. 2. Oxford: Clarendon Press, 117–34.

Magill, Kevin. 1997. *Experience and Freedom: Self-Determination Without Illusions.* London MacMillan.

———. 2000. "Blaming, Understanding and Justification." In T. Van den Beld, 2000, 183–97.

McKenna, Michael. 1998. "The Limits of Evil and the Role of Address." *Journal of Ethics* 2: 123–42.

Nagel, Thomas. 1979. "Moral Luck." In Nagel, *Mortal Questions.* Cambridge: Cambridge University Press, 24–38.

Nozick, Robert. 1981. *Philosophical Explanations.* Cambridge, MA: Harvard University Press.

Pascal, Blaise. 1966. *Pensées.* Translated by A. Krailsheimer. Harmondsworth: Penguin Books. (First published in 1670.)

Pereboom, Derk. 1995. "Determinism al Dente." *Nous* 29: 21–45.

Russell, Paul. 1988. "Causation, Compulsion and Compatibilism." *American Philosophical Quarterly* 25: 313–21.

———. 1992. "Strawson´s Way of Naturalizing Responsibility." *Ethics* 102: 287–302.

———. 1995. *Freedom and Moral Sentiment.* New York: Oxford University Press.

———. 2000. "Compatabilist–Fatalism." In van den Beld, 2000, 199–218.

———. 2004. "Responsibility and the Condition of Moral Sense." *Philosophical Topics* 32/1 & 2: 287–305.

Scanlon, Thomas, M. 1988. "The Significance of Choice." In the *Tanner Lectures on Human Values.* Ed. S. McMurrin. Cambridge: Cambridge University press, 151-216.

Schoeman, F., ed., 1987. *Responsibility, Character and Emotions.* Cambridge: Cambridge University Press.

Skinner, B. F. 1948. *Walden Two.* New York: Macmillan. Reprinted in 1962.

Smart, J. J. C. 1961. *Philosophy and Scientific Realism.* New York: Humanities Press.

Smilansky, Saul. 2000. *Free Will and Illusion*. Oxford: Clarendon Press.

Strawson, Peter F. 1962. "Freedom and Resentment." *Proceedings of the British Academy* 48: 1–25. Reprinted in Watson, 1982, 59–80.

———. 1959. *Individuals: an Essay in Descriptive Metaphysics*. London: Methuen.

Strawson, Galen. 2002. "The Bounds of Freedom." In Kane, 2002.

van den Beld, Ton, ed. 2000. *Moral Responsibility and Ontology*. Dordrecht: Kluwer.

Wallace, R. Jay. 1994. *Responsibility and the Moral Sentiments*. Cambridge, MA: Harvard University Press.

Watson, Gary, 1975. "Free Agency." In Watson, ed. 1982, 96-110.

———. ed. 1982. *Free Will*. Oxford: Oxford University Press.

———. 1986. Review of *Elbow Room* by Daniel Dennett. *Journal of Philosophy* 83: 517–22

———. 1987. "Responsibility and the Limits of Evil: Variations on a Strawsonian Theme." In Schoeman, 1987, 256–86.

Williams, Bernard. 1986. *How Free Does the Will Have to Be?* Reprinted in B. Williams, *Making Sense of Humanity: And Other Philosophical Papers*. Cambridge: Cambridge University Press, 1995.

Wolf, Susan. 1980. "Asymmetrical Freedom." *Journal of Philosophy* 77: 151–66

———. 1990. *Freedom* within *Reason*. Oxford: Oxford University Press.

12

*Free Will Pessimism**

> *The will is as free as it needs to be. That does not mean,*
> *as libertarians would take it, that it is able to meet all the*
> *demands of the morality system. . . . Nor does it mean that*
> *it is free enough to keep the morality system in adequate*
> *business, as reconcilers usually take it to mean. It means*
> *that if we are considering merely our freedom as agents . . .*
> *we have quite enough of it to lead a significant ethical life*
> *in truthful understanding of what it involves.*

BERNARD WILLIAMS[1]

THE IMMEDIATE AIM of this chapter is to articulate the essential features of an alternative compatibilist position, one that is responsive to sources of resistance to the compatibilist program based on considerations of fate and luck. The approach taken relies on distinguishing carefully between issues of skepticism and pessimism as they arise in this context. A compatibilism that is properly responsive to concerns about fate and luck is committed to what I describe as free will pessimism, which is to be distinguished from free will skepticism. Free will skepticism is the view that our vulnerability to conditions of fate and luck serve to discredit our view of ourselves as free and responsible agents. Free will pessimism rejects free

* This chapter has gone through multiple drafts and has been presented to a number of different audiences over a period of several years. This includes presentations at Leiden (2009), Budapest/CEU (2009), Oxford (2010), Arizona (2012), Delaware (2013), Montreal (2014), Chicago (2014), Aarhus/Danish Philosophical Association (2015), Gothenburg (2015), and NOWAR (2015). I am grateful to many individuals who were present on those occasions for their valuable comments and criticisms. Although I am not able to thank them all, I am especially grateful to John Fischer, Michael McKenna, Derk Pereboom, Jesse Prinz, Saul Smilansky, Galen Strawson, and Daniel Telech. (This is a slightly extended and modified version of the same chapter, as published in *Oxford Studies in Agency and Responsibility*. Vol. 4. Edited by David Shoemaker. Oxford University Press, 2017.)

1. Williams (1985b), 19.

will skepticism, since the basis of its pessimism rests with the assumption that we *are* free and responsible agents who are, nevertheless, subject to fate and luck in this aspect of our lives. According to free will pessimism, all the major parties and positions in the free will debate, including that of skepticism, are modes of evasion and distortion regarding our human predicament in respect of agency and moral life.

The argument of this chapter falls into three parts. In the first part it is argued that any plausible form of compatibilism must embrace and endorse free will pessimism. Compatibilism of this kind may be described as "critical compatibilism," in order to contrast and distinguish it from the more orthodox forms of (optimistic and complacent) compatibilism. In the second part of the chapter I offer an explanation of why it is that compatibilism has been so reluctant to embrace or accept critical compatibilism and the free will pessimism that it involves. The explanation provided turns largely on the role of what Bernard Williams has described as "the morality system," and its peculiar assumptions and aspirations. Finally, in the third and last part, I consider the general significance of these reflections and observations about critical compatibilism and free will pessimism and their implications for the free will problem itself. The conclusion I reach is that critical compatibilism and free will pessimism should not be understood as providing a solution to the free will problem but rather as a basis for rejecting the assumptions and aspirations that lie behind it—assumptions and aspirations that have been shared by all the major parties involved in this debate. What we have, according to the stance of free will pessimism, is not a (skeptical) *problem* waiting to be solved but a (troubling) human *predicament* that needs to be recognized and acknowledged.

I. *Metaphysical Attitudes and the Free Will Problem*

Before turning to the argument for critical compatibilism and free will pessimism, we need to consider the general structure of the free will problem and ask, in particular, what sort of "solution" are we looking for? On the face of it, the problem seems straightforward enough. We have an image of ourselves as active agents in the world who are, in some measure, in command and control of our own destinies and the trajectory of our lives. What we do and what we become is in some relevant way up to us and depends on our own deliberations and choices. It is on the basis of possessing powers and capacities of these general kinds that we take ourselves to be moral agents who may be held accountable for our conduct and character. Various skeptical challenges may be presented to undermine and discredit this self-image. The sorts of considerations that have been advanced include reflections about God, foreknowledge, and pre-destination; science and its implications as they concern deterministic laws of nature; and so on. The solution to the free will problem under this broad canopy would be to *defeat* the skeptical challenge and provide us with some form of "vindication" or "affirmation" with respect to our self-image as free and responsible agents in the world.

Interpreted this way, the skeptical/non-skeptical divide neatly maps onto what may be described as our "metaphysical attitudes" of optimism and pessimism. Something clearly analogous to this divide goes on with respect to the issues of the existence of God and the immortality of the soul, where the skeptical challenge is also closely associated with pessimistic worries about the human condition.[2] Viewed this way, these metaphysical concerns are not merely theoretical issues; indeed, the position that we take on such questions will shape our sense of the value and significance of human life itself. The issue of being disconcerted and disenchanted certainly looms before us under some forms of skeptical challenge. On this account, the relationship between our metaphysical attitudes and the parties involved in the free will dispute seems simple:

$$\text{Skepticism} \longrightarrow \text{Pessimism}$$
$$\text{Refutation of Skepticism} \longrightarrow \text{Optimism}$$

A particularly vivid example of this relationship is provided in the first chapter of Daniel Dennett's *Elbow Room*, an influential compatibilist work that sets about the task of discrediting the "gloomleaders" of skepticism and to vindicate the "optimistic" conclusion that free will is not an illusion.[3] On Dennett's analysis, almost all the worries associated with the free will problem involve "bugbears and "bogeymen" that have been generated by misleading "intuition pumps" employed by philosophers in the Western tradition—producing a set of groundless anxieties that require some readily available philosophical therapy for their relief.

---

2. Dennett (1984), ch. 1.

3. Dennett (1984), 169.

While libertarians and compatibilists, like Dennett, may disagree about how the skeptic can be defeated they are, nevertheless, agreed that this can be done and that this serves to secure a more optimistic view of human life.[4] However, as with the parallel cases concerning God and the immortality of the soul, not all philosophers accept that free will skepticism implies any significant or severe form of pessimism. An alternative strategy, therefore, is to defeat pessimism without refuting skepticism.[5] From this standpoint, an optimistic solution can found without following either the libertarian or compatibilist in their non-skeptical commitments. Finally, the traditional skeptic may be unpersuaded by all these strategies and insist not only that skepticism cannot be refuted, but also that this remains a basis for pessimism about the human predicament, an outlook which is indeed disillusioning and troubling because it discredits our self-image as free and responsible beings.[6] In general terms, this exhausts the various available views and strategies on free will as they relate to our metaphysical attitudes and their respective grounds. In what follows it will be argued that *all* the above positions and strategies are, in different ways, guilty of *evasion* about the real nature of the human predicament and seek a "solution to the free will problem" that precludes a truthful and accurate account of what our predicament involves. This argument will begin with an argument showing that a plausible compatibilism must take the form of *critical* compatibilism and endorse free will pessimism.

II. Compatibilism, Skepticism, and Pessimism

The best way to approach this issue is by way of considering Thomas Nagel's seminal contribution concerning the problem of "moral luck." Nagel's account of the problem of moral luck provides us with an especially powerful and pertinent understanding of the skeptical challenge in this

---

4. Kane (1996), 80.

5. See, e.g., Pereboom (2001), Pereboom (2007), Honderich (1993), and also Waller (2011). This outlook may be compared, by analogy, to the Epicurean attitude to skepticism about immortality—i.e., mortality it is not as depressing or disturbing as immortalists generally suppose.

6. Some philosophers have argued that accepting the truth of skepticism about freedom and moral responsibility would be so damaging and depressing that we should encourage the illusion that we are free and responsible agents. See Smilansky (2000). Similarly, philosophical resistance to the skeptical conclusion is often motivated by the thought that this would be a "painful conclusion to accept" [Taylor, (1959)].

sphere. The core problem in Nagel's discussion concerns the relationship between freedom and responsibility, where this is understood in terms of the relationship between control and moral evaluation. Intuitively, Nagel argues, people can only be reasonably held responsible or subject to moral evaluation for what they have control over. However, reflection on control suggests that "ultimately nothing or almost nothing about what a person does seems to be under his control."[7]This observation, Nagel goes on to argue, "threatens to erode most of the moral assessments we find it natural to make." We can categorize the various ways in which we find that control is eroded into the following four modes of moral luck.

(1) *Constitutive luck* concerns the kind of person that we are and what our moral character is like. This includes not only our dispositions of choice but also our inclinations, capacities, and temperament. To a considerable extent these matters of character and disposition do not depend on our own prior choices or decisions (i.e., for the most part we are not "self-made-selves"[8]).

(2) *Circumstantial luck* concerns the kinds of situations and choices that we face or encounter and must respond to. Obviously there is considerable variation in the sorts of challenges and difficulties that we may be presented with. Again, we have limited control over such factors even though they crucially influence the way in which we will be subject to moral evaluation and what we will actually be held responsible for.

(3) *Consequential luck* concerns how our actions and choices actually turn out, which includes upshots and results that may be entirely unintended and unforeseen. Nevertheless, the specific ways in which our actions and choices play out may greatly influence how we are evaluated and, indeed, whether we are praised or blamed.

(4) *Antecedent luck* concerns the final retreat to the agent's will as a potential source of pure, untainted control. Even here, however, we may still find that antecedent conditions influence the agent's will and, hence, in the final analysis, the agent's own will slips away from control and is vulnerable to external, alien factors.

When we consider all these various dimensions of moral luck and the limits of control we are in danger of arriving at the conclusion that, since

---

7. Nagel (1976), 176.

8. Dennett (1984), ch. 4.

nothing is properly and fully under the agent's control, there are no suitable foundations for moral evaluation or moral responsibility.

It is a notable merit of Nagel's analysis that he stops short of endorsing the skeptical conclusion. What he aims to do is to describe a problem that appears to be recalcitrant to *any* solution. Nagel is not so much concerned to generate a skeptical argument as to put his finger on the various but related ways in which *all* parties in the free will debate—including the skeptic—may be judged guilty of evasion.

(a) On the face of it, compatibilist accounts are especially vulnerable to Nagel's analysis. Although compatibilists "leave room for ordinary conditions of responsibility," they fail to "exclude the influence of a great deal that [a person] has not done."[9] That is to say, moral evaluations of conduct in these circumstances are *impure* or *tainted* because they leave scope for the influence of factors that the agent does not control (e.g., in relation to her circumstances, constitution, and so on).

(b) In contrast with compatibilism, libertarian accounts aim to secure a sharp, neat boundary between the active self, which decides what we do, and what is external and alien. But this (internal) self-image, Nagel argues, is eroded under reflection, whereby all that we are is consumed within the natural order of events—leading eventually to the disappearance of the active agent, who gets swallowed up in the causal flow of nature.

(c) Finally, despite the apparent slide into skepticism, Nagel firmly resists any easy solution of this kind because it is, as he describes our experience, impossible for us to entirely abandon or jettison our "internal" sense of self as a responsible agent, or to refrain from our tendency to extend this view of ourselves to others.[10]

According to Nagel's analysis, "solutions" in any of these directions fail to fully acknowledge that we are simultaneously pulled in *two opposing directions* that we cannot reconcile. The standard strategies that Nagel considers each try to collapse the problem by emphasizing one side of the dilemma rather than the other—but to do this is mere evasion rather than solution to the problem that we encounter.

---

9. Nagel (1976), 183.

10. Nagel (1976), 184–5

One feature of Nagel's analysis that deserves particular attention, and is especially relevant for understanding the approach taken by critical compatibilism, is what he takes to be the core requirement for any adequate attempt to preserve free and responsible agency. What is crucial, of this account, is that the active self—the free, responsible agent—must be *insulated* from the influence of fate and luck. Although Kantians and libertarians understand this general requirement in more specific terms relating to securing some form of sourcehood or ultimate agency this is, nevertheless, a requirement that *all* parties in the free will debate accept under some interpretation. It is, moreover, a key assumption that that does much to shape the entire "free will problem" and the debate that surrounds it. If this general requirement cannot be met, it is agreed by all parties, then our self-image as free, responsible agents will be compromised and will collapse.

The general requirement described above plays a key role in the core incompatibilist argument against all compatibilist strategies and proposals. Let us call this incompatibilist argument the *Basic Exclusion Argument* (BEA):

1. There is a set of conditions φ (under some contested interpretation) such that an agent is free and responsible for an action or set of actions when these conditions are satisfied.
2. There is another set of conditions β (under some contested interpretation) such that an agent's action or set of actions are subject to fate and luck when those conditions are satisfied.
*3. Any action (or set of actions) that satisfy φ cannot be such that it also satisfies β. That is to say, if an action X satisfies φ it cannot also be subject to β. <*Exclusion Premise (EP)*>
4. Any and all compatibilist interpretations of φ are such that they may be satisfied and still be subject to β (i.e., compatibilist conditions φ^* do not support or satisfy EP/ #3 above).
5. It follows that we must reject any and all compatibilist interpretations φ^*, as they are inadequate as judged by a standard that compatibilists do not and cannot reject (EP).

Libertarians believe that their own interpretations of conditions φ can satisfy EP and avoid the skeptical conclusion (although this requires the truth of indeterminism). Skeptics maintain that there is no available set of conditions φ that serve to satisfy EP and, hence, the skeptical conclusion goes through either way. In what follows I want to focus on the compatibilist response to BEA and the stance compatibilists take with respect to EP.

Proponents of BEA are entirely justified in claiming that compatibilists have consistently adhered to EP and aimed to satisfy it. What compatibilists have denied is premise #4, the claim that compatibilism fails to satisfy the standard set by EP (premise #3). Let us consider the classical compatibilist argument that is launched against premise #4, an argument aiming to show that agents who satisfy suitably interpreted compatibilist conditions (φ^*) are not subject to fate and luck (i.e., conditions β). The core feature of this argument is that the incompatibilist claim (premise #4) relies on a basic confusion between fatalism and determinism. More specifically, it is argued that if we properly interpret conditions β (i.e., β^*) then premise #4 is groundless. *Fatalism* is the doctrine that all our deliberations and actions are *causally ineffective* and make no difference to the course of events. Nothing about the thesis of determinism implies that this is the universal condition. Dennett provides a particularly vivid example of this contrast:

> Consider the man who has thrown himself off the Golden Gate Bridge and who thinks to himself as he plummets, 'I wonder if this is really such a good idea.' Deliberation has indeed become impotent for this man. . . . [11]

While conditions of "local fatalism" of this sort may occur, and deliberation and action may sometimes be futile, circumstances of this kind are "abnormal" in a deterministic world, where deliberation is generally effective. Let us call this "contributory fatalism," where this is understood to involve the *causal impotence* of the agent with respect to some outcome or upshot.

The critical compatibilism response to this line of argument, which aims at defending compatibilism and defeating BEA, tracks incompatibilist concerns. More specifically, the critical compatibilist agrees with the incompatibilist that appealing to the distinction between determinism and contributory fatalism is a shallow and evasive understanding of incompatibilist concerns. The relevant issue is not about the causal influence *of* the agent but rather the causal influences *on* the agent. On the assumption of

---

11. Dennett (1984), 104–05, 129.

determinism, however complex the mechanisms or capacities involved, the ultimate source or origin of conduct and character is external to the agent and not within the agent's control or influence. Fatalistic concerns of this kind, which we may term "origination fatalism," cannot simply be set aside or ignored on the basis of considerations relating to contributory fatalism.

What these observations reveal is that, within the structure of compatibilist commitments, whatever specific form they may take, we inevitably encounter *limits* to control and the way it is actually exercised and occasioned. Neither second-order (hierarchical) capacities nor reason-responsive abilities will enable us to evade this implication.[12] What this reveals is the fact of our finitude and contingencies—these being circumstances under which all human agents inescapably must operate. While libertarians may aspire to escape limitations of this kind (e.g., by postulating "unconditioned conditions," "contra-causal freedom," or similarly motivated forms of metaphysical apparatus of this general kind), compatibilists reject all such aspirations as illusory. Having said this, compatibilists are in no position to refuse to acknowledge the force of fatalistic concern with respect to origination issues.[13] It is at this juncture where critical compatibilists diverge from their complacent (optimistic) compatibilist brethren. At the same time, critical compatibilists also diverge from incompatibilists—libertarians and skeptics alike—in rejecting the view that considerations of this kind, relating to origination and the limits of control, license skepticism about freedom and moral responsibility. The capacities described by compatibilists (i.e. as identified by φ^*—reason-responsiveness, etc.) are, they maintain, robust and substantial enough to serve as a secure foundation for our attitudes and practices associated with moral responsibility.

At this point, the incompatibilist is sure to raise the following objection. While critical compatibilists are correct in acknowledging the force of fatalistic concern relating to origination and the limits of control, as generated on compatibilist models, the attempt to separate issues of fate and responsibility in the manner proposed cannot be acceptable. More specifically, for reasons highlighted in Nagel's discussion, the presence of conditions of origination fate bring with them worries about moral luck;

---

12. Russell (2002), 233–42; and also Russell (2000).

13. Whether we attach the label of "fate" to this concern is merely a verbal matter—the substantial concern or issue remains with us.

that is, worries relating to agents being subject to moral evaluation in ways that are sensitive to factors that they do not control. This remains the core incompatibilist objection to the compatibilist project and concessions about fate do not address or settle *this* difference. Granted that it is intuitively unjust to hold agents responsible for aspects of their conduct and character that they do not control (as per the exclusion premise), conditions of freedom and responsibility cannot be sustained in circumstances where an agent is subject to fate and luck along the lines described. From this perspective, fate and luck come together, and where such conditions hold, free and responsible agency is eroded into nothing.

The usual compatibilist reply to this, as found prominently in Dennett's *Elbow Room*, is to try to deflate the luck objection. It is Dennett's basic contention, consistent with much contemporary compatibilist thinking, that human agents are "not just lucky," we are "skilled self-controllers"—this being a theme that Dennett devotes much of his book to.[14] Once again, this general line of reply seems not to engage with the real force or basis of incompatibilist concern. Incompatibilists recognize, of course, that compatibilist accounts of self-control and reason-responsiveness do not leave us "merely lucky" or unskilled, unable to enhance our abilities and talents. The point is, rather, that the specific capacities we may have, the way we actually exercise them, and the occasions we are provided for employing them, all depend, given deterministic assumptions, on external factors and conditions that no agent ultimately has control over. In other words, from an incompatibilist point of view, even on the most generous and robust interpretation of compatibilist powers of rational self-control, we still face limits of control over: (1) the *acquisition* of the relevant capacities involved; (2) the way these capacities are actually *exercised* in given circumstances; and (3) the *occasions* in which these capacities must be employed or exercised (i.e., the sorts of moral challenges we may face or be presented with). In all these cases, what we do and will be held accountable for depends on these external or alien factors. From this perspective, moral life becomes hopelessly vulnerable to luck or the limits of control, which is not permitted by the exclusion thesis and is unacceptable to all those who endorse it. Interpreted this way, the incompatibilist assessment of critical compatibilism is that it is an inherently *unstable* effort to respond to incompatibilist concerns about fate and luck, since any effort to acknowledge and

---

14. Dennett (1984), 94.

accommodate those concerns, along the lines proposed, must discredit the compatibilist component of its commitments. More specifically, the attempt made by critical compatibilists to acknowledge and accommodate these concerns relating to fate and luck plainly violate EP (premise #3), which has hitherto been accepted by *all* parties in the debate.

It should be evident that, whatever the merits of the incompatibilist rejoinder described above, the critical compatibilist reply to BEA is very different to that pursued by orthodox compatibilism. Critical compatibilists accept premise #4—they *agree* that compatibilist conditions φ^* may be fully satisfied and the agent or actions concerned still subject to relevant forms of fatalism and luck. Critical compatibilists deny, nevertheless, the skeptical conclusion because they deny EP or premise #3 (contrary to their orthodox brethren). It is the burden of the argument, so far, that a sensible, credible compatibilism is constrained by the nature and character of its own commitments to take the form of *critical* compatibilism and thus must deny EP. Failing this, compatibilism is plainly guilty of evasion and superficiality on the matters of fate and luck, just as its incompatibilist critics have suggested.

Clearly, then, the point that needs emphasis for our present purposes, is that *any plausible* form of compatibilism must recognize and acknowledge the influence of fate and luck on the manner and context in which our capacities of rational self-control operate. In consequence of this, it must reject the EP and allow that conditions of free and responsible agency may coincide with the presence of conditions of fate and luck, understood in terms of external factors beyond our control that directly influence how our capacity of self-control is actually exercised. Nagel describes circumstances of this kind in these terms:

> A person can be morally responsible only for what he does: but what he does results from a great deal that he does not do; therefore, he is not morally responsible for what he is and is not morally responsible for.[15]

For Nagel, embracing this outlook would leave us "morally at the mercy of fate" and so must be rejected. My argument, so far, has been that this is exactly what any plausible compatibilism must commit us to, consistent

---

15. Nagel (1976), 182.

with agents possessing and exercising (robust) capacities for rational self-control.

There is another important feature of critical compatibilism that flows from the rejection of EP that needs further, independent articulation and description. This feature concerns the metaphysical attitudes that this stance naturally licenses or occasions. In circumstances where EP is not satisfied, we have (deep) reasons for being "troubled" or "disconcerted" by our predicament as this relates to human ethical life and moral agency. Even if we are "fortunate" in the particular ethical trajectory our lives may take, there is no basis (as incompatibilists rightly insist) for an easy optimism when fate and luck intrude into our ethical lives and the way we may exercise of our moral agency. These observations and reflections may and should occasion a sense of "disenchantment" about our predicament, and to this extent this will license and occasion a significant sense of pessimism (on analogy with related metaphysical issues and the attitudes that they may occasion). However, the crucial point in relation to critical compatibilism is that a pessimism of this nature is not rooted or grounded in skepticism about free will and moral responsibility. On the contrary, it presupposes that we *reject* any skepticism of this kind, since the form of pessimism that is occasioned depends on viewing ourselves and others as agents who are free and responsible but, nevertheless, subject to fate and luck in the exercise and operation of our moral capacities. Let us call this stance or metaphysical attitude *free will pessimism*. I will return in the next part of this chapter to say more about the nature and grounds of free will pessimism. For now, however, suffice it to note that even if we reject compatibilism (e.g., because we retain a commitment to EP, as incompatibilists certainly will do) it is still crucial to recognize the significance of these findings both as they relate to critical compatibilism and the free will pessimism that flows from it.

III. Compatibilism and "The Morality System"

The question I now want to turn to is why have *compatibilists* been so reluctant to embrace critical compatibilism and free will pessimism? Incompatibilists maintain that compatibilists conditions φ^* are such that they do not exclude conditions β. Whereas orthodox compatibilists attempt to refute this premise (#4), critical compatibilists maintain that compatibilists should accept or recognize the truth of premise #4 and should instead reject EP (#3). What is it about EP that orthodox compatibilists find so difficult to abandon? There are, I suggest, two considerations that run deep in orthodox compatibilist thinking that account for this resistance to jettisoning EP. The first concerns the relation between the exclusion premise and "the morality system" and the second, related to the first, concerns the question of optimism.

(1) The exclusion premise may be understood as an essential feature of what Bernard Williams calls "the morality system."[16] The morality system, as Williams describes it, places particularly heavy emphasis on the (peculiar) concept of obligation, along with the closely concepts of blame and voluntariness. Moral responsibility, as "the morality system" understands it, is taken to be primarily a matter of rational agents voluntarily violating their obligations and, thereby, being liable to blame and retribution. A further closely related feature of the morality system is that it insists that moral responsibility, interpreted in these (narrow) terms, must somehow be capable of "transcending luck," providing a purity that only genuine (rational) agency of some kind makes possible.[17] Within this framework, the aspirations of libertarianism and its commitment to EP are entirely intelligible. Although orthodox compatibilists resist the aspirations of libertarians and its efforts to secure some form of absolute or ultimate agency, they remain committed to the particular conception of responsibility encouraged by the morality system and believe that it can be satisfied within compatibilist constraints.[18] In contrast with this, critical compatibilism involves *rejecting* core features of "the morality system," including its particular conception of moral responsibility (all this being something, if Williams is right, that we have good reason to do in any case). Although abandoning EP certainly makes it impossible to salvage the particular conception of freedom and responsibility promoted by the morality system, this is not to be confused with skepticism about freedom and responsibility *tout court*. On the contrary, while proponents of the morality

---

16. Williams (1985a), ch. 10.

17. Williams (1985a), 217: "The purity of morality itself represents a value. It expresses an ideal, presented by Kant, once again, in a form that is the most unqualified and one of the most moving: the ideal that human existence can be ultimately just. . . . The ideal of morality is a value, moral value, that transcends luck. It must therefore lie beyond any empirical determination. . . . This is in some way like a religious conception."

18. Wallace (1994), 39–40, 64–6.

system tend to present the situation this way, it is generally recognized, even by the proponents of the morality system themselves, that the narrow conception of moral responsibility constructed around the assumptions of the morality system is one that is both "local" (Western, modern) and is widely contested—including within our own modern, Western ethical community.[19]

(2) There is, as already mentioned, another consideration, closely related to the first, that is also very significant in this context. The aspiration to *optimism*, in particular to tell a comforting story about the human predicament in respect of moral agency, is one that runs deep in the morality system. This deep resistance to a disturbing or troubling view of human ethical life, one where the excise and operation of our moral and rational capacities depends in large measure on factors that are not controlled or governed by those same capacities and powers, is one that is not only shared by libertarians and compatibilists but that also motivates the skeptics. All of these parties, in their various ways, hold on to EP and the form of optimism that it insists on (i.e., that human ethical life does not function or operate in violation of the constraints that EP imposes upon it). Put in other terms, the form of optimism that EP insists on is one that rejects the very *possibility* of free will pessimism, much less accepts it as the *truth* about our human predicament. It is within this philosophical fabric, as encouraged by the forms of theorizing associated with the morality system, that (orthodox) compatibilist resistance to abandoning EP should be understood and appreciated. Clearly if we allow that free and responsible action may nevertheless be infused with conditions of fate and luck, we must also abandon any form of unqualified optimism—in particular, the hyper-optimism that compatibilists such as Dennett endeavour to project.[20]

Critical compatibilism endorses no form of easy, complacent or unmixed optimism on this subject. On the contrary, in giving *weight* to the limits of control, and circumstances of finitude and contingency in the sphere of

19. Wallace (1994), 39–40, 64–5; Galen Strawson (1994), 215. Both Wallace and Strawson accept that the ideals and aspirations of the morality system are not only modern and Western but also deeply bound up with the Judeo-Christian tradition. See also Dennett's remarks in Dennett (1984), 5, 156, 165, 166.

20. Dennett (1984): ". . . my conclusion is optimistic: free will is not an illusion, not even an irrepressible and life-enhancing illusion" (169). For criticism and doubts about Dennett's optimism see Russell (2002), 249–51.

human agency, critical compatibilism suggests *a particular understanding of pessimistic concern*—namely "free will pessimism" (as opposed to skepticism about freedom and responsibility). We might describe this stance as one as that recognizes or acknowledges that conditions of freedom and responsibility do not *elude* those of fate and luck but rather *confront* fate and luck and that these conditions are, indeed, meshed and entangled together. All theories and interpretations that deny this are, from this perspective, guilty of various modes of evasion that involve some effort of one kind or another to satisfy EP and the forms of optimism associated with it. This particular aspiration is something that critical compatibilists maintain we must abandon, not only because it generates insoluble philosophical perplexities but, more importantly, because it misrepresents the (difficult and troubling) *truth* about our circumstances as human agents.

One way to resist free will pessimism is to reject the suggestion that if we abandon EP then some form of pessimism must follows from this. Perhaps, critics may argue, no relevant metaphysical attitude of this (negative) kind needs to be generated by reflections of this nature. With respect to this matter a few general observations about the nature of the pessimism involved in free will pessimism are called for. (a) We can, as we have done, distinguish critical compatibilism from its orthodox counterpart simply with reference to the disagreement about EP (and how to respond to BEA). To this extent it may be argued that no specific affective or attitudinal element is *essential* to the core distinction between these two compatibilist stances as presented. (b) Moreover, we may also concede that whatever pessimistic features may naturally accompany the rejection of EP and the associated apparatus of the morality system, there is still much to *welcome* about this shift away from these commitments and aspirations (e.g., we are better off without pernicious and destructive forms of retributivism that are grounded in these views).[21] For this reason critical compatibilism may involve elements of *both* optimism and pessimism. There is no reason to suppose that the relevant metaphysical response here must be unmixed or uniform in nature—a finding that should not surprise us since the same is obviously true with respect to other, similar metaphysical issues and reflections (e.g., concerning the existence of God, immortality, and so on). (c) The *degree* of pessimistic affect may vary depending on both our historical and cultural circumstances. For those

---

21. This is a prominent theme in many optimistic skeptical views about moral responsibility. See, e.g., Pereboom (2001 and 2007); and also Waller (2011).

who find themselves deep inside the morality system and its assumptions and aspirations, the sense of being troubled and disturbed by the thought of abandoning EP may well be amplified in proportion to the depth of their existing set of commitments. We may allow, therefore, that the sense of pessimism is likely to recede or dissipate over time as *we* (moderns, Westerners) withdraw form the morality system. All these concessions are consistent with the claim that critical compatibilism still licenses a distinct form of pessimism.

We may be pressed further here and asked to say more about the character of free will pessimism and how it relates to the critical compatibilism and the rejection of EP. In describing any form of pessimism we need to make reference to two central features: the grounds or basis of the pessimism and the quality or affective aspects that this may involve or imply. We have already been careful to emphasize that the grounds of free will pessimism presuppose that skepticism about freedom and moral responsibility is mistaken. Plainly the particular source of pessimism must be traced back to the view that free and responsible agents are, nevertheless, subject to significant forms of fate and luck (contrary to the requirements of EP). In general, pessimism is called forth or occasioned when something that we value is threatened or discredited. In this case, the significant feature of our condition that is discredited and undermined concerns our (deep) assumption and hope that there is some sort of "harmony" between our ethical life and the order of the world.[22] It is, of course, a central theme of Williams' work to argue that the ancient Greeks, unlike *we* (Western) moderns, had no such expectations about the world and how it is related to human ethical life. The important point here is that the move away from the morality system is not *cost free*—whatever gains and advantages it may involve in other respects (including that of truthfulness).

Some similar and related observations are also in order with respect to the quality or affective aspect of free will pessimism. Pessimism may take various affective forms and degrees, ranging from intense despair and grief to a milder sense of being disconcerted or disenchanted with the state of things. There is, for example, Pascal's attitude to the supposition that there is no future state, which takes the form of an extreme and

---

22. See, for example Williams' observation that "skepticism about the freedom of morality from luck cannot leave the concept of morality where it was...." Williams (1976), 39. See also Williams (1985a), 53, 170; Williams (1985b), 19–20; and especially Williams (1993), 126, 158–67.

severe pessimism that we may describe as excessive and immoderate. At the same time, we may also regard the Epicurean response of complete equanimity in the face of death as being too shallow and lacking appropriate sensitivity to features of human life that should be recognized as troubling and difficult. It is within a matrix of this general kind that we should understand the stance of the free will pessimist. The response that is brought forth on the basis of reflections about our predicament as free and responsible agents who are, nevertheless, subject to conditions of fate and luck in the very exercise of our agency, is one that falls *between* the extreme of Pascalian despair and Epicurean calm and complacency. The right response, one that is duly sensitive to the features of our predicament, is that of a moderate but engaged sense of being disenchanted or disconcerted. Not only is orthodox compatibilism in this sense philosophically *evasive* with respect to the issues that it confronts, but also the philosophical evasions concerned manifest themselves in forms of affective *shallowness* or *superficiality*—a failure to care about (problematic) features of our predicament that are or should be significant to us.

It is arguable that the preceding analysis of the source and nature of orthodox compatibilist resistance to critical compatibilism and free will pessimism still fails to identify the core concern. More specifically, it may be argued that orthodox compatibilist resistance to critical compatibilism stands at no great distance from incompatibilist resistance to compatibilism in general. The relevant issue here has to do with EP and the force of BEA itself. Orthodox compatibilists reject BEA because they reject the claim that compatibilist conditions may be satisfied when EP is violated (i.e., they deny premise #4). Their unwillingness to reject EP is rooted in the concern that if EP is not satisfied, or at least respected, then *morality itself would be unfair*. It would be unfair to endorse and apply conditions of freedom and responsibility that leave agents vulnerable to fate and luck. The thought here is one that supports much of Nagel's entire analysis of the problem of moral luck and the associated fabric of the free will problem. If fate and luck are infused into the very exercise and operation of our moral capacities as agents then all moral evaluation is tainted and impure. Morality, as it were, requires fairness *all the way down*—and that is what EP, it is claimed, secures for us.[23]

---

23. Williams (1985a): 43, 73, 215–7. Related to this, Williams also emphasizes the way in which the morality system places particular emphasis on the importance of voluntariness and blame in this context.

Clearly critical compatibilism rejects this view of things and the assumptions and aspirations that must accompany it (and which lead on to the intractable nature of the free will problem itself). For critical compatibilism, which holds that satisfying EP is not a necessary condition of sustaining human freedom and moral responsibility, the relevant standard of fairness of the attitudes and practices associated with moral responsibility are provided and adequately secured by the satisfaction of the set of compatibilist conditions identified by φ^*. The issue of fairness is *internal* to that fabric, which is itself liable to be modified, amended and corrected over time.[24] Any demand for fairness beyond this—some mode of *absolute* fairness—is liable to simply collapse under its own weight and results, ironically, in skepticism. This, at least, is where critical compatibilists (must) stand on this issue. Insisting on these observations, as they relate to human ethical life, is not, however, one that secures or encourages any simple, unmixed form of optimism. On the contrary, when we consider the various possible ethical trajectories human lives may take— especially those that are ethically unfortunate and problematic—we are confronted with an awareness of our ethical fragility and vulnerability, consistent with conceiving of ourselves as free, responsible ethical agents.[25] The very fact that we are and should be troubled by reflections of this kind is evidence that there is something deeply wrong with the assumptions of the morality system and with EP in particular. It is only on the basis of an understanding and appreciation of (the possibility of) free will pessimism that we can make any adequate sense of our response to these cases and the particular way in which we find them disturbing (i.e., that we recognize that agents are both free and responsible and subject to conditions of fate and luck, contrary to EP). Much of the resistance to critical compatibilism that comes from within compatibilism itself may be

---

24. In relation to this see Russell (2008). See also P. F. Strawson's remarks noting that inside the web of reactive attitudes and feelings "there is endless room for modification, redirection, criticism, and justification" [Strawson (1962), 78].

25. One such troubling case that helps to illuminate free will pessimism, and highlights the way in which it contrasts with theories constructed around the demands of EP, is that of "Robert Harris" (who is discussed in some detail in Watson, 1987). Harris was a vicious murderer who suffered, as Watson explains, horrific childhood abuse that does much to explain how he became a vicious murderer. Whereas EP puts pressure on any analysis to resist the suggestion that Harris was both free and responsible *and* subject to fate and luck in the way he eventually exercised his moral agency, this is exactly how free will pessimism interprets cases of this kind (and goes on to draw more general conclusions about our human predicament on this basis).

accounted for as rooted in the discomfort that is felt once we acknowledge that EP does *not* govern human ethical life. This is, no doubt, a hard truth about our ethical lives that many—especially for those who occupy a position well inside the morality system—will find difficult to accept. Indeed, many will find free will pessimism to be harder to accept—and much more disturbing—than any form of free will skepticism, since skepticism, at least, provides the consolation of ensuring that free, responsible agents are not subject to fate and luck (as per EP). There is an important sense, therefore, in which free will pessimism may be found to be much more disturbing than any form of free will skepticism—and that is especially true, of course, for those who do not find skepticism disturbing in any case.

IV. Incompatibilist Evasions and Free Will Pessimism

It has been argued, so far, that a plausible compatibilism must take the form of critical compatibilism and embrace free will pessimism. It has also been argued that the best explanation for why compatibilists have hitherto been reluctant to accept (or even consider) this view is that compatibilists have generally remained committed to the assumptions and aspirations of the morality system, including EP, which is an essential feature of it. None of this, however, in itself, shows that we should accept critical compatibilism and acknowledge that free will pessimism is the truth about the human predicament as it concerns moral agency. On the contrary, incompatibilists may *welcome* the conclusions we have arrived at with respect to the implications of compatibilism. The reason for this is that incompatibilists will suppose that the argument advanced so far, concerning compatibilism and free will pessimism, serves not so much as an effective *defense* of a (modified or refined) compatibilism as a *reductio* of the whole compatibilist project. An approach of this kind, the incompatibilist may say, is not so much a case of "biting the bullet" as of shooting oneself in the head. Since critical compatibilism concedes that compatibilism implies free will pessimism and necessarily violates EP, the correct conclusion to draw from all this is that we should *reject compatibilism*.

The argument that follows continues from where BEA, and the above line of criticism, leaves off: namely, with the claim that we must reject compatibilism because it fails the standard of EP. The right place to begin, therefore, is with the alternatives that incompatibilism offers us. From the perspective of critical compatibilism, however, none of the familiar incompatibilist strategies can survive critical scrutiny. They fail, in particular, the very standard of EP that incompatibilists appeal to in framing BEA and are no less guilty of their own distinct forms of evasion (i.e., no less guilty than orthodox compatibilism). For our present purposes, which is to identify and present the core structure of the critical compatibilist argument leading to the conclusion that we should reject EP and endorse free will pessimism, what is required is, first, a reminder of the relevant reasons for rejecting incompatibilism and the various modes of evasion that this may involve, and, second, an interpretation of the implications of this for our overall understanding of the free will problem itself. Having explained in general terms why the retreat back to incompatibilism is not a viable or credible option, we face a clear choice between EP (and the intractable free will problem that it generates) and free will pessimism. We have every reason, I claim, to opt for free will pessimism. I will call the complete argument, extending beyond BEA, *The Extended Argument to Free Will Pessimism* (FWPA).

The structure of this argument, following on from BEA and leading to the conclusion that we should reject EP and embrace free will pessimism, takes this form:

BEA (#1– #5) . . .

6. If not compatibilism (i.e., because it fails EP, as identified by BEA), then incompatibilism.
7. If incompatibilism, then either libertarianism or skepticism.
8. If libertarianism, then either (a) agent-causal or (b) event-causal libertarianism.
9. Both agent-causal and event-causal forms of libertarianism are guilty of evasion with respect to the issues raised by EP. The first appeals to unintelligible or incoherent forms of ("panicky") metaphysics; and the second is vulnerable to modes of luck of the kind that are proscribed by EP.
10. Given that both compatibilism (BEA) and libertarianism fail (FWP, #6–9), skepticism must follow. Although skepticism does not aim to *satisfy* EP (in contrast with orthodox compatibilism and libertarianism), it still *respects* EP. Since EP cannot be satisfied—that is, there are *no* conditions φ that satisfy EP—a skeptical conclusion must follow (one that is generally taken to license its own form of pessimism).

11. Skepticism is either (a) global or (b) local. Local skepticism targets modes of responsibility that are specifically encouraged by "the morality system" and that aim to satisfy EP. Global skepticism maintains that there are *no* credible accounts of conditions φ on the ground that any acceptable account of conditions φ must satisfy EP (i.e., local skepticism and global skepticism are identical).

12. Local forms of skepticism are not a threat to free will pessimism or critical compatibilism, since it also endorses local skepticism of this kind (i.e., accepts and acknowledges that EP cannot be satisfied). Global forms of skepticism are a threat to free will pessimism and critical compatibilism since they endorse the claim that any acceptable account of conditions φ must satisfy EP, which rules out the very possibility of free will pessimism.

13. Global skepticism involves "bad faith" and is itself a form of evasion with respect to (the possibility of) free will pessimism. More specifically, global skepticism involves denying the significance of moral capacities and abilities that human beings evidently possess and exercise. Skeptics generally begin by advancing global claims and then retreat back to local skepticism, manifesting their own discomfort with the evasions of global skepticism.

14. When we apply EP, and aim to satisfy or simply respect its demands, we find that it generates a range of unacceptable and unconvincing forms of evasion.

15. The free will problem structured around BEA and EP is, as Nagel's original analysis suggests, *intractable*. The root source of this impasse rests with "the morality system" and its commitment to EP, which denies the very possibility of free will pessimism (and thus critical compatibilism).

16. We are faced with a fundamental choice between EP and free will pessimism. In light of the preceding analysis, we have every reason to reject EP and embrace free will pessimism.

Let us begin with the critique of incompatibilism (#6–13), starting with the objections to libertarianism (premise #8–9).

It is reasonably obvious that if we reject compatibilism because it fails EP then we must consider one or other of the incompatibilist alternatives, libertarianism or skepticism (as per premise #6). The former believes that there is some available account of conditions φ (i.e., libertarian conditions φ#) that satisfy the requirement of EP but that this depends on the falsity of determinism. The skeptic maintains that libertarian conditions φ# fail to satisfy EP, as do compatibilist conditions φ* and there are, therefore, no accounts of conditions φ that satisfy EP. The skeptic agrees, however, with both orthodox compatibilists and libertarians that EP must at least be *respected* and the skeptical conclusion thus follows (i.e., there are no acceptable, credible accounts of conditions φ). However, skeptics may themselves be charged with embracing strong and unqualified conclusions about the "impossibility" of freedom and responsibility that are not credible and ignore crucial features relating to our interpretation and experience of agency and moral life—something that constitutes its own distinct form of evasion.

To show that FWPA is entirely sound we would need to defend each of the premises relating to the challenges facing incompatibilism (#8–13). As I have indicated, there is no reason, in the present context, to repeat and rehearse all the relevant arguments and considerations in this context. It will suffice to provide a general overview of the core concerns and objections that serve to justify and support the premises concerned. Let us begin with the problems facing libertarianism. In order to satisfy EP, with a view to overcoming the limits of control in a way that provides for genuine ultimacy (and "self-creation"), libertarianism in its classical form introduced what even its most prominent exponents have described as an "odd" set of metaphysical commitments.[26] The constructive metaphysical foundations of this theory, beyond the requirement of indeterminism, rests with the suggestion that free and responsible agents have active powers "which some would attribute only to God: each of us, when we act, is a prime mover unmoved."[27] For this we require both a conception of a person or agent that is not merely a series of events and an extraordinary conception of causation, whereby an act is produced not by an event but rather by the agent (i.e., a substance with the requisite causal power to performs the action).[28]

The theory involved here is that of agent-causation and it has been extensively and effectively criticized by compatibilists of various stripes, from Hobbes to Strawson, on the ground that it relies on "obscure and panicky metaphysics."[29] More recently, it has been described by a

---

26. Taylor (1959), 310.

27. Chisholm (1964), 34.

28. Taylor (1959), 310; and Chisholm (1964), 30.

29. Strawson (1962), 80.

prominent contemporary compatibilist as requiring that morally responsible agents must enjoy some form of "total control," which is "a total fantasy—metaphysical megalomania, if anything is."[30] This familiar line of criticism does not come just from compatibilists. It is an assessment that is also shared by many incompatibilists, including some leading representatives of contemporary libertarianism.[31] It is argued by Robert Kane, for example, that agent-causation theories land libertarianism with what he calls the "Intelligibility Problem." Although Kane also aims to find an account of libertarianism that ensures that agents are "the ultimate sources" of their actions, in such a way that EP can be satisfied, this must be done, Kane suggests, in a way that "can be reconciled with modern scientific views of human beings."[32] Kane calls agent-causation theories "extra factor" strategies on the ground that they posit some "mysterious" additional metaphysical apparatus to deal with problems about indeterminism—which, Kane claims, they do not solve in any case.[33] For this reason, Kane suggests, we need to look elsewhere if we are to find a form of libertarianism that can avoid the "Intelligibility Problem" and the various problems associated with it.

In order to avoid the "obscure and panicky metaphysics" of agent-causation theories, Kane proposes a "softer" form of libertarianism, event-causal libertarianism.[34] Event-causal theories are "softer" because they rely only on the same set of science-friendly, metaphysical commitments that compatibilists appeal to—there are no "extra factors" introduced into their ontology. What is crucial to freedom and moral responsibility, on this account, is that agents have a plurality of available reasons or motivations for acting, none of which are causally sufficient or determine that the action will occur. Nevertheless, when the agent acts on one or other of the available reasons and motives, there is a casual explanation for the action

---

30. Fischer (2007), 67.

31. For criticism of agent-causation coming from the perspective of "hard incompatibilism" or skepticism see Pereboom (2007). Among the various difficulties that this theory faces, Pereboom argues, is how it could be that agent-caused choices so neatly match "what the statistical laws predict for the physical components of our actions." A theory of this kind, he suggests, involve "coincidences too wild to be believed" [Pereboom (2007), 11–13].

32. Kane (2007), 23.

33. Kane (2007), 25.

34. The soft/hard distinction in relation to both libertarianism and compatibilism is presented in Watson (1999).

and it is rendered intelligible, since it is performed for a reason and is, therefore, neither a random or chance event. Kane's "plural voluntary control" model, as developed along these lines, relies on the notion that a prior event may cause and explain another event, even though the effect is not necessitated or determined by the prior cause. On the basis of this causal ontology, libertarians, it is argued, can offer a theory of free and responsible action that avoids objections about "chanciness" and "randomness," while still offering some account of the kind of sourcehood and ultimacy that agent-causation theorists also seek to provide. The deep motivation behind all this being, of course, the need to satisfy EP and avoid any tinge of fate and luck in circumstances in which agents are judged to be free and responsible agents.

While Kane's model is certainly metaphysically more modest than the agent-causal theory, this attempt to trim the requirements of libertarianism so they fit in more comfortably within the naturalistic framework of "the modern scientific picture of the world" comes at a cost. More specifically, as many critics have pointed out, the event-causal model opens libertarianism up to the "luck objection"—an objection rooted in the requirements of EP (as presented in BEA). It is, again, not only compatibilists who advance these criticisms. The luck objection has also been advanced by libertarians, as well as by skeptics or hard incompatibilists.[35] Derk Pereboom argues, for example, that agents who satisfy event-causal conditions of the kind that Kane outlines are *no more* in control of their conduct than compatibilist agents (even if we grant that they are no less in control). If this is the case then the conditions described fall short of the sort of control that would be required for responsibility because it fails to deliver genuine sourcehood or ultimacy. What the agent does depends, ultimately, on factors that the agent does not control. The key concern here is that, despite the introduction of some complex elements in the agents deliberative apparatus (i.e., "efforts" and "tryings"), these agents still lack control over their own will in the sense that how they actually exercise their will—what decisions and choices they make in specific circumstances, given the available alternatives—cannot be explained or accounted for in terms of any (further) control or powers that they may possess. It is for this reason that agent-causal theorists believe they need to introduce some "extra factors" to provide the sort of control that is missing from this model. It is, then, in

---

35. See, e.g., Pereboom (2001), 50–54 and Pereboom (2007), 103–10.

this sense that the agents described in Kane's event-causal model remain vulnerable to luck and so fail to satisfy EP (i.e., just as they claim that com-patibilists conditions also fail this standard). We may conclude, therefore, along with other critics of the event-causal model, that "all versions of lib-ertarianism face serious difficulties" (as per premise #9 above).[36]

Clearly, then, libertarian views, although diverse, face an unattractive choice between agent-causal theories that rely on an implausible meta-physical extravagance and the metaphysically more modest event-causal theories that fail the test or standard imposed by EP (i.e., libertarian agents of this kind are still subject to modes of fate and luck). Granted that lib-ertarianism is found wanting, this forces a further retreat, back to skepti-cism. The skeptic maintains that EP cannot be satisfied by any proposed set of conditions φ concerning freedom and responsibility. They all fail, in various ways, the standard imposed by EP and BEA. However, accord-ing to the skeptic, EP must still be *respected*, even if it cannot be satisfied. To this extent, skepticism is itself an expression or manifestation of "the morality system" and its core assumptions and aspirations. It expresses, as it were, both the disappointment that human agents fail the standard set by EP and the continued optimism that this standard, nevertheless, remains in place, even if human agents fail to live up to it. In order to sup-port this stance, the skeptic must rely on the key claim that any conception of freedom and responsibility that does not satisfy EP cannot be the "true" or "genuine" conception that we are (or should be) concerned with. That is to say, the skeptical position rests on a narrow and restricted conception of (true) freedom and responsibility that satisfies the preferred requirements of the morality system and its commitment to EP. Any alternative account must, therefore, be judged "shallow" or "superficial," such as we find in the case of "the economy of threats account."[37] From the perspective of critical compatibilism, the skeptical position is itself just another mode of evasion generated by the morality system, one that similarly seeks to rule out the very possibility of free will pessimism (as denied by any continued commitment to EP).

---

36. Pereboom (2007), 114. See also Galen Strawson (1986), 31: "If there were no libertarians left, [my skeptical argument] would be largely superfluous. But there are still libertarians. They appear to be on the increase. This is surprising in a way, because the prospects for a detailed libertarian theory seem magnificently hopeless."

37. Wallace (1994), 54–6.

Critical compatibilists will certainly agree, with the skeptic, that the particular conception of freedom and responsibility that the morality system aims to secure should be rejected and discarded. What it also denies, however, is that this licenses any unqualified form of global skepticism (i.e., as based on the general application of BEA to all proposed accounts of conditions φ). According to this view of things, we need to distinguish carefully between two distinct skeptical views: (a) a qualified or local skepticism as it concerns our modern, Western conception as encouraged by the morality system, and (b) an unqualified or global skepticism that extends to any and all proposed accounts of conditions φ. While it may be true that the narrower, local conception fails (for reasons pointed out by BEA), it does not follow from this that all proposed concepts must fail—unless, of course, we simply assume that EP holds or applies in respect of all understandings of freedom and responsibility. If this were the case, then local skepticism would directly lead to the global skeptical conclusion.

Critical compatibilists, as we have noted, are themselves committed to local skepticism as it has been interpreted above, a concession that is entirely consistent with their own compatibilist commitments (unlike orthodox compatibilists who aim to satisfy the demands of EP and the morality system from *within* their compatibilist commitments).[38] Critical compatibilists can also accept that some proposed versions of compatibilist conditions φ^*—such as "the economy of threats account"—are inadequate or insufficiently robust for the purpose of providing a substantial and credible theory of freedom and responsibility. None of this leaves them in the situation of having to accept an unqualified or global form of skepticism about freedom and responsibility, which is the only form of skepticism that is directly problematic for the critical compatibilist. The modes of freedom and responsibility grounded in the various robust, complex capacities identified and explained by (critical) compatibilism are more than adequate to the task of grounding and justifying attitudes and practices that are recognizably part of the fabric or moral and ethical life more broadly conceived (i.e., more broadly conceived than the morality system would suggest). Even skeptics generally concede this point and attempt to mask it by initially advancing strong global skeptical arguments and then retreating back to (the more modest and more plausible) qualified

---

38. Wallace (1994), 39–40, 64–6. For criticism of Wallace's "narrow" interpretation of responsibility as framed in terms of the apparatus of "the morality system" see Russell (2013).

skeptical conclusion that is limited to the local conceptions of freedom and responsibility that are encouraged by the morality system.³⁹

The general objection that critical compatibilism raises against (global) skepticism is that it is a form of "bad faith." Compatibilist models of responsible agency, constructed along the lines of rational self-control and reason-responsiveness, while they may not satisfy EP, are plainly far more robust and sophisticated in accounting for a wide range of distinctions and discriminations in this sphere than the economy of threats account. Any attempt to simply dismiss the powers and abilities described, and treat them as irrelevant to human ethical and social life, with no bearing on our reactive attitudes and retributive dispositions and practices, has more than a taint of "bad faith" about it.⁴⁰ When we take this road, the humane goal of unmasking the distortions of the morality system and its preferred account of freedom and responsibility gets turned on its head and becomes the dehumanizing hypothesis that there are no *real* or *genuine* free and responsible agents in the world. Any skepticism of this unqualified kind must inevitably face the compelling objection that it constitutes just another mode of evasion, as encouraged by the morality system itself and its attachment to EP.⁴¹

---

39. See, e.g. Strawson (1994), which was originally published as "The Impossibility of Moral Responsibility" but subsequently published under the more restricted title "The Impossibility of *Ultimate* Moral Responsibility" (my emphasis). The insertion of "ultimate" marks a drift from global to local skepticism and, therefore, a considerable shift in the significance and scope of the conclusion that is being drawn from his "basic [skeptical] argument." A similar slide or ambiguity can, perhaps, also be detected in Pereboom's contributions, where he discusses "analogues" of the reactive attitudes that survive the skeptical critique that he advances [Pereboom (2001), 97, 199–200, Pereboom (2007), 118–20]. See note 41 below.

40. Our own awareness as agents (i.e., from the first-person perspective) of possessing and exercising these powers and abilities under relevant conditions makes our *internal* sense of freedom and responsibility impossible to evade or escape by means of inflated or exaggerated skeptical arguments. It may be argued, on this basis, that it is a form of dishonesty to the facts, to treat others with powers and abilities of this nature as if they have no relevant standing as free and responsible agents.

41. It may be argued that Pereboom's "hard incompatibilism" is liable to this line of criticism. On the face of it, hard incompatibilism may be read as a combination of (global) skepticism and optimism, whereas critical compatibilism is a combination of non-skepticism and pessimism. The two theories, on this interpretation, are divergent and pull in entirely different directions. There is, however, an alternative interpretation of this relationship, drawing on the local/global skeptical distinction, which allows for a much greater degree of convergence between these two theories. If hard incompatibilism is not globally skeptical, and is only locally skeptical about "basic desert" views of freedom and responsibility (i.e., of the kind encouraged by the morality system), then the opposition between these two views is not so sharp. Hard incompatibilism should be understood, on this account, as *rejecting* global

Where do these critical reflections about the prospects of incompatibilism leave us? If we follow the argument leading from BEA and the rejection of compatibilism through to the difficulties facing the various forms of incompatibilism, we arrive back in the situation that Nagel diagnosed so forcefully in "Moral Luck," which is the intractable nature of the free will problem. All the familiar approaches and strategies are, as Nagel suggests, guilty of evasion of one kind or another. Some attempt to solve the problem by proposing conditions φ that will satisfy EP by postulating extravagant and unintelligible metaphysical apparatus. Others seek to conceal or deny the ways in which their preferred theories remain vulnerable to concerns relating to fate and luck. Skeptics, the last representatives of the morality system as it collapses under the weight of its own assumptions and aspirations, deny human freedom and moral responsibility altogether, rather than abandon their commitment to EP and the forms of optimism that it aims to secure. These modes of evasion are all encouraged by the morality system and the forms of theorizing that it generates. This leaves all those who accept EP, along with the free will problem constructed around it, trapped in a philosophical labyrinth that offers no way out.

According to critical compatibilism the insoluble nature of this philosophical conundrum serves as strong evidence that it is based on faulty assumptions and aspirations. The root source of this impasse rests with the morality system and its commitment to EP, which denies the very possibility of free will pessimism and critical compatibilism. We are, then, faced with a clear choice between EP and the morality system, on one side, and free will pessimism and critical compatibilism on the other side. How do we decide between them? Faced with this choice between EP

---

skepticism and can, therefore, accept the non-skeptical features of critical compatibilism, which can, in turn, accept the local skepticism of hard incompatibilism. Similarly, there is no reason why critical compatibilism cannot accept much of the optimistic story that hard incompatibilists want to tell about rejecting conceptions of freedom and responsibility associated with the morality system (as explained above). It follows from all this that both hard compatibilism and critical compatibilism may well be able to *accommodate* each other and are not necessarily contradictories or opposites. While this (convergence) interpretation has some merit and basis in the arguments that each side has advanced, it is still the case that, from the perspective of critical compatibilism, the (unqualified) optimistic story that hard incompatibilists want to tell is, at best, one-sided and captures only one part of the truth about our predicament with respect to issues of agency, freedom and moral responsibility. The crucial point, from the perspective of critical compatibilism, is that rejecting the morality system and its particular interpretation of freedom and moral responsibility, does not leave us in a wholly comfortable situation that licenses complacency or optimism. On the contrary, when we abandon EP, we must accept free will pessimism and the troubling predicament associated with it.

and free will pessimism we have every reason to opt for free will pessimism. One reason for this is that it allows us to set aside the (intractable) free will problem and turn our attention, instead, to the distinct questions arising from the need to provide a credible account of conditions φ—unencumbered by the (faulty) requirements of EP. More importantly, however, the right basis for rejecting EP in favor of free will pessimism is that we find, on critical reflection, that free will pessimism is the most *truthful* account of our human predicament in respect of these matters. Unlike the forms of theorizing associated with the morality system, free will pessimism involves no evasions or metaphysical fabrications. It is free will pessimism, rather than the philosophical theories constructed around EP, that most accurately and adequately capture our discomfort when we reflect on troubling cases where free and responsible agents are, nevertheless, plainly entangled in circumstances of fate and luck. Given all this, we must reject EP and accept that free will pessimism is the truth about the human predicament in respect of these matters.

Granted that we should reject EP and accept free will pessimism, there is no principled basis for rejecting critical compatibilism (contrary to BEA). That is to say, the fact that compatibilist conditions φ* fail EP, and do not satisfy the assumptions and aspiration it embodies, is not, in itself, an acceptable basis for rejecting these conditions. The conditions φ* proposed may, of course, be judged *more or less* adequate in terms of their descriptive accuracy and ability to account for the range of distinctions we need to make in this sphere but there is no basis for rejecting them altogether simply on the ground that they fail EP. While critical compatibilism certainly requires *some* (plausible) interpretation of conditions φ*—and this remains a contested matter among them—the relevant standard for this assessment is not that it both respects and satisfies EP.[42]

---

42. Critical compatibilism, so described, might be viewed as simply a version of "revisionist" theory of freedom and responsibility [e.g., Vargas (2007); and Vargas (2013)]. There are, however, a number of reasons for resisting this suggestion, including the fact that some *orthodox* compatibilist theories also present themselves as "revisionary" [see, e.g., Dennett (1984), 19]. In general, what matters for a proper assessment of any proposed revisionary theory, as it concerns critical compatibilism, is, first, where it stands in relation to EP and, second, what stance it takes with respect to the metaphysical attitudes involved. A "revisionary" theory may or may not reject EP and, even if it does, it may or may not endorse the particular pessimistic attitudes that are drawn from this by way of free will pessimism (as some theorists may regard dispensing with EP as entirely untroubling, if not liberating). Suffice it to note that most contemporary revisionist projects follow in the neo-Skinnerian tracks of Dennett's optimistic pragmatism.

V. *The Free Will Problem and Free Will Pessimism*

Now we are in a position to consider what significance the conclusion that FWPA (i.e., that we should reject EP and accept free will pessimism) has for the free will problem itself. There are two ways of interpreting the free will problem, one that is broad and general in character and another that is narrower and more specific. We may present the free will problem in the broad and general manner as being concerned with the question concerning the nature and conditions of freedom and moral responsibility. Plainly, however, viewing the problem in this more open-ended fashion does not serve to capture the more specific features of the free will problem and the standards of solution that have been set for it. As has been explained, throughout most of the modern period, the parties to this debate have enjoyed a shared understanding of the background assumptions and aspirations that frame this problem and what they would accept as an adequate solution for it. They are agreed, more specifically, that EP, as associated with the assumptions and (optimistic) aspirations of the morality system, is essential to the structure of this problem and that it serves as the relevant standard for any acceptable solution that may be proposed. In this way, the solution that all the parties to the free will problem have sought and struggled to find is to provide an account of conditions of freedom and responsibility that satisfies EP.[43] Even skepticism, which denies that any such account can be provided, accepts that this is the relevant problem that stands in need of a solution and that EP must be *respected* even if it cannot be satisfied. For the skeptic this remains the relevant requirement for any adequate theory of freedom and moral responsibility and the problem of free will must be interpreted in these terms. To *dispense* with EP, therefore, is not to propose an alternative solution to the free will problem, so conceived, but rather to *reject the problem altogether*—along with its grounding and motivating assumptions and aspirations. These are, however, the very steps that FWPA takes and, therefore, free will pessimism should not be understood or interpreted as any kind of solution to the free will problem (i.e., given this stricter, narrower interpretation).

On the narrow understanding of the free will problem, all the parties involved in this dispute are agreed that free will pessimism cannot even be

---

43. As we have noted, this includes (orthodox) compatibilists [e.g. Dennett (1984) and Wallace (1994), 64–6], among others.

considered an available *candidate* for a solution, since it depends on rejecting the very assumptions that generate the problem in the first place—namely, EP. Considered from this perspective, the correct understanding of critical compatibilism is that it aims to replace the free will problem with an acceptance of free will pessimism, understood as a more truthful account of the human predicament. This predicament, along with its distinct pessimistic implications, is not a *problem* to be solved but a *predicament* waiting to be recognized and acknowledged. Taking this step involves abandoning the evasions and fabrications of the morality system and the various modes of theorizing associated with it. When we abandon these assumptions and aspirations of the morality system, we do not solve the free will problem so much as cast it aside.

What, then, does free will pessimism contribute to the free will problem more broadly conceived? Even if we discard EP, and reject the free will problem as narrowly interpreted, we still cannot present free will pessimism as a *solution* to the free will problem more broadly conceived. Any solution along these lines would require a complete and convincing account of conditions φ^*. Although we may be fully persuaded by FWPA, we still face any number of significant issues and difficulties relating to the (contested) interpretation of conditions φ^*. While the narrow free will problem should be cast aside, and we can agree that accounts of conditions φ^* cannot and should not be rejected on the ground that they fail the standard of EP, critical compatibilism must still develop and defend its own preferred interpretation of conditions φ^*. Clearly, then, a defense of free will pessimism does not, by itself, provide us with a complete theory of critical compatibilism. Many suggested accounts of conditions φ^* may be found wanting and should be discarded. Even the most promising may still require further refinement or better articulation.[44]

Having identified the limits of FWPA, we may now summarize its key claims and contributions. There are three interconnected components to this argument that are especially significant. First, the FWPA provides a diagnosis of why (orthodox) compatibilists have resisted the critical compatibilist approach and the free will pessimism associated with it. The fundamental source of resistance, it is argued, has its roots in the assumptions and aspirations of the morality system. Second, the FWPA makes clear that any adequate solution to the free will problem broadly conceived,

---

44. For two important and impressive recent contributions that offer (compatibilist-friendly) accounts of moral responsibility see McKenna (2012) and Shoemaker (2015).

as provided by some satisfactory account of conditions φ^*, will not deliver wholly optimistic conclusions about our human predicament in respect of these matters. On the contrary, free will pessimism is the troubling and difficult truth about our predicament and any credible account of conditions φ^* must recognize and acknowledge this. Third, and most importantly, the FWPA makes clear that any adequate and acceptable solution to the free will problem, broadly conceived, does not and cannot turn on a solution to the free will problem narrowly interpreted in terms of EP. The free will problem, more narrowly understood, has been generated by the faulty assumptions and illusory aspirations of the morality system. When these assumptions and aspirations are set aside we are better placed to recognize and acknowledge the (difficult) truth about the human predicament, without the evasions and fabrications that are encouraged by the morality system.

BIBLIOGRAPHY

Chisholm, Roderick. (1964). "Human Freedom and the Self." Reprinted in Gary Watson, ed., *Free Will*. 2nd ed. Oxford: Oxford University Press (2003), 24–35.

Dennett, Daniel. (1984). *Elbow Room: The Varieties of Free Will Worth Wanting*. Oxford: Clarendon Press.

Fischer, John. (2007). "Compatibilism." In Fischer, Kane, et al. (2007), 44–84.

Fischer, John, and Kane, R., Pereboom, D. and Vargas, M. (2007). *Four Views on Free Will*. Oxford: Oxford University Press.

Honderich, Ted. (1993). *How Free Are You?* Oxford: Oxford University Press.

Kane, Robert. (1996). *The Significance of Free Will*. Oxford: Oxford University Press.

———. (2007) "Libertarianism." In Fischer, Kane, et al., 5–43.

McKenna, Michael. (2012) *Conversation and Responsibility*. New York: Oxford University Press.

Nagel, Thomas. (1976). "Moral Luck." Reprinted in Russell & Deery (2013), 31–42.

Pereboom, Derk. (2001). *Living Without Free Will*. Cambridge: Cambridge University Press.

———. (2007). "Hard Incompatibilism." In Fischer, et al (2007), 85–125.

Russell, Paul. (2000). "Compatibilist Fatalism." Reprinted in Russell & Deery (2013), 450–68.

———. (2002). "Pessimists, Pollyannas and the New Compatibilism," in Robert Kane, ed., *The Oxford Handbook of Free Will*. Oxford University Press, 229–56.

———. (2008). "Free Will, Art and Morality." *Journal of Ethics*. 12: 307–25.

———. (2013). "Responsibility, Naturalism and 'The Morality System.'" In D. Shoemaker, ed., *Oxford Studies in Agency and Responsibility*. Oxford University Press, 184–204.

Russell, Paul, and Oisin Deery, eds. (2013). *The Philosophy of Free Will: Essential Readings from the Contemporary Debates.* New York: Oxford University Press.

Shoemaker, David. (2015) *Responsibility from the Margins.* New York: Oxford University Press.

Smilansky, Saul (2000). *Free Will and Illusion.* Oxford: Oxford University Press.

Strawson, P. F. (1962). "Freedom and Resentment." Reprinted in Russell & Deery (2013), 63–83.

Strawson, Galen. 1986. *Freedom and Belief.* Oxford: Clarendon Press.

———. (1994). "The Impossibility of [Ultimate] Moral Responsibility." Reprinted in Russell & Deery (2013), 363–78.

Taylor, Richard. (1959). "Determinism and the Theory of Agency." Reprinted in R. Shafer-Landau, ed., *Ethical Theory: An Anthology.* Oxford: Wiley-Blackwell.

Vargas, Manuel. (2007). "Revisionism." In Fischer, Kane, et al. (2007), 126–65.

———. (2013). "How to Solve the Problem of Free Will." In Russell & Deery (2013), 400–16.

Wallace, R. Jay. (1994). *Responsibility and the Moral Sentiments.* Cambridge, MA: Harvard University Press.

Waller, Bruce. (2011). *Against Moral Responsibility.* Cambridge, MA: MIT Press.

Watson, Gary. (1987). "Responsibility and the Limits of Evil." Reprinted in Russell & Deery (2013), 84–113.

———. (1999). "Soft Libertarianism and Hard Compatibilism." Reprinted in G. Watson, *Agency and Answerability.* New York: Oxford University Press (2004), 197–215.

Williams, Bernard. (1976). "Moral Luck." Reprinted in B. Williams, *Moral Luck.* Cambridge: Cambridge University Press (1981), 20–39.

———. (1985a). *Ethics and the Limits of Philosophy.* With a commentary by A. W. Moore and a foreword by Jonathan Lear. Routledge: London & New York. (Routledge Classics edition 2011.)

———. (1985b). "How Free Does the Will Need to Be?" Reprinted in B. Williams, *Making Sense of Humanity.* Cambridge: Cambridge University Press (1995), 3–21.

———. (1993). *Shame and Necessity.* Berkeley, CA: University of California Press.

Wolf, Susan (1990). *Freedom Within Reason.* New York: Oxford University Press.

List of Related Publications and Interviews

Below is a list of publications by Paul Russell relating to free will and moral responsibility that are not included in this volume.

BOOKS AND EDITED BOOKS

Freedom and Moral Sentiment: Hume's Way of Naturalizing Responsibility (New York & Oxford: Oxford University Press, 1995).

Free Will and Reactive Attitudes: Perspectives on P. F. Strawson's "Freedom and Resentment." Introduced and edited with Michael McKenna (Farnham: Ashgate, 2008). [Reprinted in paperback by Routledge 2016.]

The Philosophy of Free Will: Essential Readings from the Contemporary Debates. Introduced and edited with Oisin Deery (New York & Oxford: Oxford University Press, 2013).

PAPERS AND ARTICLES

"The Naturalism of Hume's 'Reconciling Project,'" *Mind* 92 (1983), 593–600.

"Hume's 'Reconciling Project': A Reply to Flew," *Mind* 94 (1985), 587–90.
  [A reply to Anthony Flew, "Paul Russell on Hume's 'Reconciling Project'" *Mind*, 93 (1984), 587–8.]

"Hume on Responsibility and Punishment," *Canadian Journal of Philosophy*, 20 (1990), 539–64. Reprinted in (a) *Hume: Great Political Thinkers*, edited by John Dunn and Ian Harris (Cheltenham: Edward Elgar, 1997), and (b) *Hume and Law*, edited by Ken Mackinnon (Farnham: Ashgate, 2012).

"Hume's *Treatise* and the Clarke-Collins Controversy," *Hume Studies*, 21 (1995), 95–115.

"Free Will," in *The Encyclopedia of Empiricism*, edited by Edward Barbanell and Don Garrett (Westport, CT: Greenwood Press, 1997), 107–11.

"Smith on Moral Sentiment and Moral Luck," *History of Philosophy Quarterly*, 16 (1999), 37–58.

Critical Notice of *Responsibility and Control* by John M. Fischer and Mark Ravizza, *Canadian Journal of Philosophy*, 32 (2002), 587–606.

"Moral Sense and Virtue in Hume's Ethics," in *Values and Virtues: Aristotelianism and Contemporary Ethics*, edited by Tim Chappell (Oxford: Clarendon, 2006), 154–66.

"Hume on Free Will," in *Stanford Encyclopedia of Philosophy*, edited by Edward N. Zalta (Winter 2007; revised September 2014). http://plato.stanford.edu/archives/win2007/entries/hume-freewill/.

"The Free Will Problem" [Hobbes, Bramhall, and the Free Will Debate], in *The Oxford Handbook of Philosophy in Early Modern Europe*, edited by Desmond Clarke and Catherine Wilson (Oxford University Press, 2011), 425–44.

"'Hume's Lengthy Digression': Free Will in the *Treatise*," in *Hume's Treatise: A Critical Guide*, edited by Donald Ainslie and Annemarie Butler (Cambridge: Cambridge University Press, 2015), 230–51.

"Free Will and Moral Sense: Strawsonian Approaches," in *Routledge Companion to Free Will*, edited by Meghan Griffith, Neal Levy, and Kevin Timpe. (New York: Routledge, 2017), 96–108.

Review of *Conversation and Responsibility*, by Michael McKenna, *Philosophical Review*, 126 (2017), 285–95.

"Free Will and 'Affirmation': Assessing Honderich's Third Way", in *Ted Honderich on Consciousness, Determinism, and Humanity*, edited by Gregg Caruso (London: Palgrave, 2017).

"Moral Responsibility and Metphysical Attitudes", in *The Oxford Handbook of Moral Responsibility*, edited by Dana Nelkin and Derk Pereboom (Oxford University Press, forthcoming).

INTERVIEWS

"Seven Questions About Free Will and Moral Responsibility," *Methode—Analytic Perspectives*. No. 3 (2013), 170–78.

Five Books, interview on Free Will and Responsibility, December 2013. http://five-books.com/interviews/free-will-and-responsibility-on-paul-russell.

"Hume's Irreligious Core," interview with *3: am. Magazine*, May 2016. http://www.3ammagazine.com/3am/humes-irreligious-core/.

Index

Watson, Gary, 44n16, 74, 87–88, 91,
148n20, 151n24, 168n12, 191n7,
194n13, 199n20, 201n24, 205n29,
215, 232, 234n31, 260n25, 265n34
Williams, Bernard, xvin3, xx, xxi, 98,
105n3, 108–10, 118, 124n5, 128,

149n22, 203n26, 206n33, 229,
243–44, 255, 258, 259n23
Wittgenstein, Ludwig, 20n2
Wolf, Susan, 80–81, 89, 159n1,
191n9, 219
Woody, J. Melvin, 139n8